TROUT STREAMS
OF MICHIGAN

By Janet D. Mehl and Company

Foreword by Robert Traver
Illustrations by Mitch Smith
Cover painting by Ed Sutton

©Copyright 1998 by the Michigan United Conservation Clubs
ISBN 0-933112-38-6

MUCC

TABLE OF CONTENTS

Southern Lower Peninsula Streams

A foreword
by the author of
"Anatomy of a Murder"

Kenneth S. Lowe

A big part of the fun of fishing is getting to know the quirks of the water one fishes, which can vary enormously. This is especially true of trout streams, with which Michigan luckily abounds, and the reader of this book, whether fisherman or not, will be charmed and enlightened by this engaging report on the variations of the makeup of some 50-odd trout streams scattered throughout the state.

Buying this book may also help preserve these and other waters from those overzealous souls among us who are excessively devoted to progress at any price.

—ROBERT TRAVER
1903-1991

INTRODUCTION

In the late 1970s the Michigan United Conservation Clubs published the first volume of *Trout Streams of Michigan*. The second volume followed in 1983. Both publications proved very popular and when they became out of print the organization decided to reissue them together in a single volume as a service to sport anglers and to raise additional funds for MUCC's conservation efforts.

Most of the stream descriptions in the first volume were prepared by fisheries biologists of the Michigan Department of Natural Resources. MUCC commissioned Janet D. Mehl, a seasoned trout angler, to write the second volume.

The result is a book that describes in detail the characteristics of the major trout streams in a state that is favored with an abundance of prime trout waters.

Whether you are a veteran trout fisherman or fisherwoman or a beginning angler, MUCC believes *Trout Streams of Michigan* will add immensely to your enjoyment and knowledge of trout fishing in Michigan waters.

—Kenneth S. Lowe
1921-1996

THE LAST FRIDAY IN APRIL
By JANET D. MEHL

It wasn't that first trout fishing trek at the age of seven that has since made every last Friday in April a sleepless night for me. Nor the next. Nor the one after that, when the wind-tussled tag alders and chanting saw grass lining the Cedar River near my childhood home clawed tenaciously at my earthworm. At last the bait would **ker-plunk!** into the water, sounding every finned and feathered creature within 50 feet. I quickly cranked up the slack line, anxious to feel the **tap, tap, tap** of a thriving trout darting for cover, only to find that my hook still lay where I had heaved it, the slinking current having swept it beneath the brush-choked bank and driven it fast into a cedar root. The chill, sinister water curled in a devilish smile at my feet, and the dark cedars looming over my head seemed to flaunt a fiendish mockery.

But finally, many lessons later, the magic moment arrived: My worm was swept not into a cedar root, but into the mouth of a small, hapless trout. I skittered the tiny splattering prize to my feet and hoisted it into the tall grass, where it flopped frantically and then lay still, gaping gills gasping their last breaths. I hunkered down to admire the spritely brookie, its sides a brilliant vermilion backdrop for the red spots ringed in blue, the tail edging the seven-and-a-half-inch mark on my tape measure. At that time—in the infantile stages of trout anglerhood before creel limits and great fish lengths lost their undeserved priority—seven inches was a legal length for brook trout in Michigan's Lower Peninsula. And so, with the care of a mother holding a newborn baby for the first time, I carried home my testimony to the trouting fraternity and prepared for a grand feast.

At first glance, the name Cedar **River** seems deceitful, for along much of "my" stretch—the West Branch in eastern Clare County—I can touch both banks with my ultralight spinning rod, standing in water ankle-deep. Upon careful perusal, however, one soon learns that this wily serpent defies the wits of even the most adept of trout anglers, be he fly or spin or bait fisherman. For between the intermittent flat spots of placid, gliding fluidity or tailing sparkling riffles, the stately current spills over cedar roots and fallen logs, somersaulting to dark, covetous depths that can fill an angler's waders, gouging the earth from beneath the banks, carving protective haunts for wary browns, the most elusive of trout. And that, my friends, is what distinguishes the venerable Cedar as a brown trout "river."

A 10-minute drive from the Cedar puts me on the upper reaches of the Tobacco, its gurgling waters ambling merrily through cedar-scented swamps. Fallen cedar logs crisscross the swirling ribbon of water, which yields indigenous brookies in the headwaters before it slackens below, forming dark pockets for wary browns. I approach "my" stretch of the stream with great fervor, for it is superb trout habitat. The spring-fed seepages common to cedar swamps provide the high oxygen levels and cooler water temperatures required by the finicky brook trout. Also known as the **speckled trout** in central Canada and as the **squaretail** in parts of the Northeast, the brook trout requires cleaner, colder water than that inhabited by other trout. It thrives in temperatures of 57° to 60° and is seldom found where the

mercury exceeds 68° for any length of time. The brookie is not actually a true trout (genus **Salmo**) but a char of the genus **Salvelinus (S. fontinalis)**, as is the Arctic char and the lake trout.

A fall spawner, the brook trout can spawn over much finer gravel—often coarse sand—than the brown or rainbow can. Such fine-gravel areas frequent much of my Tobacco trouting paradise, cleansed of debris and oxygen-suffocating silt by the stable current.

Cover is plentiful, and I still marvel at the number of trout that a small given section of the stream will hold. Any object that prevents the fish from being seen by bank-treading predators, deflects the current for less resistance, or funnels food into a feeding lane may harbor trout.

The object need not be much larger than the fish itself. I first learned this when I caught my first legal brown trout from the Cedar. I had meant to cast to the edge of an undercut bank, but my crawler had landed nearer the middle of a flat, barren stretch. But, following the cardinal rule of angling, I followed through with the cast, allowing the bait to tumble along the stream bottom toward me. To my amazement, a brown charged out from beneath a small cedar stump not 12 inches in diameter, devoured the wriggling crawler, and erupted the glassy surface in a shower of spray. This incident illustrated another indelible lesson of the angling world, one that defies the laws of probability: An unusually large number of "trophies" are taken by quirks or strange twists of fate. But as William Carlos Williams said, "Memory is a kind of accomplishment," and I suspect this is true regardless of fate.

I now live hundreds of miles from the Cedar and Tobacco rivers in what is dubbed the richest, most dazzling, most exciting cultural center in America, certainly the epitome of wealth and ruin among mankind—New York City's Manhattan. Yet, amid the noise and flurry of activity, just knowing that through the familiar cedar-scented lowlands and rolling farmlands of Clare County the Cedar and Tobacco flow placidly, eternally, makes everything in my life a little easier. Each year I return to these tiny rivulets, vestiges of my childhood, a feeling of homecoming, to tempt their feisty trout, to feel their cool waters hug my waders, to be comforted by their soul-filling grandeur. To see a panicked whitetail bounding up a hillside, to hear a low rumble in the distance—thunder? A second later I smile as I recognize the drumming of a partridge's wings.

Certainly it is these smallest of waters that command the greatest respect and stealth from the trout angler. The key to reaping their harvest consistently lies in a single word: patience. Trout in small streams are spooked far more easily than those in larger rivers since they are more vulnerable to birds and other predators. The slightest motion, vibration, unnatural shadow or glare of metal or any disturbance of the environs will send small-stream trout streaking far upstream for cover. In larger rivers, with more water to maneuver in and above-surface visibility obscured by depths, trout may simply flee upstream to the nearest pool. Several minutes later these same fish may drop back to their respective lies, providing the angler with another opportunity to present a lure to them. A small-stream trout that has been frightened however, will take much longer to return to his former lie, and the angler might as well leave him for another day. No matter, for the next outing will find the same trout in the identical lie.

Obviously, it is also much harder to present a lure in tiny flowages. Some lend themselves to bait fishing only, in which, if an angler is skillful enough to get the offering to reach a fish, the trout is sure to have encircled most objects in the stream before the hook is set. But "**If you don't get hung up, you're not getting to the fish**"—I still hear my stepfather's words of many years ago echoing in my mind.

Ask any trout fisherman to name the finest trout angler/mentor he knows and nine out of 10 will answer that it is his own father. I am no exception. Many years and hundreds of trout later, I still watch his intense concentration, his presentation,

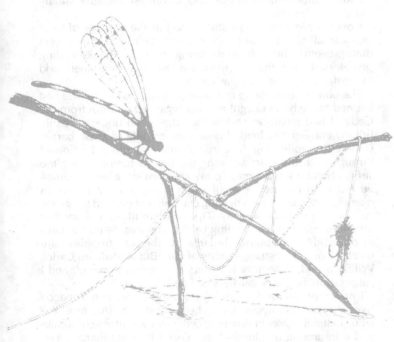

his efficiency with awe. His graceful fly casts reach 70 feet or more. He drops a spinner beside a log near the opposite bank, deftly skipping it over numerous logs, allowing it to settle into dark pockets, and still manages to guide the flopping quarry to net. But his skill far exceeds casting accuracy: It is understanding his quarry, knowing how to entice strikes when fish are not interested in feeding; this is what separates the good trout anglers from the great ones.

Shortly after my trouting initiation on the Cedar, he "graduated" me to the Manistee, which, he assured me, was a wide-open river that could easily be fished with a fly, thereby issuing me a fly rod and box of flies and sending me on my way. Matching the hatch was somewhat like a game of 20 Questions—if it wasn't bigger than a breadbox, I could eventually reach a conclusion through the process of elimination and flailed away with this cumbersome outfit. Gradually, I too learned to love this angling art, although I am not a fly purist but respect fly-casting as another means to the end sought by all trout fishermen, a purpose that is universal among the sect yet individualistic and not adequately described by words.

The Manistee is indeed an open, easily fished river, offering

a vast expanse, an exhilarating freedom, an unleashing of spirit and of splendor not felt on smaller creeks, as well as all three trout species in a given stretch, in places at least. Its shifting bottom contour rises and falls abruptly, adding, in part, to its great diversity of holding water. Dark, secluded pools harbor elusive brown trout, **Salmo trutta**, while gravel-bottomed, fast, riffly runs hold rainbow trout, **Salmo gairdneri**.

The brown trout is certainly the most wary and hardest to catch, but its superior intelligence is a misinterpretation of its reclusiveness. It is the most highly sought trout and provides unmatched challenge, particularly during nighttime fly hatches. The slow, deliberate **slurp** of a rising brown—in contrast to the rapids **splat** of a snatching brookie—will put goosebumps on any fisherman's flesh. A late fall spawner, the brown trout's preferred temperature range is 54° to 63°, with the lethal limit about 75°. Because it has a greater tolerance of varying temperatures and lower oxygen levels than the brook trout, because it is much more difficult to catch than the vulnerable brookie and grows to much larger sizes, preying on other trout, brown trout populations naturally succeed brook trout numbers in natural environments.

Rainbow trout, spring spawners, prefer coarse-gravel bottoms and fast, bubbly current. Because of their migratory inclination they are not planted in small streams in near the numbers that brown trout are. Brook trout are seldom planted in Michigan. Trout planted by the Department of Natural Resources are fingerlings—three- to six-inch fish.

After months of research and interviewing literally hundreds of Michigan trout anglers in writing my articles for this book, I was both amazed and proud at the number of those who release every fish they catch. To you I tip my hat with its 14 flies, for much of our future trout fishing relies on such conscience. I, however, find the delicate orange flesh just too delectable to release **all** of my fish.

Even among members of the trout-fishing fraternity—a relatively small segment of the angling world—is a vast array of schools and philosophies. There are the small-stream pursuers, the big-water hounds, the worm dunkers, spinner flingers, and fly purists, and even among the latter the match-the-hatch proponents versus the presentation theorists. Often our methods are not founded on biological rationale but on habit or recommendation or superstition. In fact, many of the most popular fly patterns, wet and dry, do not even resemble anything in the natural world. Perhaps the trout are as fickle as anglers. I suspect we could eliminate nearly half of the infinite multitude of flies available and still take good catches efficiently and consistently in varying combinations of angling ability, holding water, and natural fauna.

But it is the perceptive angler who can determine the trout's mood and how and when to select just the right pattern to entice temperamental fish to strike. It is this infinite variety that makes each trout fisherman his own, that adds to the fun, the mystique, and, pardon the pun, the lure—and the quirks—of trout. And for this reason I hope we never have to part with even the most scraggly, obsolete, or absurd of patterns.

For despite these differing methods and lures, among us all is a common bond, that same passion which makes that last Friday night in April one sleepless with anticipation, visions of five-pound browns flashing in our heads. That same zeal which, even now, leads me back to the Manistee for each opening day, even though I **know** its trout will lie unseen, lethargic, ghostlike in the icy, swollen deluge, traces of winter too soon past, my heart still dancing with excitement.

And **that** is why we fish for trout.

THE TROUT OF MICHIGAN'S STREAMS
By TOM HUGGLER

Your first "trophy" trout might well have been a rambunctious brookie—a little blur of native beauty as it nailed the worm you offered from a brush-choked stream bank. Or it could have been a cartwheeling rainbow that smashed the spawn sack you had bounced fast along the gravel stream bottom and that had come to net only after an exhausting battle that wound up far downstream. Another angler's first trophy might have been a foraging brown that sucked in the imitation from among hundreds of mayflies that littered the stream surface at night and then, rampaging through the shallows, churned those waters to a froth while the angler held on and tried to steady himself in his canoe.

I've never taken a trout that wasn't a trophy—no matter the size. And it's hard for me to believe that the fabulous trout fishing we enjoy in Michigan today is largely a phenomenon of this century.

The silver steelhead that ascends our rivers from the Great Lakes by the thousands in spring and fall and the chunky brown trout found in waters across the state are not native to Michigan. Only the dainty, jewel-like brook trout, originally found only in the Upper Peninsula and now established throughout the northern Lower Peninsula and in some southern Michigan streams, is a true Michigan native.

Experts tell us that all trout are of Arctic marine origin. The fish migrated south ahead of the descending glaciers and became established in freshwater lakes and rivers of North America and Europe. Rainbows and cutthroats moved south through the Bering Straits of the Pacific Coast. Cutthroats found the rushing waters of mountain streams and the cold depths of high country lakes much to their liking, whereas the rainbows fed heavily in the ocean before mounting their spawning drives up the huge West Coast rivers from Alaska to California. The same ice movements pushed brown trout south between Norway and Greenland as far as Spain and sent the char-like brook trout as far south in North America as temperatures would allow him to live.

Fishing was tremendous a hundred years ago too, but the game species were lake trout, whitefish, and the now extinct grayling. Michigan Indians and early settlers had long speared spawning lake trout in the shallows of bays and had netted the abundant whitefish as they schooled along river mouths. Lake trout to 50 pounds were sometimes caught, and there were some reports of 100-pounders being taken by early commercial netters. One commercial fisherman reported that "in the early part of the week ending October 23, 1824, at the fishery on Grosse Ile, 30,000 whitefish were caught in a single day." Another commercial netter three years later commented that he had taken 15,000 whitefish with a single seine in five hauls.

Fishing for grayling was equally fantastic a hundred years ago, and at one time the mighty Au Sable was one of the very few Michigan rivers that harbored this colorful game fish. Now found only in remote Montana rivers, the Northwest Territories, and elsewhere in the Arctic, the grayling is a species of trout with

a high dorsal fin, a variety of iridescent colors and white flesh of delicious quality.

The fish in Michigan were not large—10 or 12 inches being an average size, although two-pounders were sometimes taken—but were very easy to catch. Grayling would strike at anything resembling a fly, be it a piece of squirrel's tail or a blue jay feather, and anglers often fished with leaders containing three or more flies. Sometimes two or more fish were caught at once.

Anglers from Chicago, Detroit, and the eastern states, as well as from foreign countries, told of catching up to 100 pounds of grayling daily. Many were left along the shores of the Au Sable to rot, and thousands were shipped to the southern markets, where they brought the unheard of price of 25 cents per pound. It seemed as though, like the plains buffalo and the immense flocks of passenger pigeons, the grayling supply was inexhaustible. History teaches a different lesson.

But just as deforestation in the East was ruining the quality brook trout habitat, so too lumbering in the Michigan northwoods not only scarred the land but destroyed the quality of rivers like the Au Sable. Like trout, grayling needed precise living conditions of cold, highly oxygenated, clean water.

The stripping of the streamside forests caused erosion which put huge quantities of silt into the Au Sable. This silt smothered the gravel bars where grayling spawned. Deforestation also caused the river to warm up beyond the grayling's tolerance, but the final blow to these delicate fish came when thousands of logs were run through the Au Sable system. Anglers complained of finding grayling suffocating from fine particles of bark meshed into their gills and there's no question that the huge logs raked the spawning beds, rendering them sterile.

Early in this century the grayling disappeared from the Michigan scene, although an attempt was made to restore them in the U.P. (see chapter on the Otter River), and now they are extinct in the state except in a half dozen lakes in the northern two-thirds of Michigan where they have been planted.

The introduction of brown and rainbow trout to Michigan in the late 1800s helped restore quality fishing, and the steady plants of both trout and salmon, especially the latter in the past decades, has once again given our state worldwide recognition as an angler's mecca. A good argument could be made that fishing in the Great Lakes state today is better than it ever was and that "the good old days" are right now.

Native brook trout from the U.P. spread south to replace the disappearing grayling, and by the end of the century were well-established in northern Michigan streams and ponds. Brookies like the colder 60 to 65 degrees water of small, spring-fed streams and the colder headwaters of larger waters. Many streams in the Lower Peninsula were ideal for brookie transplants. In 1879 the first plantings went into Cass, Berrien, and Kalamazoo counties in southwest Lower Michigan.

In 1885 a Grayling man named Rube Babbitt put 20,000 brook trout fry into the Au Sable, and brookies (along with rainbow trout) began to replace the fast-disappearing graylings as the river's calling card. William B. Mershon, a prolific outdoor writer and conservationist at the turn of the century, kept a diary listing accurate records of the number and size of grayling and trout caught by him and his friends. On May 4, 1900, Mershon himself caught 41 big trout from the Au Sable (there were no creel limits then), and his party of 10 collectively took 1,038 fish.

"The best day of fishing I ever enjoyed," Mershon wrote.

Brook trout did equally well anywhere the water was clear, fresh, and sparkling. Beaver ponds of the northwoods and well-shaded farm streams of the southern counties are both home to this handsome fish whose flesh is a pink-orange and is delicately delicious.

Most won't argue that brook trout are the most colorful of trout/char species. Their dark, olive-green backs and upper sides are marked heavily with light marbled, wormlike patterns, changing to lighter flanks with spots of blue and green and two or three rows of red dots. The belly is generally white, although there may be traces of red-orange about the gills and pectorals. Native brookies often have more red to their bellies—occasionally being entirely blaze red in color.

Michigan brook trout as a rule don't grow large. An eight- to 10-inch fish is about average, although anglers in the know can take brookies from 12 to 16 inches. These larger fish often come from secluded beaver ponds or hard to find freshets back in the woods. A few lake-run brook trout wax fat in the fish-rich Great Lakes (particularly Lake Superior) and return to run tributaries in the fall. These lake-run fish, called "coasters," generally run from two to four pounds and can be taken by spin-casting or trolling small spoons in silver, gold, or copper color around river mouths and in shoal water. The state brook trout record is a six-pound, two-ounce fish.

The Michigan Department of Natural Resources annually plants several hundred thousand brook trout in state streams and lakes. Still, a large amount of the brook trout population is sustained through natural reproduction, particularly from the smaller, cold feeder streams.

Steelhead and rainbow trout are one and the same species; the main difference lies in the habits of the fish. Rainbows live in inland lakes and rivers and do not migrate long distances when they spawn. The steelhead, on the other hand, chows down in the Pacific Ocean or Great Lakes, putting on important spawning weight, and then runs the rivers as a brawling mature fish.

When the West Coast steelhead were brought to Michigan (the first release was of California fish in 1876), they adapted well to fresh water and found plenty of streams and lakes where food was abundant and water temperatures in the preferred 60° to 70° range. It didn't take these early fish long to find their way into the Great Lakes, and the basis of a tremendous fishery was established. Runs quickly developed on both sides of the state, and by the 1920s were occurring in all of the Great Lakes.

Michigan anglers enjoyed good steelheading until the 1950s. By that time the sea lamprey and uncontrolled commercial netting nearly wiped out the Great Lakes trout fishery. Since then, these problems have been brought under control, and once again the steelhead is providing an excellent Michigan sport fishery.

Rainbows or steelheads are a silver-sided fish with upper flanks and backs of gray-green, often dappled with black spots. They can be told apart from the sometimes look-alike coho and chinook salmon by their white mouths, black spotted backs, and anal fin rays, usually fewer than 12. By comparison, cohos have 12 to 15 rays and chinooks have 15 to 17 rays.

Fish in the river for long periods of time often are darker than fresh-run steelies, and they usually display the pink-red stripe along their sides characteristic of the rainbow trout. Spawning males usually show a heavy crimson or bright orange-pink streak and dark bodies along with a prominent hook jaw. Steelheads vary in shape from long, cylindrical fish to those with fat, football shapes, especially the small-headed females.

Young Michigan steelheads often stay two years in the stream of their birth or where they were released as fingerlings. Then they move into the Great Lakes to feed, put on weight and mature—a period of from two to four years. Their diet is largely alewives, which, according to some estimates, constitute 90 percent by weight of all Great Lakes species. As mature spawning adults, steelheads average eight pounds, with many fish from

10 to 15 pounds taken each spring and fall. The state record is a whopping 26-pound, eight-ounce fish.

The DNR has long been committed to steady plantings of rainbow and steelhead trout, although some natural reproduction occurs. Hatchery-reared numbers have varied from a half-million to 2 million annually.

The brown has been the most controversial of the three trout species found in Michigan streams. In 1884 the Pere Marquette was the first major American river to receive the transplanted European browns offered by Baron von Behr, president of the German Fishery Association. Loch Leven brown trout were planted in the Pere Marquette and in Coldspring Lake near Harrison the following year. By the end of 1896, more than 1.7 million were planted. Stockings of brown trout increased around the country and 15 years later, at the end of the century, 38 states had received browns.

In 1897 the Michigan Fish Commission banned further plantings, saying the brown trout was, overall, an inferior species. Others condemned the brown as well, claiming that the fish were too difficult to catch, too expensive to rear, and cannibalistic by nature.

These fears are largely unfounded, however, and the brown trout has come to be a highly respected, much sought after fish. Browns are wary in streams where they feed in the shallows at night and in the shoal water of the Great Lakes, but anglers have discovered special tactics for taking these handsome game fish. Two of the brown's best features are his ability to withstand warmer temperatures (up to 75°) than most trout and his habit of growing to tackle-busting size. The state brown trout record is a 34-pound, six-ounce bruiser caught by Vestaburg angler Robert Henderson in Arcadia Lake in Manistee County on May 16, 1984.

Brown trout get their name from the overall appearance of the fish. They are a light to dark brown with greenish-brown on the back, lighter brown sides, and a creamy yellow belly. The sides, back, and dorsal fins are spotted with brown or black marks, often ringed with a halo of white. Lake-run fish are silver in appearance and lack the characteristic red splotches of river browns. The flesh is firm and white and excellent to eat.

Like brook trout and rainbows, brown trout maintain some natural reproduction in Michigan streams, but the DNR continues to stock heavily. A solid brown-trout sport fishery is developing on the east side of the state in Lake Huron and is rivaling the hot action in Lake Michigan on the west side. Brown-trout plantings have tapered off from a peak of about a million and one half fish in 1973 to about 300,000 annually since then.

Many of these fish planted in the open waters of the Great Lakes run up tributaries in the fall and, like the mighty steelhead, provide tremendous sport. A large number never see a lake and grow fat in rivers, dining heavily on minnows and insect life, especially the giant mayflies that hatch in late June.

Quality trout fishing is available nearly everywhere in the state, and access and accommodations are excellent for anyone who wants to go. The cost to fish trout is as expensive as the angler wants to make it. The sometimes trout fisherman on a small back stream with his old waders and simple spincast outfit can get just as much enjoyment as the "every weekender" who prowls the Great Lakes shorelines with his depth finder and downriggers. Both are in search of a quality experience and a trophy trout, and each has an excellent opportunity to get both in Michigan.

It is hoped that the trout angler will be conscientious as he borrows a piece of river for a few hours of personal use. The fisherman who cares will not litter the stream bank and will return fish he doesn't plan to dress for the table. He will show courtesy and respect to fellow anglers. He will not trespass and he will use sporting methods for taking his trout.

In the back of the conscientious trout fisherman's mind will stir the story and lesson of the Michigan grayling, and he will pledge himself never to allow such a rape of the resource to occur again.

When he has taken from the river whatever he came to get, he will have left no mark for unborn generations of trout fishermen to find.

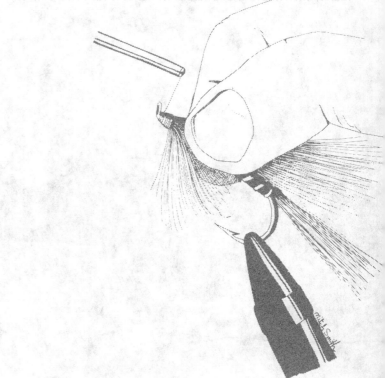

TROUT-FISHING TECHNIQUES

By DALE RIEGER

Trout have captured the fancy of fishermen for hundreds of years. Their widespread distribution in Europe and North America is part of the reason. Others include the trout's impressive list of credentials. To most anglers, he is the prize of prizes and highly respected for his fighting ability, natural wariness, overall handsome appearance, and excellent taste.

Reams have been written about these popular game fish, and as more and more information about trout and how to take them is acquired, more written materials will appear in magazines and books. What fly-rod and reel combination is best? How do you match the hatch on a particular stream? What are the best trout recipes? What methods work best? The list is endless. This chapter will attempt to touch upon the many options of technique open to the trout fisherman.

To me, the most important consideration of trout fishing is to know the trout's habits and habitat. If you don't have a clue as to why trout lie in certain pieces of water and don't develop the ability to recognize these places, you'll never understand how to catch them with regularity.

Avid fishermen call it "reading the water," and it's something that anyone can learn with experience. Trout are found in fast-flowing streams where shade and the river's gradient help keep summer temperatures down. Insect larvae along the stream bottom and small minnows in the stream contribute to a trout's diet, so these organisms must be present in the river you plan to fish. A fast current often flows over a bottom of gravel, cobble, or bedrock. These structures, as well as boulders and logs, help provide resting areas and safety for trout. In addition, fast water mixes with the air and helps provide an oxygen-rich environment for trout.

This doesn't mean that trout aren't found in quiet pools of water, though. Generally, if stream temperatures are below 70° and some fast water and suitable gravel beds for spawning are available, trout will use the river. Trout like the long, quiet stretches as nesting areas. This is especially true of migrating steelheads and browns, which can often be seen stacked up like so many logs in such northern Michigan rivers as the Little Manistee, Platte, and sometimes the Au Sable.

I first began to understand something about trout and their preferred living conditions by going after brookies in small streams. This is an excellent way to begin trout fishing because all of the important considerations (a wary stalk, proper reading of water, careful presentation of the bait) are necessary, even though the quarry may be a seven-inch brookie and not a 10-pound steelhead or brown at the moment.

Brookies in the generally clear small streams are exceptionally wary fish. If you can catch them consistently, you can take the larger browns and steelheads, often under more difficult and trying conditions.

When checking out a prospective trout stream, it's best to do so during low-water conditions, preferably in the late summer when lack of rain makes for a clear, shallow stream. During high-water conditions, trout rivers often become roily, and the fish are well distributed throughout, making it difficult to spot the best places. During the low-water period of late summer, trout move into the pocket water formed by underground structure or are found in riffle areas where oxygen content is high. At these times they also hang out under overhanging banks where shade helps keep water temperatures down.

Learn to think like a trout, and remember three things when trying to figure out where a trout might lie in a stream—food, safety, and favorable current. I like to fish pocket water, which is simply a small pool of water or depression caused by some structure in the stream. Current passing over a submerged boulder, for example, often will scoop out a small hole just downstream, a perfect spot for a trout to lie. Trout rarely lie in the open current unless they are actively feeding or oxygen content in the stream is low.

As water flows around logs and large rocks, trout often will lie in the edges or breaks in current caused by such obstructions. When wading upstream, I make it a point to first fish the pocket water just below such structures and then make a cast or two on each side. Often more than one trout can be caught this way. Changing position a little and casting to the water immediately in front of the structure can be a good bet too, as sometimes larger trout will hold right in front of such cover, especially if they are feeding.

Trout like to lie along ledges and drop-offs too, and these can be found by wearing polarized sunglasses and watching the bottom. Pay particular attention to the current as it will follow the bottom contour. Current and structures are the clues that spell out what's underneath. Move slowly and when you spook trout, make it a point to check out where they were hiding. Commit this knowledge to memory, and you'll begin to catch trout.

Other good places to catch trout are under bridges where shade cools the water and just below tributaries, as the stream temperature may drop a little from the cold addition.

Although some purists won't touch live bait, I use it a great deal with success and believe that beginners should start with it. In small streams brookies and browns readily wallop worms, grubs, grasshoppers, and crickets. I like to use an ultralight spin-cast outfit with closed-face reel (the brush-choked banks of typical small streams in Michigan make the open-face models not as practical), but others prefer the short fly-rod (about seven feet) or cane pole. Use light line in two- or four-pound test and a small hook with medium or no shank in size 8 or 10.

I like large leaf worms or night crawlers cut in half. A gob of red worms is good too, especially in the early season. Use no weight, unless the stream is really fast, as weight will cut down on the natural effect of drifting bait. Fish upstream or down, but allow your bait to drift through the pocket water and other likely trout haunts as described above. Move slowly, especially if walking the bank, as trout will spook when they feel tremors from shore fishermen, and try not to cloud up the water, if fishing downstream, any more than is necessary.

Bait fishing is particularly good in early and late season for brookies and browns. In midsummer try yellow grasshoppers, grubs, and crickets, or you might want to turn over rocks in the streams and dig out insect larvae as bait. The best nymphal creatures to use are caddis worms, damselfly nymphs, dragonfly nymphs, stonefly nymphs, and hellgrammites.

When bait fishing I usually fish downstream and point my rod at the bait as it works downstream with the current. This action takes tension from the bait and allows it to work freely.

Night crawlers will take migrating steelheads and brown trout as they move upstream to spawn, but the best natural bait for these species is the spawn sack or single salmon egg.

Spawn sacks can be bought for about $1.50 per dozen, or the enterprising angler can tie his own. Make them about the size of a marble (larger if the stream is dirty), using the commercially prepared netting or a piece of head scarf silk. Tie them up in a tight ball with strong thread and sink a sharkless hook into the sack just below the knot. This is the strongest part of the sack. The juice that runs out will scent the water, but check the spawn bags every few minutes or so and change them when they are ''milked out.''

Steelhead spawn is best as the eggs are smaller than those of the salmon and brown trout and they last longer. Some anglers lay clusters of spawn from fresh-caught steelheads on a rock to dry out in the sun. Then they thread the clusters on a bare hook, but spawn used this way will not last as long as when tied up in a sack.

Throw the spawn sack to a likely looking hole in the river after having weighted the rig with a triangle or bell-shaped

sinker. Some anglers put a swivel about two feet above the spawn bag and just ahead of this attach a barrel sinker or slip sinker. The swivel keeps the sinker from slipping down, and a steelie picking up the bag can't feel the telltale weight.

Another way to fish the spawn sack is to cast quartering across the rod tip right at the bag and, on a tight line, allow the sack to tumble along the bottom. You'll feel the characteristic tap-tap-tap of the spawn sack. Set the hooks hard if the sack stops.

The single salmon egg can be deadly on migrating steelheads and browns. On a shankless hook, thread a single salmon egg with one or two split shot above the hook for weight. Throw a small handful of eggs into the head of a likely looking hole or pool, count to five, and then send your bait into the hole. This method is called "chumming." You can buy commercially prepared salmon eggs that are "extra firm" for stream fishing with this method.

Spin-casting artificials is another excellent method for taking trout. Tiny gold- or copper-colored spoons, flatfish in fly-rod size, and miniature spinners and colorful blades have suckered many a small brookie and brown into slashing strikes. One problem, however, is that these small lures often can't be cast and worked properly in small streams, and they have to be fished much the way that worms and other natural bait are.

One of the best methods for taking steelheads and browns, however, is with artificials. These migrating fish normally don't strike out of hunger but out of aggravation. The key is in getting the lure to the fish and offering it just in front of him again and again. Colorado and Mepps spinners work well this way. Like the spawn sacks, they should be cast quartering across the stream and upstream from the angler. Allow the offering to sink on a tight line and crank slowly, allowing the blades to just turn over. If you've spotted a fish resting in a hole or lying over a bed (in this latter case try for the male, not the female), work the lure to him over and over until he strikes savagely.

This method works equally well for the imitation spawn lures. The Okie Drifter (especially in chartreuse with red spots), Cherry Bobber, Cherry Drifter, Gooey Bob, Egg Drifter, and Spin N Glo come in various sizes and shapes.

Don't overlook plugs for steelheads and browns and even large brook trout. One angler I know consistently catches big brown trout on the Sturgeon River near Wolverine each summer by using Rapalas. He fishes in the dead of night with a floating model tied directly to his line without benefit of swivel. He casts across the river and retrieves slowly, jerking the lure at intervals as though it were an injured bait fish.

It's tough fishing this way, and he loses more fish than he catches because playing them in the open river and netting them alone is difficult. Some of the lunkers I've seen him bring home, though, more than make up for the frustration.

A good steelhead technique using plugs is called the dropback method. This is especially effective on large, unclear streams in the spring like the St. Joseph and Manistee. Find a likely hole where steelheads will be resting and anchor upstream. Using a rubber core sinker or split shot or no weight, depending upon the lure's action, release line and allow the lure to work downstream with the current.

As the deep-working lure enters the hole, hold the line tight with your thumb and let it wiggle for a moment. Then release three or four feet of line and, again, let the lure shimmy in the current. Sometimes steelheads can't resist smashing the tantalizing offering. Fireplugs, River Runts, Tadpollys, Rapalas, and small Ping-a-Ts work well with this method.

Fly-fishing for trout is a completely different method and possibly the most effective. It involves a balanced rod and reel, a stream large enough to backcast without getting tangled in the brush, and intimate knowledge of a trout's eating habits. Dry flies that resemble the adult insects native to the stream are used with a floating line and fine leader. Or streamers that resemble nymphs or other emerging larvae or small minnows are tied to fine leaders attached to sinking fly lines. Both techniques work well depending upon what the trout happen to be eating at the moment in that stream.

Some anglers open the stomach of their first-caught trout to determine what the fish are feeding upon. The fisherman then attempts to match the fare with an artificial.

Another form of fly-fishing is for migrating steelheads. With this method the angler does not attempt to match the steelie's food. He simply uses a bright-colored fly or piece of yarn, weights it with split shot, and then works it repeatedly just in front of a bedding steelhead. Dazzled by the fly dancing in front of him over and over, the steelie eventually rushes at the lure. Two anglers double-teaming such fish often can get a strike in a couple of minutes.

The beginning and experienced trout angler should consider some of the fine literature available on this subject. There is always something new to learn about trout fishing, and new books are coming off the market each year.

One popular volume is Dave Richey's "Steelheading for Everybody" (Stackpole). A highly touted outdoor writer and Michigan river guide, Richey tells the complete how-to and where-to story on catching Michigan steelheads. This book is a must for all steelheaders.

Peter Barrett's "In Search of Trout" (Prentice-Hall) is primarily on fly-fishing but also contains much useful information on bait-fishing for trout. Another must book for fly fishermen is Joe Brooks' "Fly Fishing" (Outdoor Life). Former fishing editor of **Outdoor Life**, Brooks was a world renowned trout fisherman until his death a few years ago. "Trout Fishing" (Harper & Row) written by Brooks is also a fine addition to any trout fisherman's library.

Nighttime brown-trout anglers will want to read Jim Bashline's "Night Fishing for Trout" (Freshet Press). An expert on this subject, Bashline discusses methods of presentation, flies, wading at night, trout feeding habits, and tackle selection.

One of the best overall books on trout fishing is "Trout Fishermens Digest" (Digest Books), edited by Richey. It includes 50 contributing authors and covers every known facet of the sport. From picking out rods and reels for fly-fishing, bait-casting, or spin-casting to special trout tactics, this book tells it all. Some of the chapters include: "How To Read a Trout Stream," "Backwoods Beaver Pond Brookies," "Bait Fishing for Stream Trout," and "How to Choose Proper Fly Tackle."

If you like good literature along with basic trout-fishing facts, be sure to include Robert Traver's "Trout Magic" and "Trout Madness" in your library. These books, published by Crown, are full of gentle humor and amusing anecdotes of Upper Peninsula trout fishing, told by the author of "Anatomy of a Murder" who also is the author of the foreword of this book.

Read some of the materials described to improve your trout-fishing techniques. Glean from all possible sources everything you can about this exciting sport and these remarkable game fish. Michigan trout fishing has never been better, and anglers shouldn't miss the tremendous opportunity now offered.

DRIFT-BOATING FOR STEELHEADS
By MIKE GNATKOWSKI

There is more than one way to catch a steelhead in Michigan. Members of the steelheading legion include bottom-bouncers, light-liners, fly advocates, hardware specialists, drop-back trollers, and bobber addicts, to name a few. All of these techniques take their share of fish. But without a doubt the most exciting and enjoyable method of doing battle with these silver bullets is from the business end of a McKenzie drift boat.

Before I risk being drowned next time on the river, I should say that I had my own personal doubts about what could be more thrilling or awesome than tangling with Mr. Steelhead armed with a long, limber rod and hair-thin monofilament. Friend and river guide Joe Schwind assured me that one trip in his West-Coast-style drift boat would convince me that drift fishing is the number one method for battling Michigan's number one game fish. He was right.

The new year was barely a day old when we hit the launch site near Croton Dam on the Muskegon River. Joe had invited Ron Gloss to accompany us on my maiden voyage. While we strung the rods and readied other essentials for the drift trip, Joe filled me in on the history of the drift boat.

Its origin can be traced to the New England Coast where North Atlantic cod fishermen devised the first functional facsimile commonly referred to as a bank dory. When the pioneers began settling the Pacific Northwest and discovered the tremendous salmon runs which the region was once famous for, they thought about the stable, seaworthy dories of New England. The transplanted dories proved to be the perfect craft for cutting the onshore breakers to reach the salmon runs. As time went on, the need for a stable craft for running the treacherous whitewater rivers arose and the result was the drift boat as we know it today. With the passing of time, the West Coast ocean dories were redesigned and modified from a deep, full displacement hull to a wide, shallow displacement hull, with a flat bottom for running rocky, white-water rivers. Further modifications were made by increasing the rocker or upward curve fore and aft. The sides were also flared to ward off the crashing waves. All of the early drift boats were constructed of cedar planks.

Credit for the first McKenzie-style river boats and their design is given to two Eugene, Oregon, boat builders, Woody Hindman and Tom Kaarhus, who produced their initial boat around 1939.

Today there are two main classes of drift boats whose hull designs are named after the rivers on which they were used—either the McKenzie or the Rogue, and the Rapid Roberts. Most of the drift boats in use today are of the McKenzie or Rogue style. The Rapid Robertses resemble a huge bathtub characterized by the broad stern, with the pointed bow to the oarsman's back. While the bow of both classes are to the oarsman's back, which would be upstream, the bow of the McKenzie has been squared off to accept a small motor. Only the stern of the McKenzie now remains pointed. Although a few of the wooden models are still in use, fiberglass and aluminum have replaced wood as building materials.

Drift boats have only been on the steelheading scene in Michigan for a short while. With the resurgence of the Great Lakes fishery and the consequent comeback of the lake-run rainbows, it was natural that Michigan anglers take a page from the West Coast steelheader's book and discover the exciting method of fishing from a drift boat called plug-pulling or, more commonly, hot-spotting. Each spring and fall Michigan's rivers are seeing more and more drift boats, and it's no wonder. Drift-fishing has proved to be equally exciting and deadly on Great Lakes steelhead and salmon.

After Joe's briefing, we were ready to begin our float, which would end some eight miles downstream. As we pushed off, the sensation of floating above the water, hanging motionless in the swift currents, was akin to the feelings one gets on his first small airplane ride. Everything goes rushing by as you sit suspended over the swirling surface, and it is the ability of the boat to hold stationary in the conflicting currents which makes the craft the fishing machine that it is.

As we started our drift, Joe pointed out that the technique we were using was similar to the drop-back method made famous by river guide Emil Dean years earlier but with a hitch. Not only does the drift boat allow the angler to gradually drop his lures back to the fish, but the lures can also be swept towards and away from the fish, rather than just dropping the baits straight back. In this way the fish can be antagonized into striking by appealing to their territorial instincts. Or sweeping the lures away may trigger a response that an easy meal is about to get away. Either way, the drift boat has the added advantage of mobility and the ability to cover a lot of water in a day's fishing.

Generally, drift-fishing takes place on Michigan's larger rivers such as the Muskegon, Big Manistee, Au Sable, and St. Joseph, and this points up a problem that many small-stream steelheaders like myself will have on the big rivers—reading the water and picking out fish-holding lies. Joe explained that locating the isolated pockets where steelheads and salmon hold in big water is just a matter of looking at the river on a smaller scale instead of trying to analyze and then fish the entire river. This means looking for the same type of fish-holding structure that you would on any steam. Current-deflecting rocks, protective logjams, calm eddies, deep holes adjacent to riffles, and shelves which break the flow are places to look for big-river steelheads and salmon. With this knowledge in mind, it didn't take long to begin recognizing likely hot spots.

A surprising number of boats were on the river for a blustery January day and it was several bends before Joe decided we had enough room to begin fishing. Ron and I allowed the Daiwa level-wind reels to freespool out about 50 feet of line before engaging the brake and positioning the rods in the holders. The tips of the eight-and-a-half-foot custom-made Sage rods began to pulsate and dance as Joe dug into the current with the oars and the #20 Hotshots and Hot-N-Tots responded with their enticing wobbling and jitterbugging action. Joe pointed out that the rod tips were his key to what the lures are doing, and the minute the rods quite working the lures had either picked up some debris or were hung on bottom, and that was our cue to bring them them in and get them working again.

With the rods working their tantalizing dance, I pointed out a good-sized boulder in midstream that looked particularly "fishy" and Joe responded by sliding the boat sideways, allowing the lures to swing close to the rocky lie.

I had slipped into a state of semidaydream, entranced by the winter beauty of the Muskegon, when Joe roused me from my mental lapse with a call to action, "Fish on!" The No. 2 rod was bucking and creaking under the strain of a tail-walking steelie that was trying to rid itself of the Hotshot firmly notched in the hinge of its jaw. Before long, the leverage of the powerful but limber rod turned the tables and the quarry lay exhausted on the surface where Ron deftly scooped up the prize.

Joe seemed disappointed by the smaller-than-average three-pounder and indicated that as a general rule steelies caught while drifting with plugs run much larger, but I didn't care. The first steelhead of the year is always a special fish, one that is remembered months later, regardless of size. And besides, the silvery rainbow was just right for the table.

While the battle was going on, Joe had maintained our position upstream of the rock and I hurriedly sent the wiggling chartreuse-and-orange Hotshot back out into the strike zone. Joe proceeded to let the drift boat slip-slide down the edge of the run coming off the right-hand side of the rock this time. The rods had just begun the rhythmic quivering when the same rod directly in front of me shuddered and then arced into a reverse downrigger position, and the steelie was cavorting downstream before I could free the contorted rod from the holder. Constant bulldogging and short but powerful runs made for some anxious moments before a hook-jawed mate to our first fish was added to the box. Two winter steelheads in less than a half-hour is fantastic fishing any time, any way you do it, but doing it from the warm, comfortable seat of a drift boat makes it all that much more enjoyable and rewarding.

Successful drift-boat fishing requires some teamwork when it comes to putting fish in the cooler. Anglers manning the rods in the two seats in the bow of the boat are responsible for making sure the baits are performing their tantalizing dance. Should the rods "go dead" it is the bow-positioned angler's chore to quickly retrieve the fouled lure and remove any "salad" or debris inhibiting the bait's action and then to get the lure back in the water. Once one of the rods slaps down under the pressure of an enraged steelhead or salmon, the angler closest to the bucking rod must free it from the holder with an up-and-out motion. The next move is to stand and get the rod high and then determine the direction the battle is taking so the other fisherman can clear the remaining lines according to which side of the boat the fish is on. As the fight progresses, the fishless angler readies the net at the side of the boat where the spent trophy can be brought into the mesh with a steady, even sweep of the rod.

Slugging it out with powerful steelies and salmon from a drift boat has many advantages and few drawbacks. One distinct plus of the drift tactics is that anglers can get away with heavier line than when using conventional stream rigs without sacrificing strikes. This is because as the lures are dropped back through the run or hole the first thing the fish sees is the bait and not the line as its sweeps past. Generally, 10- to 14-pound line is the standard and the stronger mono is an advantage when tangling with these wild fighters. A high-abrasive line such as Maxima or Trilene XT is preferred.

The mobility of the drift boat is an added plus when a fish streaks off on a 100-yard run and you have to be in hot pursuit or risk losing the fish. Time wasted pulling the anchor or fiddling with balky motors results in plenty of lost fish, and the responsiveness and maneuverability of a drift boat can put you in the best position for fighting and landing big fish. Sharp hooks and the correct drag setting are little things that will go a long way towards improving your fish-hooked versus fish-landed ratio.

While the anglers in the front of the boat enjoy the thrill of fish brought to net or disappointment over broken lines or hooks that pulled free, it is the man on the oars, the "stickman," who must be given credit for battles won and lost. Without his stream-reading savvy and ability to work the boat near prime lies, there would not be any hookups to rejoice or cry over.

Joe Schwind is a master at reading the water, sorting prospective hot spots, and then "ferrying" the drift boat back and forth across the stream to secluded pockets where he "feathers" and works the oars against the currents, giving the lures the enticing wiggling action that drives the anadromous species crazy. Besides his stream knowledge, Joe is a stickler for details such as good, strong knots, fresh line, and a good selection of baits. Two of his most productive drift-boat baits are the #20 Hotshot and the one-half-ounce size Hot-N-Tot in gold, silver, and chartreuse. Other deep-diving crankers such as Tadpollies and Wiggler Warts can trigger explosive strikes. In fact, just about any bait that dives deep and shakes up a storm will produce at one time or another.

Because the lures used for drifting require the force of the current to start them dancing, the best drift-fishing takes place when water is being released from upstream dams or rains or melting snow raise river levels and result in stronger-than-normal flows. Besides supplying the necessary current, the higher water stimulates feeding and fish will move into the edges of runs and tails of holes where they can intercept dislodged morsels. Steelheads and salmon are also less spooky when the river is high and discolored and can be approached more easily. The heavier flows also bring fish out of hiding from under blowdowns, logjams, and other "trash," as drift fishermen call it, to holds where they can see your baits and you can keep lost lures to a minimum.

Because prime drift-boat time is when conditions are less than ideal—i.e., high, off-colored water—fishing from one can add days to our fishing season. Winter fishing which requires wading can be a frigid, if not downright dangerous, affair. But from the comfort and safety of a drift boat and with the help of a small, portable heater, winter fishing is not only bearable, but a heck of a lot of fun. The rushing torrents brought on by spring thaws and fall downpours are cussed by wading fisherman and called a blessing by drifters.

December rains had answered our prayers by bringing in fresh runs of bright fish to complement the darker holdovers from the fall salmon run, and even though January's frosty nights had chilled the Muskegon, the fish were still aggressive and willing, as our initial action could attest.

Ron and I were just giving some thought to firing up the heater when Joe started slowly easing the boat through a swift waist-deep run flanked by calmer, swirling eddy. A stately cedar sweeper provided overhead cover near the middle of the run. The spot nearly shouted "**Steelhead!**" Right on cue, one of Ron's rods doubled over and it was all he could do to free the buckled rod from the holder and hang on for dear life as the steelie charged off on a freight-train-like tear. The icy-cold water prevented the brute from clearing the surface and the fish relied on strength rather than acrobatics. Ron played the prize gingerly, handling it with kid gloves before I could slip the mesh under the exhaused steelhead. The fish, a beautiful 11-pound hen, was just taking on its winter colors and the gill plate reflected a rainbow of purples and blues, complementing the faint pink slash dissecting its chrome flanks.

About the only things that could rival the natural beauty and awesome coloring of winter steelheads are the breath-taking scenes encountered while floating Michigan rivers. Fall's radiant crimsons and ambers provide a startling backdrop for battling the tackle-busting chinooks and cohos. Wintering turkeys scratching for acorns on a melting slope and transient goldeneyes whistling overhead are common sights on winter forays. The incessant hammering of pileated woodpeckers and the frenzied drumming of grouse have a way of intensifying the thrill of stalking steelies on the beds in spring. Unlike Great Lakes trolling, where the seascape can sometimes prove to be boring, each bend in the river reveals something different—be it flora or fauna. And that seems to be what makes drifting more than just a fishin' trip.

By day's end the wintery landscape and wildlife gracing the banks of the icy Muskegon had cured any tinges of cabin fever Ron and I might have had. Joe added the real topper by enticing 18 different steelheads into smacking our plugs and the thrills

and memories provided by a limit of steelies would go a long way toward pacifying our fishing appetites until winter melted into spring.

Although a drift-boat excursion is the perfect way to shake the winter doldrums, fall and spring provide better fishing, depending on the species you're after. Anglers planning a drift trip can count on salmon action in September through early November. Steelheads begin making an appearance in October and continue plentiful as long as the river and access points remain open. March finds fresh runs of spawning steelies entering the rivers, and fishing remains excellent for them into May.

Anglers wishing to experience a drift trip while foregoing the $2,000 investment in boat and equipment can contact Joe Schwind, 4189 Meadow Brook, Freeland, Mich. 48623 (517/781-4925), or Gnat's River Charters, 6934 West Illinois St., Ludington, Mich. 49341 (616/845-1158).

Drift-fishing has got to be the most exciting and innovative method for tangling with Great Lakes trout and salmon, bar none. Yet there are still those die-hards who refuse to try anything except the tried-and-true. But I'd be willing to place a small wager that one trip down the river in a drift boat and you might be convinced into swapping your waders for a pair of oars.

NIGHT FISHING FOR TROUT

By GREG BOLAK

"Looks like an omen," I thought as I carefully picked the mayfly off my shirt. The delicate wings and gracefully curved body rested in my hand. I flipped the Isonychia spinner into the breeze coming off Grand Traverse Bay. "Let's see," I mused, "20 minutes back to the cottage and another 20 minutes to grab the gear and drive to the river. It's after 8 now." I estimated that I'd be on the river by 9 o'clock.

The ride home was quick and the ride to the river was even quicker. I remember Tom White's words from the other day, "Try for the big brown near the birch slanted over the water. It broke me off twice this year." The sun had set and darkness was enveloping the path. It was still early, but good fish began to work the first pool before dark. I had timed it just right.

The Boardman flowed clear and swift, barely discolored from the afternoon rains. The pool was long, ending in a narrow gravel run with high banks on both sides of the river. There was a splash across the stream, just before the flat water gave way to the riffles. I lost one fish that would easily have gone over two pounds here. It smashed a nymph on the first cast and cleared the water by a good two feet. Would I really have set the hook better if it weren't the first cast? No sense rationalizing now; it's another night.

I false-cast parallel to my bank and made a change of direction to shoot the Tellico to the far rocky bank. A strike if coming would take place as the fly began its swing toward the surface. Not very traditional, probably better for streamer fishing, but it works. Two, three times I repeated the cast and finally felt a jolt. Not the fish I was hoping for, but a 12-inch brown is better than a log.

Darkness came quickly as I worked downstream. A bit after 10, fish started working along the banks. Unfortunately, this meant options. Should I put on a big dry and fish the water, try to match the hatch, or play the percentages? I decided on the latter as I tied on a Muddler. Cast and quarter. It worked for many years and I hoped it would tonight.

I waited only minutes for results. As the fly began to drag, it was intercepted by a brown 14 inches long, fat and colorful.

Slow and cautious wading brought me to a deep pool that washed up to a long shallow gravel area. I knew a good fish was along the opposite shore since I spooked it a couple days earlier. The Muddler cut a wake across the pool and stopped a foot from the gravel. The rod curved deep to absorb the strike, and I hoped that leaving on the 4X tippet wasn't one of my bigger mistakes. That loud splash in the darkness was connected to the fly, to the leader, to fly line, to rod, to me. Again a heavy splash and silver droplets glistening in the moonlight. A run toward the bank was snubbed and the fish sped across the riffle. The Hardy buzzed its resistance more than once. Back to the pool, back to the gravel, but the runs had become shorter. The fish was close and pretty well spent.

Now for the net. "Great," I thought "I've got the net, now if I could see the fish, I'd be all set." But the fish was netted all right, all 16 inches of it. It was admired and released.

A couple 10-inchers were caught before the big one struck. I knew it was a dandy because it felt as though I had hooked the bumper of a logging truck going downhill. Its first jump and landing sounded like a small tree falling into the water. For once, I'd like to lie and say I caught it, but I'm too worried about repercussions of the fish gods. It got away like a few others past and probably a few others to come. But it's anticipation like this that brings us back to stalk trout in the dark of the night.

Night fishing is not a panacea for waning hatches or fishless days. It is another option in the fly fisherman's repertoire, and what an option it can be! I remember leading my father-in-law down a stretch of river with my fly line dragging downstream of us. In the hundred-foot stretch I helped him through, three out of the six fish that struck were landed. There was a brown on the Manistee that almost took my rod. I was holding it very loosely and I'm glad that my finger got caught between the reel and the reel seat. You can ask Tom White about a certain stretch of a certain river where in 45 minutes he caught and released 20 fish from 12 to 14 inches and then stopped counting. The South Branch is filled with legends of huge browns. I believe that if I put in my time a 20-incher will eventually come to net. Big trout are nocturnal, so it may be wise to fish for them on their schedule.

How do you begin night stalking? First, wade the stretch you plan to fish at least once and preferably more times during the day before venturing out after dark. If you never believe anything you read, believe this.

Here's an example. Tom and I stopped at Bob Summer's and he mentioned a bridge-to-bridge stretch of water that was productive. We neglected to mention that we'd be fishing at night. I began by ripping my waders and wading semiwet for close to four hours. About two hours after dark (after Tom and I split up), I came to a big gravel bar, so big that it looked like the shore of a lake. Strange things happen at night. I thought I missed a fork in the river and ended up on a lake.

I began to contemplate building a fire and sitting it out until morning. There was a current and I followed it. Hey, I thought, with a little luck I could be down in Grand Traverse Bay by 9 the next morning. Pressing on for another hour brought waist deep fast water and incredible pools. The banks were so brush-choked that they were impenetrable. Finally a house came into sight and that meant a road out. Unfortunately, sounds like those from a Vincent Price movie echoed in the night. "I'm not going past any place where they lock up crazy people, or torture trespassers, no matter what," I said to myself.

I then saw the oil rig on the opposite bank. I went downstream a bit to cross, but the water only got deeper. Then I saw the trestle. The banks were too steep and brush-filled to climb on my side, so I grabbed the rails. If you have never gone hand-over-hand across a bridge with a full tackle vest and a couple of gallons of water in your waders, you aren't missing anything.

I found Tom, who was cursing a hole deeper than his eight-foot rod. The doctor in him spoke, "You can get hypothermia when you're that wet and it's this cold."

I looked at him, lay on my back, and let the water rush out of my waders. "Let's get back to the cottage and Grand Marnier," I said. We caught nothing that night, but I think I made my point about unexplored stretches at night.

One of the most important aspects of fishing after dark is safety. Those stretches that are simple during the day pose hazards to self and tackle. To overcome these obstacles, several things should be done.

Waders should definitely have felt soles. The added traction is not only a blessing but a necessity. If you have those with the inflatable chamber, so much the better. A wading belt will keep the water out but can pose severe problems if you are swept up in the current.

Lights should be carried, and I always carry two. One is the flex-light used for tying on flies and the second is a small disposable one with a bigger beam. Check the batteries on both before you go out.

Insect repellent is also a must, and one that doesn't come off when you sweat is the most effective. Don't forget a hat; it's better to have those little creatures that fall from the trees bounce off it rather than get tangled in your hair, especially if you are not really sure what is crawling around up there.

While in the stream think before you move. Wade sideways to lessen your resistance to the current. Always be sure of your balance and slowly use your foot to probe before making a step. Remember, you can't see that log or rock the way you did during the day. Under most circumstances, stay away from the outside bends of streams. It is here that the current does its damage. I have waded many stretches where the current on an outside bend was easily four feet deeper than the water opposite it. Don't take chances. If you think that the water may be too fast, too deep, or the bottom too mucky, chances are you're right.

Many anglers I've talked with don't care to night-fish because they can't see their flies. This is a valid point. You are fishing the water near cover but by feel. An advantage is that you will have fish that will move out from cover a bit and you can get extremely close to rising fish. With an eight- to nine-foot rod, you can just about dap for some fish. I've talked to anglers who have fished the Hex hatch and experienced fish rising three feet away.

To keep out of trees and bushes you should fish with the same amount of line out on each cast and move yourself rather than stripping out more line or shooting line. I also have found it effective to tie my flies with stiff and a bit oversize hackle that can serve as a weed guard. On my Muddlers I tie the bottom deer hair in such a way that it will deflect off logs or branches.

Presentation methods vary when fishing at night. Staking out an area where you know there are big fish is a common technique. For those of you who enjoy waiting, go right ahead. I know of anglers who arrive at a spot as early as 5 in the evening during the Hex hatch to "claim" it for when the fish start to rise. This gives you plenty of time to consider every angle and drift.

Another technique is to fish upstream using a short line. As you spot rising fish, you cast to them. If the fish seems large, spend time with a cast-drift, cast-drift procedure. At times you may spend quite a bit of time on one fish, but it could very well be worth the time.

In either type of fishing, see if there is a rhythm to the feeding and time your cast accordingly. These techniques are especially effective during the Hex hatch but can be used with large flies throughout the season.

The last technique is the one I use most frequently. Since I seldom hit the hatches of large mayflies and the majority of my fishing is done from mid-July through August, I have had to adapt. I needed a technique that could be used effectively while covering as much water as quickly as possible. I have used the above techniques, but the vast majority of my outings find me fishing wet. At about dusk I'll use a streamer to imitate either brown or brook trout as well as large nymphs, the Tellico or Yellow Stone being, for me, the most effective. When darkness comes, on goes the Muddler. You can fish it dry, just under the surface, subsurface, or in any combination. The cast is made directly across stream from my position and allowed to swing directly below me. Most strikes come midway through the drift. This method is so simple and so effective that it still amazes me. Two things must be remembered when using this technique—one, always cast as close as practical near fish holding cover and, two, allow the fly to complete its swing.

On the nights when I hurry the retrieve I am not as successful as on those when I allow the current to do the work. Aside from log jams and holes, you should fish shallow gravel areas nearby. Sculpins and crayfish are abundant here at night. One fish that I kept was autopsied and found to have three three-inch crayfish in its stomach. You may want to dig around the debris before you start fishing. You'll be surprised at what you find.

A few last notes that should be considered. Go with a minimum of 4X tippet. I prefer 3X under most circumstances. Keep your rod tip up to absorb the shock of the strike. Carry a net with a good-size opening. When landing your fish, you have to make a decision. Will you do it in pitch dark and risk knocking it off or will you turn on the lens light and possibly spook it into a fearful run? I try never to shine a light on the waters I plan to fish when changing flies, but if I think the fish is played out, I feel it's better to be sure to get the net around the fish than the fish under, over, or on the net. That decision I'll leave up to you.

Fishing at night is exciting and addicting. It may give you a chance at a fish too difficult to take during the day or to latch on to one of those big nocturnal feeders so often heard about.

If you have any apprehension of the dark, try uttering this little prayer (the origin of which I have forgotten):

From ghosties and ghoulies,
And long leggedy beasties,
And things that go bump in the night,
Good Lord deliver us.

THE CHOCOLAY RIVER
By JANET D. MEHL

The Chocolay River is one of the Upper Peninsula's most scenic and prolific rivers, offering a variety of excellent trout-fishing opportunities. It is also one of the Upper Peninsula's most popular rivers, crossed by US-41 and M-28, and flows into Lake Superior at the community of Harvey four miles southeast of Marquette. The largely undeveloped system offers fine fishing for all three species of trout all season plus runs of steelheads, coho and chinook salmon, anadromous browns, and a few "coasters" or lake-run brook trout. Several cold, bubbly, spawning tributaries flow into the river, one of which is the site of the Marquette State Fish Hatchery and Research Station.

The East and West branches of the Chocolay join to form the mainstream near Skandia. Silver Lead Creek draining Stump Lake flows through the K.I. Sawyer Air Force Base to the headwaters of the West Branch northeast of Gwinn. The West Branch is a rather remote, gurgling brook trout stream, part of which is accessible only by foot trails. John Driver, Marquette hatchery supervisor, said the adverturesome angler willing to walk a mile or two for small stream fishing would be surprised by the size and number of chunky brookies in the West Branch. Its sparkling water spills over a small bedrock cliff—Frohling Falls—about two miles below its origin, forming a natural barrier to migrating steelheads. The West Branch is quite small, 20 to 25 feet wide at the mouth, six to 24 inches deep with three- and four-foot pools, and ripples over a bottom which alternates between sand, gravel, and rock. Brush, log jams, undercut banks, rocks, and pools provide good cover. It is accessible from County Road 545.

The East Branch arises near Carlshend and flows northerly to Skandia. It is much like the West Branch—a good brook trout stream—but smaller, about 15 to 20 feet wide at the mouth. It ripples from pool to pool although cover is not as abundant as it is in the West Branch. About midway through its course, the East Branch takes a 10-foot plunge over rock—the Upper Chocolay Falls. Access is available from County Road 545 and from two small tracts of state land below the falls.

The two branches converge into the narrow mainstream channel which is about 35 feet wide, creating a large, deep pool. The gradient is steep and the current is very swift, rushing over rock, gravel, and sand bottom to US-41. This is an excellent stretch in which to fill a creel with brookies, browns, and an occasional rainbow. The banks are almost entirely undeveloped, forested with elm, poplar, and hardwoods. The stretch is accessible from US-41 and from state land adjacent to the jog in Backman Road (Section 14).

Below Yalmar (US-41), brown trout become the dominant species, closely followed by brook trout and then small rainbows. The stretch of river between Yalmar and Green Garden Hill Road (the next road crossing the river downstream) is a favorite among many anglers due to the variety of trout available, the trophy brown trout found in the deep pools and log jams near Green Garden Hill Road, and the picturesque environs.

Mike Anderegg of Marquette, an avid Chocolay River fisherman, said many brook, brown, and rainbow trout are taken from the rapids between US-41 and Green Garden Hill Road, his favorite stretch. He suggested parking at Green Garden Hill Road and walking down the railroad tracks about one-and-a-half miles to the wide bends approaching the tracks. The wide bends create deep pools holding big fish and flow through state-owned land. A lone cabin known to locals as Jack's Camp sits on a bluff near the tracks overlooking the river. An angler might also drive one mile north on Camp 4 Road (located one-and-a-half miles east of Yalmar), park on the state land there, and walk down the railroad tracks about one-half mile to the bends. Access is also available at US-41 and at public fishing easements near the mouths of Foster and O'Neil creeks.

Anderegg said there are pools below US-41 which are too deep to wade while the river channel remains quite narrow. Below Jack's Camp the river straightens for a mile or so before gliding through several wide, sweeping bends again near the mouths of Foster and O'Neil creeks.

Below Green Garden Hill Road the gradient decreases and the current slows. Many hefty brown trout are taken from here to the railroad testle below Mangum Road, but it is a difficult area to fish. Portions of the stretch are too deep to wade, but the river banks are generally high, often too high for an angler to climb out of the river, Anderegg said. Below Mangum Road the river flows through state land to the tráin trestle, is deeper, and contains many log jams. Not far below the trestle, the river enters a cedar jungle, splitting into several narrow channels which creep through the darkness of the cedars for about one mile to the Lake Kawbawgam outlet. Driver warned against trying to canoe these "spreads" as it is impossible to determine which channel is the main river and most canoeists become lost. He suggested the stretch between US-41 and Mangum Road for a pleasant canoe trek.

LeVasseur Creek is a lengthy tributary and flows largely through state land but is too warm to be trout water. The Lake LeVasseur wildlife flooding is impounded just above Lake Kawbawgam. Both contain warmwater fish.

Below the Lake Kawbawgam outlet, the river is slow and deep with a sand and mud bottom. Big resident browns are taken from the exceptionally cold water, particularly near Beaver Grove Road leading north from County Road 480 just east of US-41. The river is 50 to 60 feet wide with pools up to 10 feet deep. Several swift, crystal-clear, spawning tributaries enter the river, particularly Big, Cedar, Cherry, and Silver creeks. Their bottoms are primarily sand and host hundreds of spawning steelheads, lake-run browns, and coho and chinook salmon in addition to resident brook, brown, and rainbow trout. The creeks offer excellent fishing during the summer for browns, the dominant species, and rainbows, many of which will become steelheads. Cherry Creek, the site of the hatchery, has as great a flow as Big Creek—10,000 gallons per minute of 20cfs, Driver said. The tributaries increase the flow of the mainstream by 50 percent, creating a powerful attraction for anadromous fish.

Spring steelhead runs peak about May 1. The runs are believed to be increasing due to the removal of lamprey-control weir in the late 1970s, allowing all anadromous fish access to much more spawning gravel in the upper river. Ten thousand steelheads were planted in the Chocolay in 1980. Salmon runs are excellent. Most anglers fish the lower river with boat and outboard motors, launching from the public fishing site at M-28 and fishing downstream to either the Harvey Marina or the township park one-half mile above the mouth. Steelheads are caught in the river all winter, especially during thaws.

Since natural reproduction in the river is very good, plantings are generally not made. Jerry Peterson, fisheries biologist at the DNR's Escanaba office, said brook trout were planted in the river until 1964. During the 1950s, the DNR began planting brown trout in the previously all-brook-trout stream until they were well established. In 1976, 9,000 Atlantic salmon were planted in the Chocolay, the only Lake Superior tributary in Michigan to receive Atlantics, but the plant was considered a failure. Splake were planted in the mouth of the river in 1981. Summer

steelheads (14,000 per year) have been introduced since 1985. Results to date have been very favorable both in Marquette Bay and in the Chocolay River. The hundreds of thousands of lake trout, brown trout, coho and chinook salmon, and steelheads planted in Marquette Bay have a direct influence on anadromous runs in the Chocolay.

Streamer flies (Royal Coachman, Muddler Minnow, Spruce fly), spinners, and spawn are commonly used to fish the Chocolay. Mark Trotochaud, Jr., of Marquette has fished the river regularly for about 25 years using these lures. In May 1981 he caught a six-pound brown below US-41 and has taken a few coasters weighing up to two-and-a-half pounds.

The Chocolay also hosts some good fly hatches, particularly in June and July. There is a variety of caddis and smaller mayfly hatches such as the Hendrickson. Others include the Light Cahill, Blue-winged Olives, March Brown, and Quill Gordon. Don Beaudoin of Marquette, a loyal Chocolay River fly fisherman, said March Brown hatches occur in June between 10 and 2 during the day, with spinner falls at night. Hatches of Tiny White-winged Blacks and most drakes are nearly nonexistent. Hatches of **Hexagenia limbata** on the lower river are very poor.   □

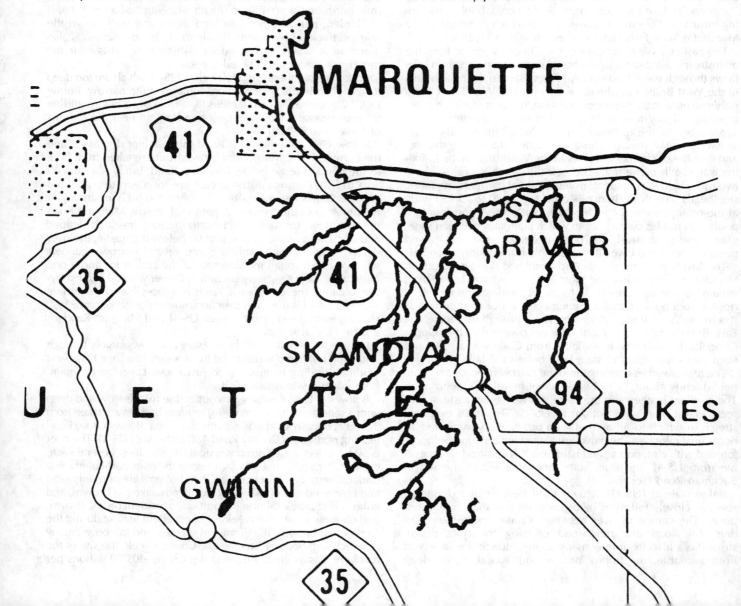

THE OTTER RIVER
By RAYMOND P. JUETTEN
Fisheries Biologist

The Main Branch of the Otter River begins at the confluence of its North and West branches (its major tributaries) near the Houghton-Baraga county line northwest of Pelkie.

The 40- to 60-foot- wide stream flows northeasterly across a glacial flood plain (used for forestry and farming) to Otter Lake in Houghton County. The banks, although quite eroded in some areas, are lined with grasses, evergreens, and broad-leaf trees. The bottom is hard sand, and there are many deep pools with limited cover.

There are very few resident trout in the Main Branch, and the stream's popularity stems from its fine spring and fall steelhead runs. This is the only area of the Otter River system open to the special extended trout and salmon season. Anglers successfully use spawn bags as bait in the spring, whereas minnows, night crawlers, and artificial lures provide the best results in the fall.

The average size of the steelheads running the Otter is three to five pounds; however, local residents claim a few steelheads in the 10- to 12-pound class are taken here annually. These fish spawn in the North and West branches. The primary factor limiting trout production in the Otter River is the occasional severe spring floodings, which cause stream-bank erosion and channel degradation.

Many canoeists use this stream during the summer months. Its moderate flow is ideal for beginners. The maple, aspen, and balsam forests and farm fields to either side are picturesque, and many people picnic along the river.

The North Branch rises from swamp seepage in southeast Houghton County. This gentle, clear-water stream flows southerly across a glacial flood plain until it joins the Main Branch 2½ miles northwest of Pelkie. Forest is the primary land use on this floodplain, but there are some farms southwest of Tapiola.

The North Branch receives a fine steelhead run each spring and anglers concentrate their efforts downstream from the bridge on the Donken-Tapiola Road. The river has a sand bottom in this area and is 30-40 feet wide. Pools are abundant, and the banks are lined with tag alder and grasses.

Upstream from the Donken-Tapiola Road bridge, hardwoods and evergreens border the North Branch. It is 15-30 feet wide here and has extensive areas of gravel riffles and many deep, fast pools.

Brook trout and small rainbows abound in this area. There is a small population of browns here too.

Most of the brook trout come from the cold-water tributaries, namely the Little Otter River, Slates Creek, Sante River, Bart Creek, and Ebers Creek. These streams are five to 10 feet wide and have extensive spawning riffles. Most receive little fishing pressure although some limit catches of brook trout are taken on the Sante River.

Many county roads cross the North Branch, making it easily accessible and although most land bordering the stream is

privately owned it is not posted, and most landowners allow fishermen to cross their lands.

The North Branch from the mouth of Slates Creek downstream is open enough for fly fishing and can be waded. Fair hatches occur; however, area anglers are mostly bait fishermen. Limit catches of eight- to 12-inch brook trout are quite common, and occasionally a 16-inch brookie is caught.

The West Branch of the Otter River rises from several small, unnamed ponds and swamp seepage in southwest Houghton County, west of Nisula. The headwaters above Otter Siding Road are lined with tag alder and the stream flows across a waving plateau of mixed hardwood and evergreen forests mixed with swamps. The rest of the stream flows through hilly forestland. Most of the stream border is in state ownership.

Vehicular access is quite limited, but the upper section can be reached via the Otter Siding Road off M-38, two miles west of Nisula.

The Pike Lake Road crosses the stream two miles north of Nisula, and the Limestone Mountain Road crosses the stream about 2½ miles northwest of Pelkie.

The picturesque stream, which flows through a semi-wilderness area, has a moderate flow, very clear water, and is 15-40 feet wide. The upper limits feature an abundance of pools and cover. On the other hand, the lower stream has little cover, numerous pools, and extensive riffle areas, many of which are suitable trout-spawning areas. The banks downstream from the Pike Lake Road are 200-300 feet high in places. Because the soils are clay-sand variety, the stream becomes quite clouded after a rainfall.

The odd steelhead is taken here, but the West Branch supports a fair brook-trout fishery too. The best brook trout fishing is found downstream from the Pike Lake Road. There are caddis hatches on the stream although most of it makes for tough fly fishing. Local anglers mostly fish bait and because of the clarity of the water they are most successful during and after periods of rainfall and high water. Brook trout up to 10 inches are common here, and a few up to 14 inches are caught.

Bruno Creek, Lake Fifteen Creek, and the outlet of Pike Lake are the main tributaries to the West Branch and all have extensive areas of spawning riffles and abundant cover for young trout. Some legal-sized brook trout also inhabit these streams, but due to limited access and overabundant cover they receive little fishing pressure.

The Otter River is the only known Upper Peninsula stream to be once inhabited by the Michigan grayling, and this was the last stream in the state to contain grayling.

Fred Kroll, a fur buyer, discovered grayling in the Otter in 1884, and local Indians told him these fish were river herring. In later years they were called bastard whitefish by lumberjacks.

In 1914 the Michigan Fish Commission stocked 25,000 grayling fry in the Otter. The results of the 1914 plant could not be determined, however, and this last attempt at artificial propagation failed.

Walter Erickson, a lifelong resident of the Otter River Valley, mentioned, ''They sort of floated up to a fly, delicately dimpled the water in taking the fly and when hooked they raced nearly on the surface, downstream.'' The largest grayling he took was 19 inches, but most averaged 10 to 12 inches. In 1934 he took his last grayling from the North Branch. The fish was 11 inches and he caught it several times that summer before finally keeping it.

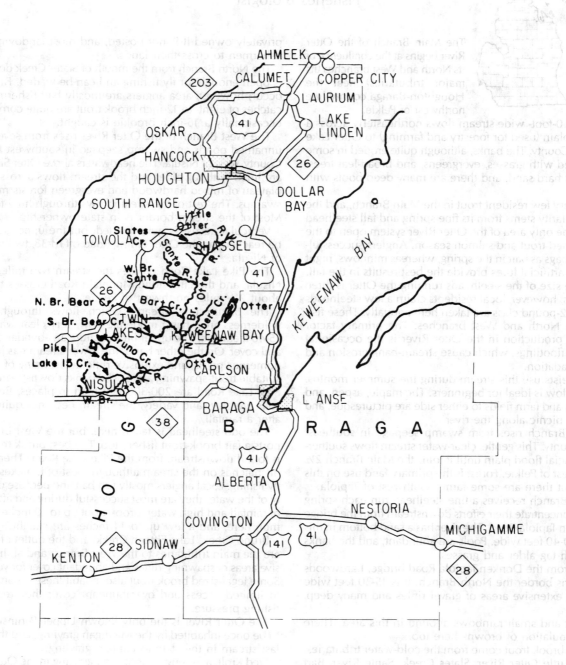

THE PAINT RIVER

By DELL SILVER
Fisheries Biologist

The Paint River is the dominant river system in Iron County. It has been of prime importance to the area since the first explorers arrived about 1840. It was first used by exploring trappers and traders and then by loggers, to whom it was so essential. Presently it is used as a source of electrical power.

The name Paint is derived from the Ojibway word "Miskua," meaning "it is red," and this evolved to Paint. The red color is actually a rusty brown which the river picks up from the many lowland areas that it drains.

The mainstream of the Paint is formed by two branches approximately equal in size, the North Branch and the South Branch. These two streams flow easterly through Ottawa National Forest and then join to form the mainstream near Gibbs City. The mainstream continues southeast until it meets the Brule and the Michigamme rivers, amid a mass of power dams and big water, to form the Menominee.

The most commonly accepted origin of the North Branch is the spring which drains into the head of Mallard Lake impoundment. The stream flowing from Mallard Lake dam tumbles over rocks and boulders for a mile or so before it takes on the characteristic slow, quiet flow of the upper North Branch.

The remains of a rustic sluicing dam dating back to the "pine days" are visible from the USFS Road 362 crossing. Thirty-Three Creek joins the North Branch about a mile and a half below Mallard Lake. It is a slow-moving silt and sand bottom creek that abounds with beaver dams and brook trout. The entire North Branch is primarily a brook trout stream in contrast to the South Branch, where browns are quite common.

The brown waters of the North Branch are then strengthened by a second sizable tributary, Paint Creek, a fast-flowing stream. For the next seven or eight miles the North Branch flows east through low-lying wild country. The bottom type is largely sand and silt with a few scattered rocky areas. Beds of tape grass are common in the silted areas. Lowland conifers and tag alder line the shore. The river starts to change character gradually below USFS Road 147.

The bottom type becomes increasingly rocky here and the gradient increases. In 1989, in a 1,200-foot section here, sky hook beam covers were installed to increase available cover and holding capacity. The river turns south in the area of Stump Creek and broadens out considerably. Long, straight, shallow stretches of slow water broken occasionally by narrow gravel ledges appear unproductive, but brook trout are quite numerous along the tag alder edges and at the foot of the gravel ledges until early June when warming temperatures cause the trout to seek cooler waters. Most of the North Branch receives only light fishing pressure. During the week a fisherman is likely to have the whole stream to himself.

Brush Creek, a sizable tributary just above the confluence with the South Branch, is a slow-moving, brushy steam with many tributaries. It drains a large area between the two branches and is stalked regularly by local bait fishermen.

At the forks where the branches meet, there is a small national forest campground, the only designated campground above the mainstream.

The water of the South Branch originates in the southeast corner of Gogebic County at a place called "Paint River Springs." Except for US-2 there is very little public access to the stream before it reaches the Elmwood area. This stretch undoubtedly supports a good brook-trout population judging by its remoteness and quality of downstream waters, but, practically speaking, canoeing and fishing waters begin at Elmwood.

Good catches of brook trout are taken between Elmwood and the first bridge downstream (USFS Road 149). The stream itself is very rocky with tag alder edges to the mouth of Cooks Run. The South Branch has a trout population split about equally between browns and brooks with an odd rainbow. The lower six miles of stream are easily accessible to fishermen, and the portion below Forest Highway 16 is canoeable except during periods of unusually low water.

This quaint little trout stream is fast moving and well suited to both fly- and bait-fishing.

A few years ago an extensive stream improvement program was completed on the lower six miles of Cooks Run. The purpose was to increase the average size of the fish by providing instream cover of the type preferred by large fish. The deep, slow-flowing meadows area, starting about one-half mile below Forest Highway 16, is in contrast with the rest of the stream, but it is a preferred place for the evening brown-trout fisherman. Good-size brown trout are present throughout this tributary. The upper limit of the brown-trout waters in the South Branch seems to be the mouth of Cooks Run. Below this area the South Branch is broad, shallow, and rocky for several miles. Fishing improves as you progress downstream until the river turns north. The remains of old stream-improvement structures are evident in this area. Many of them still provide good fish cover. Occasional rainbows may be picked up from here down to Crystal Falls on the mainstream.

One of the major landmarks on this section of the stream is Uno Dam. It is a picturesque old logging dam flanked by large rock outcrops with an immense hold below. This area is privately owned which makes a canoe necessary for access. Below Uno Dam the river turns and flows north for about three miles.

Gold Mine Hole, another South Branch landmark, is located just downstream from the USFS Road 151 bridge. It is a large-bend hole noted for its lunker browns and brooks. Below the Gold Mine Hole the river slows down a bit and the bottom type changes gradually toward sand. The river soon turns east again in the final stretch before it meets the North Branch. Fishing is fairly good in this easterly-flowing portion, but access is a problem.

When the two forks meet, the darker water of the North Branch seems to predominate. This is known as the Gibbs City area.

This is big water with many deep holes. The river broadens out and slows down about 20 minutes float time below the Gibbs City bridge. Good fishing for browns, rainbows, and smallmouth bass picks up between Blockhouse campground and the mouth of the Net River. The water gets quite warm through this area during the long, hot summer days and it is probably marginal for trout. The smallmouths found in the Paint are fighters, though, and will put most trout to shame. Look for areas with large submerged rocks for best smallmouth action.

There is a lot of slow, broad water between the mouth of the Net and Paint Dam. Fishing in this area is fair. If canoeing, three rapids between Paint Dam and the Bates-Amasa bridge must be run. The first is a short one that should cause no problem for the experienced canoeist. The second rapids is called Upper Hemlock Rapids. It is quite long and should be floated only by experienced canoeists with their life preservers securely fastened. The bottom stretch, Lower Hemlock Rapids, is very long (¼ mile) and should be shot only by those with a strong death wish. Portage trails exist around all rapids, but it is pro-

bably easier to "line" your canoe down using a pole to keep it off the rocks. The portage trail runs along the right bank on Upper Hemlock and along the left bank for Lower Hemlock. Fishing in the area of the rapids is reported to be good for rainbows and browns early in the season.

The Hemlock River, a major tributary, joins the Paint just above the Upper Hemlock Rapids. The Hemlock is a brook trout stream and is accessible for two or three miles along County Road 643 and northeast of Amasa.

Canoes can be launched at Paint Dam and taken out at the Bates-Amasa bridge for fishing in this area. Between Lower Hemlock Rapids and the bridge, fishing is fair for large trout early and good for smallmouths later. The stream is quite broad and rocky. Below the bridge the river slows down for about a mile, then broadens out and speeds up a bit. This area is shallow with scattered boulders protruding above the water surface. The slow water just below the bridge is fairly good for northern pike and smallmouths. Trout diminish steadily between here and Erickson's landing.

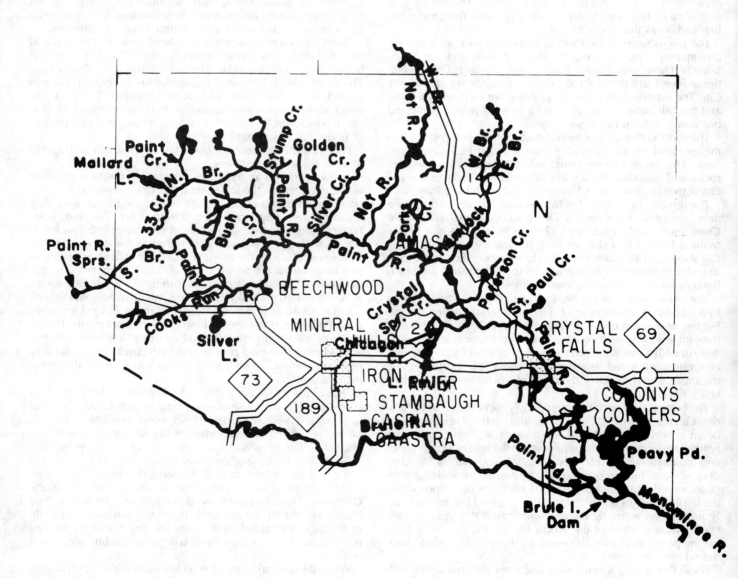

THE ONTONAGON RIVER
By RAYMOND P. JUETTEN
Fisheries Biologist

The mainstream of the Ontonagon River begins near the village of Greenland in northeast Ontonagon County and flows northeasterly for approximately 15 miles before reaching Lake Superior. It is fed by three major tributaries, the East Branch, the Middle Branch, and the West Branch.

The width of the mainstream varies considerably. In the upper reaches near the Military Hill it is 60-125 feet wide, and the lower area near Ontonagon is 400-500 feet wide.

The current from Greenland downstream to Grand Rapids is swift, and from Grand Rapids downstream to Ontonagon it is sluggish. The bottom has some gravel near Grand Rapids, is swift, and from Grand Rapids downstream to Ontonagon it is sluggish. The bottom has some gravel near Grand Rapids, but over the remainder of the stream it is clay or a clay-sand mixture.

The stream banks slope gently away from the river through steeply rolling hills that vary in height, usually averaging 15-30 feet. Some banks southeast of Grand Rapids are nearly vertical and range in height from 15 to 100 feet.

The old saying, "too thick to drink, too thin to plow," is a fitting description for this stream. The water has a red clay color, and the bottom is not visible even at a depth of a few inches. The stream is shallow enough for wading in most places southeast of Grand Rapids; however, because of this extreme turbidity deep pools cannot be easily distinguished. Therefore, bank-fishing is recommended. Downstream from Grand Rapids most anglers use boats as the stream averages over six feet deep.

The Ontonagon supports a warmwater and anadromous (sea-run species such as steelheads and salmon that return to the rivers to spawn) fishery.

In the spring anglers concentrate their efforts on steelheads. A variety of methods and lures is used, but spawn-bag fishing is the most popular. Most steelhead fishing is done near the Military Hill area, where US-45 crosses the stream, downstream to the Rockland-Victoria Road. Fishermen usually still-fish the deep pools. Steelheads up to 10 pounds have been reported, but the average size is three to six pounds. The run usually begins in mid-April and extends through mid-May.

In late May and extending through mid-September, anglers begin fishing walleyes, northern pike, and suckers in the lowermost eight miles of the river.

During the fall the brown trout migrate upstream from Lake Superior, and anglers turn out in large numbers to catch these prized game fish. The area around the US-45 bridge is the most popular fishing spot. The run extends from late August through October. Still-fishing from the bank with spawn bags is the most popular angling method. These browns average two to five pounds, and occasionally one of the eight- to 10-pound class is caught.

The East Branch of the Ontonagon River rises from Spring (Jingle) Lake located in northeast Iron County. The stream in this headwater area is generally less than 30 feet wide, is quite shallow, and brown in color. It flows through areas of extensive tag alder-spruce swamps which are spaced by many beaver meadows.

The East Branch from Spring Lake to Lower Dam Impoundment was once prime brook-trout water. Heavy siltation caused by the many old beaver dams and Upper Dam Impoundment makes it presently unsuitable, though, for trout production. These blockages probably warmed the river here, making it more suitable to warmwater species than trout. The silt covered many trout-spawning areas, and the brook trout disappeared. To return this section of stream to trout water would require chemical reclamation and channel clearing. As this system is almost completely inaccessible, with the exception of Upper Dam Impoundment and Lower Dam Impoundment, the costs are currently judged prohibitive.

The East Branch below Lower Dam flows through hilly hardwood forests on sandy loam soils. Tag alder and grasses line the stream banks.

The stream runs 30 feet wide with a rapid current. Its water is light brown in color and the stream bottom is gravel and rock rubble. Except for several miles of stream east of Haystack Mountain, cover is adequate and features logs, rocks, and some undercut banks. There are many riffles and deep, fast pools suitable for trout spawning. The bottom type east of Haystack Mountain is rock rubble and boulders and several stream-improvement devices (rock deflectors) installed in this area in the 1950s are still serving their intended purpose.

This part of the East Branch is prime brook- and brown-trout water, and steelheads migrate upstream as far as Lower Dam. It is open enough to permit fly fishing, and caddis and mayfly hatches occur here.

Brook and brown trout up to 15 inches are not unusual although the average brookie taken by anglers is seven to 10 inches, and the browns average 10-11 inches. Occasionally during the summer a brown in the three- to four-pound class is taken.

The stream is open to the extended trout and salmon season from the M-28 bridge at Kenton downstream. The spring steelhead run, which peaks at the end of April, attracts anglers from long distances, and success in the vicinity of Kenton is good. The fall brown-trout run does not attract as many fishermen here as on the mainstream; however, success is usually good for the few anglers who participate.

The rapid-flowing Jumbo River is the largest tributary entering the East Branch in this section. Its average width is 25 feet, logs and undercut banks are plentiful, and the bottom is sand and gravel. The Jumbo receives a steelhead run each spring. These fish usually spawn between M-28 and Jumbo River Falls two miles upstream. There is good resident population of browns in the lower reaches of the Jumbo but very few brooks. However, the East and West branches of the Jumbo both contain good populations of brooks and some brown trout. Caddis hatches occur on this stream and there are mayfly and caddis hatches on the West Branch. The stream generally is not open enough for easy fly fishing.

Smith Creek, Spargo Creek, and Stony Creek enter the East Branch upstream from the mouth of the Jumbo. These three streams flow rapidly over a sand and gravel bottom and are 10 to 15 feet wide. In the lower reaches of Smith Creek the bottom is clay which causes the stream to have murky color. It clouds the East Branch for several hundred yards downstream from its mouth. These three tributaries contain brooks and browns, with Smith Creek having the largest population.

Downstream from Sparrow Rapids the East Branch begins to pick up the red clay color characteristic of much of the Ontonagon system. The stream has a sand and grvel bottom with some clay.

Brook and brown trout and resident rainbows inhabit the stream near Sparrow Rapids, but the trout population thins downstream until it finally gives way to warmwater species near the mouth of Newholm Creek. Here the stream becomes sluggish.

Access between Sparrow Rapids and the mouth of the East Branch is limited and this may explain the light fishing pressure the stream gets. Most angling occurs near the mouth during the steelhead and brown trout runs where access is gained from US-45.

Beaver Creek is the primary tributary below Sparrow Rapids, and its color is quite murky as the bottom is primarily clay. A fair brook-trout population is present in the lower reaches of this five- to 10-foot-wide stream which is seldom fished.

The Middle Branch of the Ontonagon River begins at Crooked Lake in eastern Gogebic County. Between Crooked Lake and US-2, it is 15-20 feet wide and quite warm and shallow, making it marginal for trout. Near US-2 the stream enters a lowland area, and the banks become lined with tag alder. Its average width is 20 feet with a gravel and sand bottom. Current velocity slows and the numerous deep pools have silted bottoms. Water temperature decreases here, and brook, brown, and rainbow trout are quite numerous with brookies being the most plentiful. Caddis hatches occur here, but because of the overhanging tag alder, fly fishing would be difficult.

The stream is not wadable from US-2 downstream to the mouth of Wolf (Ma-In-Gan) Lake Creek. Most anglers use canoes or rubber rafts to fish this stretch (canoes can be rented at a livery located on US-2 about one mile west of Watersmeet). Wolf Lake Creek is a warmwater stream and has no trout.

Below the mouth of Wolf Lake Creek to USFS Road 171, the stream widens to about 40 feet and is wadable although deep pools are common. The bottom is a mixture of sand and gravel. Banks are lined with tag alder, but these do not extend too far out over the stream and it can be easily fly-fished. Cover consists mostly of logs and undercut banks. Brook trout are the most abundant species and they average seven to nine inches although some are taken in the 12- to 14-inch class.

Browns up to four pounds are taken here, but they usually run 10-12 inches, as do the rainbows.

Duck Creek joins the Middle Branch at Watersmeet. This is a small coldwater stream which rises from Duck Lake and flows roughly seven miles through lowland choked with tag alder. It has an excellent population of large brook trout and some large browns. (A Watersmeet angler caught a nine-pounder from the Duck in 1971.) Special regulations for Duck Creek stipulate a 10-inch minimum size limit for brown trout, a five-trout limit, and artificial lures only.

Boniface Creek also enters the Middle Branch near Water-

smeet. Warmwater species are abundant here, and few trout are found. From USFS Road 171 downstream to the mouth of the Tamarack River, the current velocity slows down considerably, and trout fishing is poor. The Tamarack River itself is too warm in the summer for good trout fishing. In the winter, however, brookies up to two pounds have been caught through the ice.

Below the mouth of the Tamarack River the gradient of the Middle Branch steepens. From this point to Bond Falls the river averages 40 feet wide and has a sand-gravel bottom with some rock rubble and boulders. Cover in the form of logs and undercut banks is abundant, and the stream is wadable although frequently anglers must leave the stream to get around deep pools. The upland is covered with hardwoods, and tag alders line the banks.

A USFS campground at Burned Dam located near Mex-i-min-e Falls is a scenic spot and the starting point for float-fishing trips downstream five to six miles to USFS Road 172 (also called Interior Road after the now abandoned town of Interior). The stream is wadable, but floating is the only means of access between these two points.

Mayfly and caddis hatches occur and this is an area easily fly-fished, although bait-fishing is preferred by local anglers. This is beautiful trout water with a good population of brookies and browns and a small population of rainbows. Brook trout in this region are often larger than those caught elsewhere in the Middle Branch.

The quality of trout fishing from the Interior Road bridge decreases downstream toward Bond Falls Basin. The dam at Bond Falls has a bottom release, and river temperatures below the dam are up to 10°F cooler than temperatures upstream on the Middle Branch near the Interior Road bridge.

The Middle Branch from Bond Falls to Agate Falls is highly regarded by trout anglers. Avid fly fishermen from many states make annual fishing trips to this stream. One Illinois angler wrote that he had fished here annually for the past 50 years, a Wisconsin angler wrote that he had been coming here for 30 years, a New York angler said he has fished the river since 1954.

This section is famous for its brook- and brown-trout fishing. It has good hatches, and this scenic stream is easily fished and is wadable. The flow is rapid and cover consists of boulders and logs with a good mixture of deep, fast pools and riffles. The banks are lined with cedar, balsam, pine, maple, and some tag alder. The six-mile stretch is quite inaccessible, however, with most fishing done upstream from M-28. It can be reached elsewhere via logging trails.

Agate Falls located about one-quarter mile downstream from M-28 is a barrier to upstream migration of steelheads. This beautiful falls attracts many visitors each summer and is a popular steelhead fishing spot.

For one-half mile below Agate Falls the stream has the appearance of a beautiful trout water, but few trout other than steelheads are taken here although the water yields browns in the fall.

Brook trout and browns are abundant about a mile downstream where the velocity moderates. The topography here is more gentle and the soils are red clay. The stream color now changes from light brown to the red color typical of much of the Ontonagon system. The stream has good cover, and the bottom is gravel.

As the stream flows northerly it is fed by several small, cold tributaries. These feeder streams are used by brookies and browns for spawning. The Baltimore River and Trout Creek are the biggest, and they have good populations of brook trout.

Access is by logging roads or trails and, therefore, fishing pressure is low. Trout populations give way to warmwater species near South Military Hill, and from this point on, suckers are the primary species of fish present.

The West Branch stream begins at Lake Gogebic in western Ontonagon County and flows easterly through mixed hardwood forests of maple and aspen for approximately 20 miles (lineally) until it joins the Ontonagon River near Victoria. The West Branch supports a warmwater fishery, and with a couple of exceptions is not suitable for trout.

Cascade Creek, the only coldwater tributary, enters the West Branch upstream from the Norwich Road. It is a small, swift trout stream, six to 20 feet wide, featuring banks lined with tag alder and excellent rock and log cover. Some beaver dams are present and contain brookies up to 10 inches. There is very little spawning gravel in Cascade Creek, but Bush Creek, its major tributary, has extensive gravel spawning riffles. Cascade Creek is accessible via USFS Road 22. It is not open enough for fly-fishing.

The South Branch Ontonagon River from Eighteen-Mile Rapids downstream to the West Branch is classified as a top quality warmwater mainstream. All the tributaries entering the South Branch below Eighteen-Mile Rapids are warmwater streams and this is the reason for the sudden change in classification.

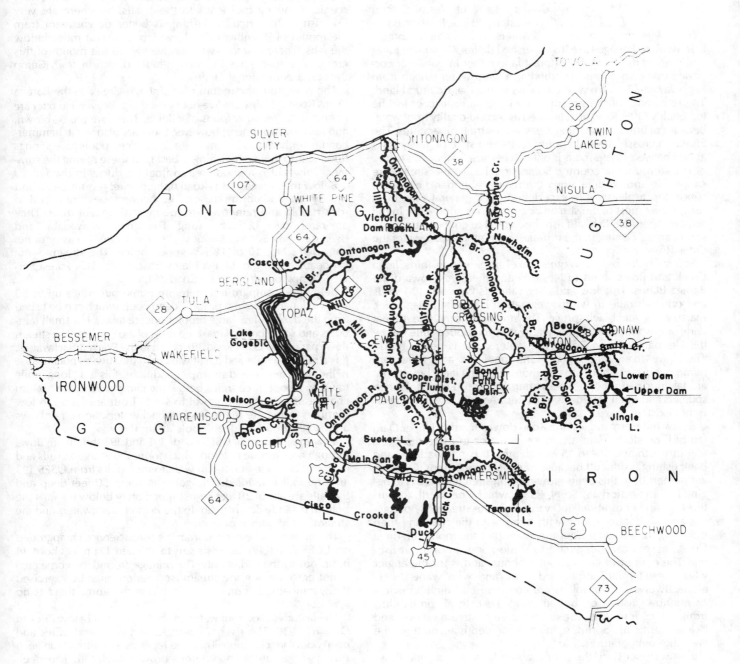

THE STURGEON RIVER
(Baraga County)
By RAYMOND P. JUETTEN, Fisheries Biologist

The Sturgeon River arises in Wagner Lake in central Baraga County. It flows southerly to the village of Nestoria, then westerly to the Prickett Backwaters in Houghton County, then north to Portage Lake. Its watershed drains 705 square miles and it flows mostly through forest land either in public or corporate ownership. It is classified as a warmwater stream from Highway M-38 north, where it flows through agricultural land. The remainder of the stream and all tributaries except for the top-quality Otter River are classified as second-quality trout water because of limited spawning areas and warm temperatures. The Sturgeon crosses several county roads and state highways, but access between these roads is difficult because of the wild nature of the surrounding country. Some stretches of the stream are canoeable and wildlife along the river is abundant, making a canoe trip a pleasurable experience. As a general rule, trout fishing over most of the stream above M-38 is good early in the season. After that, fish and fishermen tend to concentrate in the spring areas. Fishing in the tributaries with the exception of the Otter River is poor.

Several miles below Wagner Lake the Sturgeon joins Tama Creek and flows south to Nestoria and then west toward the Baraga Plains. This lowland river valley is between 100 yards and one-half mile in width. Vegetation is primarily tag alder, marsh grass, and black spruce. The stream is from 20 to 40 feet wide and wadable from the headwaters to about a mile below the Herman-Nestoria Road. The water color is nearly black. There are many deep pools and boulders and riffles are numerous. Creek chubs are common, but some large brook trout are taken for about two weeks after the season opens. French spinners and small Daredevls work best. Aquatic insects are nearly nonexistent.

Below the Herman-Nestoria Road downstream to Upper Dam (an old log sluice dam) the river increases to more than 100 feet in width and 10- to 15-foot depths. It is not wadable and bank fishing is difficult because of marshy conditions. Oxbows are numerous in this deep, slow-moving stretch. There is a logging trail in Section 35, T49N, R33W which goes north toward this area and ends about 100 yards from the stream. By portaging a small boat or canoe with a motor to the river and then motoring for about an hour upstream past the mouth of Tioga Creek, access can be gained to some good brook trout fishing. The entire trip takes about 12 hours and is for the angler who doesn't mind some hard work and who wants to be alone. Twelve-inch brookies are common and night crawlers or minnows fished on bottom work best. In all probability, trout move into this stretch when the stream above and below warms up. Spring seeps and the depth account for the favorable temperatures.

Below Upper Dam the river is about 50 feet wide and flows through hardwood forests. It is wadable to US-41, but the bottom is slippery and felt-soled waders are recommended. Rock riffles and pools are numerous and boulders provide good cover.

Canyon and Upper falls downstream from US-41 are very scenic. A hiking trail leads to these falls, but there are very few fish in this vicinity. Fishing is better downstream from the mouth of Plumbago Creek, which is several miles below the falls. There is a four-wheel-drive trail to the mouth of this creek. The road goes in the southerly direction from Camp Baraga, a correctional facility.

The river from the mouth of Plumbago Creek to the Baraga Plains Road is a pleasant five-hour canoe trip. Beaver and otter are numerous as are other forms of wildlife. There are brook, brown, and rainbow trout here; however, there are also some hammerhandle northern pike. Many of the large, deep pools have springs flowing into them and fishing is best near these during the summer. This is also a good area to float for ducks in the fall.

Below the Baraga Plains Road upland relief is quite steep and the stream gradient increases. The bottom goes from sand to rock rubble and rainbows are the most abundant trout. They are rarely over 12 inches long. The stream is wadable and because of its 50- to 75-foot width, fly fishing is easily done. An Adams No. 10 or 12 is a good choice. The stream is not canoeable from the Baraga Plains Road to the U.S. Forest Service campground on USFS Road 191.

Below the campground there are numerous riffles up to 50 yards in length followed by long, deep pools which can be fished from the bank. A few large brook trout are taken, but small rainbows and some browns make up most of the catches. The stream flows parallel to USFS Road 191 down to the Prickett Backwaters. It is a mile to a mile-and-a-half walk in to the stream, but because of the steep terrain and swampy conditions, this is a "long" mile to walk. About three miles below the campground the bottom changes from rock and gravel to sand. Trout are found in low numbers from here to the Prickett Backwaters. Some rainbows are caught in a few deep pools along the way.

Near the junction of USFS Roads 191 and 193 the stream flows through a sandstone outcrop which forms the Sturgeon Falls and Gorge. It is a mile-and-a-half walk to these falls from USFS 193 and the trail is marked. The gorge is about 50 feet deep and the falls are about 20 feet high. Immediately below the falls the bottom is sandy downstream to the Prickett Backwaters and the stream is too warm for trout.

The stream can be canoed from the Forest Service campground on USFS Road 191 downstream to Prickett Dam in about 14 hours during the spring only. The portage around the gorge area is not posted along the stream, so caution must be exercised if any canoeing is done, as once inside the gorge there is no way out.

The last stretch of trout water on the Sturgeon is below Prickett Dam to M-38. The river is about 75 feet wide and riffles and deep pools are common. This area receives a steelhead run each spring and a run of anadromous browns each fall. The steelhead run begins in early April and the brown run usually in early

September. These fish are caught mostly on spawn bags.

During the summer months fishing for browns is very good here. There are few brook trout as temperatures are marginal. The stream and its tributaries provide little trout reproduction, so in 1974 a brown trout stocking program was resumed. By the fall of 1976 the 1974-planted fish were 19 to 22 inches long and those planted in 1975 were in the 15-inch class. The fishery is well accepted, but local anglers are quite secretive about their success.

Here the river flows through hardwood forest and the bottom is 60 percent sand and the remainder is gravel and rock rubble. It is about an eight-hour canoe trip from Prickett Dam to M-38. There are rapids about four miles below Prickett Dam at the lower end of which is a three- to four-foot falls. The stream is subject to daily flow functions because of the operation of Prickett Dam, a hydroelectric generating facility. When the gates are closed the river is generally about two feet lower than when they are open. Canoeists should check at the dam before going downstream because when the dam is closed the stream is too shallow for a pleasant trip.

THE FOX RIVER
By WILLIAM H. GRUHN
Fisheries Biologist

The Fox River is a picturesque stream with its headwaters located in Alger and northern Schoolcraft counties. It flows generally southeasterly through flat sand plains and lowland swamps to its confluence with the lake branch of the Manistique River.

The Fox became included in the Michigan Natural Rivers Program in 1989. The river now enjoys more protection from development. Department of Natural Resources director's orders issued in May 1989 prohibit or restrict launch and recovery of motorboats on parts of the river system.

This system has enjoyed a colorful history, being widely used to transport logs downstream to mills located in Seney on the Fox River and Manistique on the Manistique River between 1880-1900. The locations and, in most instances, remains of eight old logging dams can still be found on the Upper Fox River and its branches—East Branch, West Branch, and Little Fox River.

The Fox River watershed encompasses approximately 270 square miles. The water temperature rarely exceeds 68°F and offers some of the finest brook trout fishing in the U.P. Roughly, 80 percent of the adjacent lands are under public ownership, providing many recreational opportunities in the area. A number of public roads cross the river and its tributaries.

There are four campgrounds located on this river system. The East Branch Fox River Forest Campground is located at the old Fox River Rearing Station along M-77, just 8.5 miles north of Seney. The Seney Municipal Campground is found on the Fox River just three-quarters of a mile northwest of Seney on the Fox River Road. The Fox River Forest Campground is situated on the Fox River just four-and-one-half miles northwest of Seney on the Fox River Road. Stanley Lake Forest Campground on Stanley Lake Flooding, Little Fox River, is 13 miles northwest of Seney and 1.5 miles from the Fox River Road. All four campgrounds provide good rustic camping facilities and access to the Fox River system.

The Fox River originates in a semiopen marsh a quarter-mile west of Deadman Lake. It flows south through Casey Lake to its confluence with its west branch. The surrounding land is typically light sandy loam covered with lowland hardwoods, plus scattered swamp conifers. The stream bank is lined with a tag alder thicket.

The stream here is small with moderate to rapid flow, a sand and silt bottom, and enough scattered gravel to provide adequate brook-trout spawning habitat. Fishing pressure is light with success fair for brook trout under 11 inches. Primary trout foods available include muddlers and stone-fly larvae.

Several small lakes of 10 to 40 acres drain into the Fox River in this area, but they are surrounded by private ownership and contain warmwater species.

The headwaters of the West Branch are a semiopen marsh, Mallard Lake, and Beaver Pond in eastern Alger County. This is flat sand plains country with the open Kingston Plains to the west and upland hardwoods plains to the east. The river bottom is narrow and covered with lowland hardwoods and conifers.

This river has a maximum width of about 30 feet, depth of six feet, is light brown in color, and flows in a series of riffles and pools. The bottom is a sand and clay combination with enough gravel here and in Spring Creek to sustain a good brook-trout population. It receives light fishing pressure with good success.

The West Branch has four feeder streams—Pelican, Loon, Grass, and Spring creeks. All are warmwater streams except Spring Creek.

From here the Fox River flows south through some four miles of flat sand plains, covered with grass and scattered red-pine plantations to its confluence with Little Fox River. The river bottom consists of sand and sandy loam, and the stream edge is lined with dense tag alders.

The stream here is about 30 feet wide, and the maximum depth is approximately four feet. The water is clear, light brown, and flows along in a series of slicks and riffles. Cover in this area is fair and there is sufficient spawning habitat for brook trout to maintain a healthy natural population. Brookies taken commonly run up to 12 inches with 16-inch fish being taken frequently. Access is excellent with only a few 40s along the stream under private ownership.

Eight miles northwest of Seney the Fox is joined by the Little Fox River. This 10-mile-long stream originates from springs above Stanley Lake and flows southeast through flat, sandy grass plains that are dotted with aspens and white birch, plus scattered red and jack pine plantations. Along the east side of the stream there are occasional hollows of the original sandy loam covered with swamp conifers. The river bottom is this same soil upon which grows an assortment of lowland hardwood. A dense thicket of alder borders the stream.

The Little Fox is a clear-water stream ranging from eight to 25 feet wide and up to four feet deep. Its bottom is 70 percent sand/silt and 30 percent gravel. Stream flow and water color are similar to the West Branch. The cover is good, having been supplemented by stream-improvement structures and the river supports a good brook-trout population.

Fishing is difficult because of dense tag alder growth along the banks. However, a recent brush removal project has helped remedy the problem. All of the adjacent lands are public.

The Fox River from the mouth of the Little Fox River crosses eight sections of flat, grassy sand plains with scattered red, jack, and white pine stands, plus a few aspen and white birch to reach Seney.

The river in this segment is 30 to 40 feet wide and flows in a series of slicks and pools, with occasional riffles. It has a light brown color. The bottom composition is mostly sand and silt with some gravel sections.

This portion of the stream receives moderate fishing pressure with good success. Brook trout range in size from legal to two-and-a-half pounds. The most popular means of fishing is wading, but floating is also productive. Three tributaries entering the Fox River above Seney—Hudson Creek, Two-Mile Ditch, and Granden Creek—also contain brookies.

An abrupt change occurs in the river below Seney. The topography between Seney and the Manistique River is made up of low, flat cattail bog and black spruce-tamarack swamp with scattered sand ridges of red and jack pine and loamy sand ridges of aspen and swamp hardwoods. The river bottom is still sandy loam covered with lowland hardwoods and alder thickets.

The river has now become a long, glassy slick splitting only briefly to form an area called the "spreads," converging to flow leisurely to its confluence with the Manistique River. The area above the spreads is about 40 feet wide, two to six feet deep, and has a sand/silt bottom. The spreads are made of several broad, "false" channels while the river below is broad and deep flowing over compacted sand and hard pan.

The water is clear and brown, but, because of depth and overhead shade, it appears dark brown to black. Instream cover consists of an abundance of windfalls, log jams, undercut banks, overhanging brush, and deep pools. Because of the bottom type, very little, if any, good brook-trout spawning habitat is available.

Access to the river is very poor, due to the swampy conditions; thus, fishing pressure is light but success is good for those willing to trudge through the swamp and cattails. Of particular interest is fishing in the spreads. Fishermen park along M-77, just a half-mile south of Seney, and walk in to the river. Some very nice catches of eight- to 14-inch brook trout are taken with an occasional fish up to 18 inches.

The East Branch empties into the Fox River about a mile above its mouth. While the East Branch is a tributary, it is nearly equal in watershed, discharge, and length to the Fox River, and it is even more popular as a trout stream. Its watershed makes up 37 percent of the entire system.

The East Branch begins in a series of small spring lakes. The river flows about six miles to the M-77 crossing. The steam in

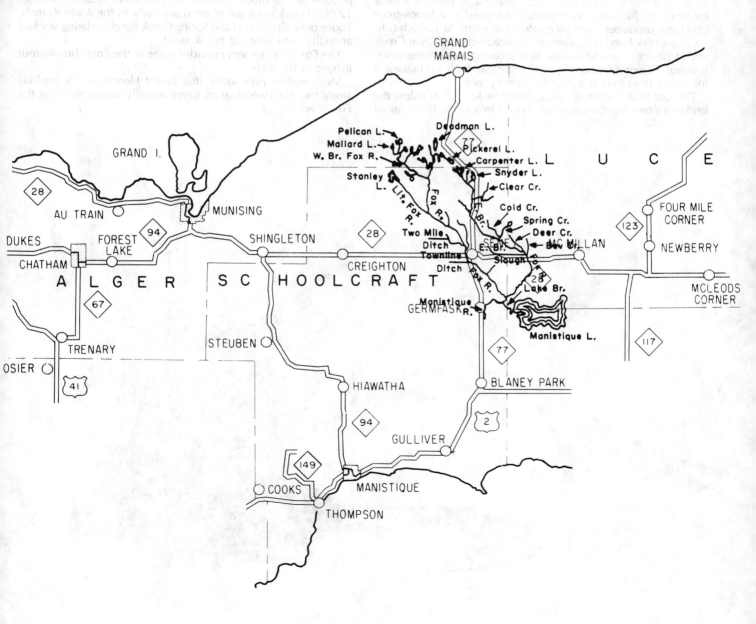

this area is from 10 to 30 feet wide, has a maximum depth of eight feet, and the bottom is sand (80 percent), gravel/rubble (19 percent), and silt (one percent). The clear water flows along in a series of riffles and slicks until it meets Clear Creek. From there, it flows in a series of slicks and pools. The East Branch is a good trout-fishing stream that improves below the junction of Haymeadow Creek.

Haymeadow, Snyder, Clear, and Camp Seven creeks empty into the East Branch in this segment. All are small and shallow and have sand bottoms. They receive light fishing pressure and produce only fair catches of small brook trout (less than 10 inches in length). Several small lakes and ponds in this area produce fair to good brook trout fishing.

Haymeadow Pond is a four-acre, shallow spring pond at the head of Haymeadow Creek. It contains a small population of brook trout and produces some nice catches at times.

On the East Branch Fox River Forest Campground is Kings Pond, a five-acre impoundment that was once used as a rearing pond by the state. This pond has a series of boiling springs at its head that supply it with cold, clear water, making it ideal for trout production. It is presently managed as a brook-trout pond and produces some nice catches of eight- to 12-inch fish.

Clear Creek Pond is located on the headwaters of Clear Creek and at the site of an old beaver dam. It covers about three acres, is about 12 feet deep, and is cool and clear. It also is managed for brook trout and is a popular fishing spot.

The East Branch changes abruptly below M-77. Just below the bridge it flows from a grassy sand plain in a sandy loam cattail bog. The stream below the bridge is a series of slicks and pools, but in the spreads it splits briefly into several broad, shallow, sandy channels, which unite at the mouth of Cold Creek. The stream then continues down to M-28, a distance of roughly 14 miles. The bottom is sandy with a few scattered gravel areas. The water is very light brown, and the land is about 50 percent privately owned. Fishing pressure in this area is moderate, probably the heaviest in this system, and excellent catches of brook trout up to two pounds and an occasional brown trout are taken. The best fishing is obtained by parking on the west side of the M-28 bridge, motoring a small boat upstream to the spreads, and then fishing the holes and undercuts back down to the Soo Line Railroad bridge. Minnows, worms, spinners, lures, and flies are all used.

Cold Creek, Spring Creek (a tributary to Cold Creek), Deer Creek, Bev Creek, and East Branch Slough all enter the river in this area. Cold and Spring creeks are top-quality trout streams and the others are good.

Natural reproduction is more than sufficient to maintain good populations of brook trout in the Fox River system although 12,000 brook trout are planted annually in the Main Branch. Today only Kings Pond and Spring Creek Pond are being stocked annually with yearling brook trout.

The Fox River system provides some of the finest brook-trout fishing in the state.

Most anglers now agree that Ernest Hemingway's exploits along the Big Two-Hearted River actually occurred along the Fox River.

THE WHITEFISH RIVER

By JEROME H. PETERSON
Fisheries Biologist

The Whitefish River of Marquette, Alger, and Delta counties is one of the larger river systems of the central Upper Peninsula. It drains an area of 300 square miles.

The East Branch and mainstream of the Whitefish River flow southward through an expansive valley which was carved by a glacial stream that once flowed from Lake Superior's Au Train Bay to Little Bay de Noc on Lake Michigan. Final retreat of the glacier and "tilting" of the land mass opened the St. Marys River system and closed this "outlet" of Lake Superior via the Whitefish Valley.

The East Branch of this river system begins with multiple springs in central Alger County only 13 miles south of Lake Superior. The West Branch of the Whitefish River commences with a series of spring-fed tributaries in west-central Marquette County and drains southeasterly through the "Trenary Tillplain." Both branches unite in extreme north-central Delta County to form the mainstream which in turn flows south and empties into Upper Little Bay de Noc.

The East Branch of the Whitefish flows through land chiefly under the control and ownership of the USFS. Considerable private timber-company land and small individual ownerships also exist.

The major recreational uses of the East Branch are canoeing and sport fishing. The stream is navigable from the headwaters at Trout Lake, and canoeing is quite popular during the summer months. Access to the lake is gained via USFS Road 2273. The stream below Trout Lake is as much as 100 feet wide with holes to four feet deep. There are numerous riffles and minor rapids, but no actual waterfalls exist on this branch nor are there any log jams or necessary portages. Limestone bedrock, rubble, and cobble comprise the stream's bottom.

The stream flows in a southerly direction through Alger and Delta counties for a distance of about 10 to 11 miles, until the "Buckeye Grade" or USFS 2236 is reached. This is an old railroad grade heavily used during the logging days at the turn of the century. It is a day's leisurely canoe and fishing trip from Trout Lake. The scenery is tremendous, some fast water exists, and good brook trout fishing is available. Another three miles or so of quite faster water is found until the East Branch merges with the West Branch to form the mainstream. There are no developed campsites along this branch of the Whitefish, but natural facilities are more than adequate.

Mosquitoes, blackflies, no-see-ums, and deer flies are a problem from the middle of May through the 4th of July. Canoeists, fishermen, and others venturing upon this stream are advised to bring plenty of bug dope.

There are five tributaries to the East Branch of the Whitefish River. Dexter Creek is the first of these that enters from the west and is the largest and most important. About 15 miles in length, it joins the East Branch two miles below Trout Lake. It is fed by numerous springs along its length. Riffles and pools alternate in an almost ideal sequence. Reproduction of brook trout is good, and some steelheads and lake-run brown trout use the stream for spawning. The Dexter probably contributes some trout recruitment to the East Branch.

Of note, but of lesser importance as one proceeds downstream, are the Squirrel, Unnamed, Spring, and Pole creeks. The former three are small with sandy bottoms. Brook-trout reproduction is minimal, making little contribution to the East Branch and providing little sport fishing in the streams themselves.

The Trout Lake complex and the East Branch of the Whitefish are quite cold, and the water is of high quality. Brook trout are native to the watershed, and considerable natural reproduction occurs in the Trout Lake and the associated springs area. Rainbows were introduced in the mid-1960s but have since been discontinued. Introductions of brown trout began in 1970 with fair to good results. Occasional adult coho salmon have been noted in the upper parts of the East Branch and Trout Lake area.

Access by the public is limited, and this adds a definite "quality" to the river. Only one private hunting camp is found alongside the whole stream. County Road 509 and USFS Road 2234 parallel the river on the east at a distance of one-half to two miles. A couple of trail or logging roads head toward the river but can only be traversed on foot.

The entire East Branch is fishable with flies, artificial lures, or live bait. Flies are most popular in the late spring and early summer, while artificials or live bait seem to work better in midsummer or early fall. All things considered, fishing is fair to good throughout the East Branch.

The West Branch of the Whitefish system begins as lowland drainage in extreme southeast Marquette County near the village of Dukes. Within a few miles a series of small tributary streams—McMasters, Dems, and Sucker creeks—unite with the West Branch to form a fairly good-sized stream. A general south to southeasterly direction is followed through Alger and Delta counties before union with the East Branch. Six miles of stream exist in Marquette County, 35-40 miles in Alger County, and 15 miles in Delta County.

The West Branch has eight tributaries. All are designated trout waters except a small portion of Dorsey Lake outlet. All have natural reproduction of brook trout and to a lesser degree, steelheads and brown trout. Scotts, Werner, Dems or Huber, and the Casey are good brook-trout producers and are believed to contribute significantly to the West Branch's trout population.

The West Branch of the Whitefish in Alger and Delta counties is a series of pools and riffles over a limestone bedrock, rubble, gravel, and cobble bottom. A falls of three to four feet exists in Section 10 and is a barrier to upstream fish movement. The deep pool below the falls provides good steelhead fishing each spring. An attractive state forest campground is also found here. US-41 crosses the river about one mile south of Trenary. For the next couple of miles the stream's gradient is considerable and riffles and rapids common.

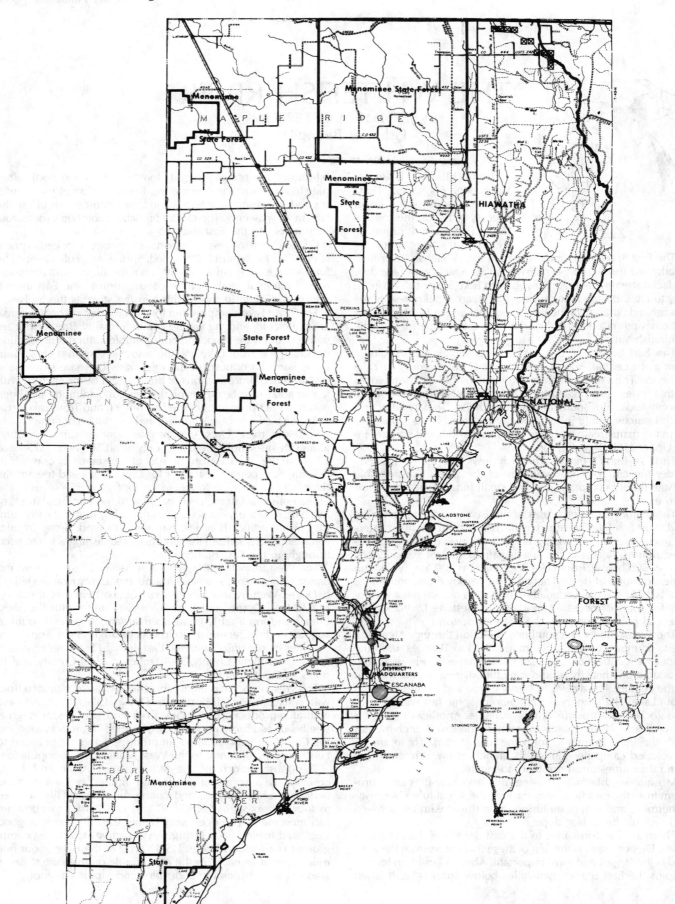

The West Branch slows down considerably in Delta County, and depths to several feet are common. Casey Creek enters a short way above the "Buckeye Grade" or USFS Road 2236. Below USFS Road 2236, one encounters the rapids on the Whitefish system known as Flynns Rapids. It extends for perhaps one-half mile. Quite good brook trout and steelhead angling exists below Flynns Rapids, the lower end of which has a sharp bend known as "Deadman's Curve." The Little West Branch flows south for several miles and rejoins the stream a mile or so below the junction of the East and West branches. Beyond Deadman's Curve it is but a couple of miles of alternating short pools and riffles to the union with the East Branch.

Most of the West Branch is canoeable and quite popular in May and June or September and October. Best put-in point is the public access site above Kiva in Alger County. A small portage is necessary around the falls, and log jams, deadheads, and boulders are occasional above Trenary.

Brook trout are native to the system and intensely sought after by the angler. Introductions were discontinued in 1965 because tributary streams provided adequate natural reproduction. Recent increases in steelhead and brown trout runs are apparently due in part to natural reproduction and large plants in Little Bay de Noc.

The water quality of the West Branch and tributaries is quite good. It is slightly alkaline, moderately hard, and abundantly supplied with oxygen. Midsummer stream temperatures for the most part are below 72°F, but extremes in the upper 70s have been recorded.

The mainstream averages 100 feet in width in the upper reaches but widens to several hundred feet near the mouth. It is a series of long rapids or riffles and deep pools over a limestone bedrock or cobble bottom. The first major riffle encountered when moving downstream is found about one-half mile below the East and West branches and is known as Johnson's Rapids. Then comes Blacks Rapids, about a half-mile above the mouth of the Haymeadow Creek. Hales Rapids, a quarter-mile above the mouth of the Chippney Creek, is quite popular in May and June with trout fishermen. The Flowing Well Rapids is found about one-quarter mile above the mouth of Bills Creek, and along with Bills Creek Rapids is becoming popular for steelheads and browns in the fall. The lowermost riffle is also called Johnson's Rapids and is found about a half stream-mile above US-2.

The mainstream is classified as second-class trout water with a number of good trout-producing tributaries entering along its length. The stream is large enough and provides an environment suitable for trout, but natural trout reproduction from the mainstream is limited because of the lack of suitable spawning conditions, competition, and predation. Haymeadow and Chippney creeks produce good numbers of brook trout and lesser numbers of rainbows and browns.

Spring steelhead and fall brown-trout runs increased on Chippney, Haymeadow, and Bills creeks during the late 1960s and early 1970s. Small numbers of coho and chinook salmon also ascend these streams in the fall. Natural reproduction of these species occurs and is best in the Chippney and Haymeadow creeks.

The lower two miles of stream are slow, and depths of six to eight feet are common. Grassy islands, bays, and sloughs occur. The entire mainstream is a good canoeing stream in the spring and fall. Low water levels in some summers, however, make for poor canoeing. The rapids throughout this stretch make the trip interesting, and one does not have to be an expert to navigate them. The mainstream flows southwesterly through very scenic hardwood ridges and brooding evergreen swamps.

The USFS owns considerable frontage on the mainstream. Also of note are the fishing and hunting camps evident along both sides of the stream. Usually the camps are found at or near rapids or fast water and often account for the names given to the individual rapids.

Access for the public is limited to putting in on either the west or east branches of the Whitefish off the Buckeye Grade (USFS 2236) or at the mouth near the US-2 bridge. It is a good day's canoe trip to the mouth from either branch on the Buckeye Grade.

THE ESCANABA RIVER
By CLIFFORD LONG
Fisheries Biologist

In northern Marquette County, just a few miles northeast of eastern tip of Lake Michigamme, the outlets of Brocky, Wolf, Long, and Clear lakes join to form the Middle Branch of the Escanaba River. From here it flows south and east to Gwinn, a distance of about 75 stream miles, where it is joined by the East Branch to form the Main Escanaba River.

From Gwinn the stream flows southward another 25 miles to Boney Falls Impoundment on the Marquette-Delta county line. Halfway through this stretch, it is joined by another major tributary, the Big West Branch of the Escanaba. Below Boney Falls Impoundment, the Escanaba flows southeast for another 20 miles before it empties into Little Bay de Noc just north of Escanaba. There are three dams in the lower five miles of stream with the lowermost one less than a mile from the stream mouth. U.S. Geological Survey figures indicate a total drainage area of 923 square miles.

The four lakes whose outlets form the Middle Branch are trout lakes being managed primarily for rainbows and brook trout.

In this rugged terrain, the outlet streams tumble over rocks and riffles, glide along the base of cliffs, and rest in pools populated with brook trout. Brook trout are the most abundant. Though the streams are not too far from traveled roads, the rugged terrain screens out all but a few local fishermen whose knowledge of the country leads them directly to the most productive pools. There is some natural reproduction, but the size of the feeder streams limits the production of larger fish and seriously handicaps the fly fisherman.

As the Middle Branch flows south, its volume is increased by groundwater seepage, springs, and small tributaries.

The Greenwood Reservoir (2,400 acres) has been built on the Middle Branch. The best canal access now is off County Road 581 south of Ishpeming. Canoeists are cautioned that the upper portion of the Middle Branch contains some hazardous "white water." Though the stream flows through rugged and relatively undeveloped country from Humboldt to the Cataract Basin, it is crossed by five bridges, and there are several other access points all fairly evenly spaced. Therefore, the entire stretch can be negotiated by a series of short trips tailored to fit the time available to the canoeist. *Portaging is necessary around several waterfalls.*

A healthy brook-trout population dominates the headwaters of the Middle Branch and its tributaries below Humboldt. They include Bell Creek, Black River, West Branch Creek, and several smaller, unnamed streams. These augment the flow in the Middle Branch, sustain some excellent brook trout fishing of their own, and provide recruitment to the mainstream below. Spawning success in the mainstream, judging from fish collections, does not appear to be very impressive. Except for this one factor, the habitat is excellent for trout, and a good fishery for large brown trout is maintained

via a stocking program. The many riffles and rapids with quieter waters at their lower ends and the pools below the waterfalls provide excellent opportunities for fly fishermen and spincasters.

The water in the main stream and some of the tributaries, particularly the Black River, has a brownish cast from swamp leachings and iron deposits in the area. The waterfalls, the heavily wooded areas, and the bald knobs of Canadian Shield rock over a half-billion years old make this a most scenic area to traverse.

Between the dam and its junction, with the East Branch at Gwinn (about five stream miles), the Middle Branch courses swiftly between high banks over a bottom consisting chiefly of large boulders. Wading this stretch is treacherous at best. The river's width spans 75 to 100 feet, and, due to the operation of the power plant, flow fluctuates widely. Some good trout fishing is available here, but the flow characteristics make it unpredictable.

The East Branch of the Escanaba River is formed by the junction of Warner and Schweitzer creeks about four miles southeast of the village of Palmer. Both creeks are coldwater streams with good brook-trout populations maintained by natural reproduction. Both flow through rugged, rocky country timbered with hardwood and pine. Streambank cover is mostly tag alder which limits fly fishing, but bait fishermen enjoy some excellent fishing for trout running 12 to 13 inches. Warner Creek flows unobstructed, but Schweitzer has a 48-foot head dam about five miles above its mouth.

The East Branch flows east for three or four miles, then swings gradually to the south toward Gwinn and its junction with the Middle Branch. Its total length is approximately 18 to 20 miles, and it flows through less rugged country than does the Middle Branch.

Goose Lake, until the 1950s, received sewage effluent from Negaunee. The upper two or three miles of the outlet is marginal for trout because of the higher temperatures of the groundwater seepage. The lower three-quarters of the stream (five to six miles), plus the East Branch below its mouth, produces sizable brook and brown trout. Gravel riffles and frequent pools provide excellent opportunities for both bait- and fly-fishing.

The East Branch from Goose Lake outlet to the junction with the Middle Branch is one of the most popular trout streams in the Upper Peninsula. Reproduction in the mainstream and in the tributaries (Uncle Tom's Creek, O'Neal Creek, Halfway Creek, and several unnamed) is more than adequate to maintain a good trout population.

The stream lies almost entirely within the boundaries of the Copper County and Escanaba River state forests. Approximately four miles of frontage is in state ownership. This ownership is scattered with stretches of private ownership in between; but since the stream is both wadable and canoeable, all of it is fishable by the public. Fishing pressure is fairly heavy, and success is above average. Most of the stream lends itself well to fly-fishing, but most of the pressure is from bait fishermen.

In the southwest part of Marquette County directly east of Republic and in the north part of Dickinson County within the boundaries of the Michigamme Forest, the land is level to gently rolling and the soils are sandy. The area is wooded to semiopen with an array of small lakes in the extreme northern part. It is traversed by two-rut sand plains roads with a short stretch of county-maintained gravel road in the southeast part. In this area, a number of small streams find their sources in the lakes and in springs and groundwater seepage percolating through the porous sandy soils. Most of them cross the Marquette-Dickinson county line between tiers 44 and 45 north; and in so doing, some of them have their names changed so designation by name, in many instances, is confusing to one not familiar with the area.

In southeastern Marquette County several coldwater streams converge to form the West Branch. Brook trout predominate, and in spite of the shifting sand bottoms, there is enough gravel to provide for adequate spawning and there is no lack of natural reproduction or fish food organisms.

These small drainages represent well over one hundred miles of stream and, though they are difficult to fish, they produce some fine catches of brook trout for those hardier fishermen who are willing to fight the brush and shifting sand in pursuit of these handsome fish. Conditions dictate natural baits and short rods.

The three- to five-mile stretch of the North Branch of the Big West Branch beginning at the county line and extending to the mouth is only occasionally fished by canoe or small boat, but it seldom fails to produce. Fishing this stretch by any other means is essentially impossible.

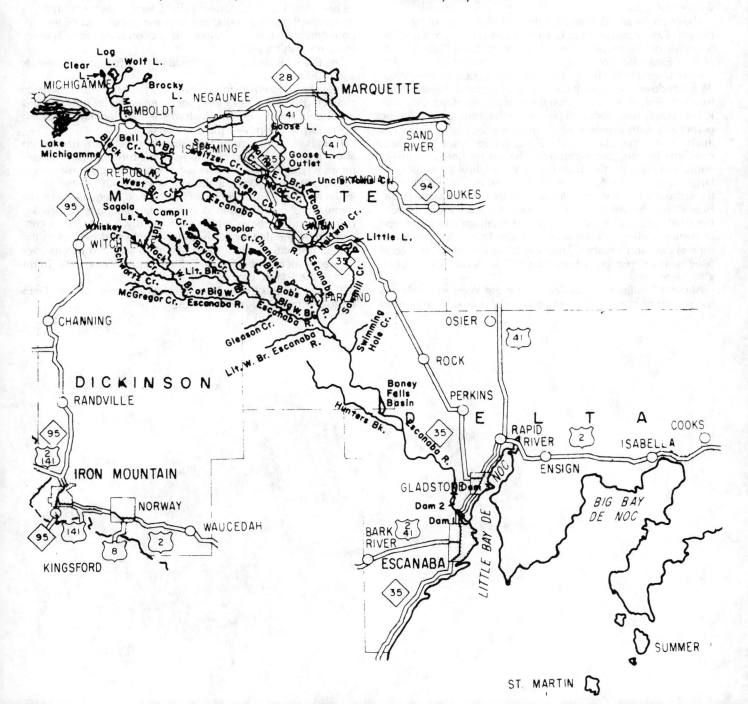

The Big West Branch of the Escanaba River begins with the confluence of the West Branch and the North Branch in Marquette County. It flows eastward for eight to 10 miles to the Escanaba River. It is large enough to be negotiated by canoe or small boats which can be lifted over logs or log jams. It yields brook trout, brown trout, and rainbow trout in that order of abundance and is well suited to fly fishing. Chandler Brook, which originates in Pike Lakes seven miles to the north, is its largest tributary with Gleason Creek, from the southwest, the only other tributary. Both are brook-trout streams with fair to good natural reproduction which contributes to the population in the mainstream.

The Big West Branch is in the Escanaba River State Forest and like all the waters above, most of the frontage is in public ownership and retains most of the natural beauty associated with wilderness areas.

The Main Escanaba River, formed by the junction of the Middle and East branches near Gwinn, flows southward for 45 to 50 miles before emptying into Lake Michigan's Little Bay de Noc at Escanaba. Four impoundments interrupt this stretch.

From Gwinn to the Boney Basin (the first impound, about 25 miles downstream from Gwinn), the Escanaba flows through forested land, most of it within the boundaries of the Escanaba River State Forest. About 75 percent of the frontage is in public ownership with usable access points spaced about five miles apart. It is a popular stretch of stream for trout fishermen, campers, boaters, and sightseers. The stream bottom consists entirely of rock, ranging from coarse gravel through rubble and large boulders to solid bedrock. Gradient is quite even throughout with short runs of rapids separating the many pools. Brook trout, brown trout, and rainbow trout are found in both the rapids and pools; and their relative abundance in either type of habitat varies with the season, water levels, temperatures, time of day, and weather. Trout foods are abundant, and good fishermen are frequently rewarded with limit catches of "bragging"-size fish.

About 12 miles south of Gwinn the Big West Branch joins the stream from the west and adds a considerable amount to the volume of flow. There is a convenient access point a short distance below the mouth of the Big West and some good trout-fishing waters in the immediate vicinity. About two miles farther downstream on the east bank is the mouth of Sawmill Creek with areas suitable for an overnight stop. The Sawmill is a small but excellent brook-trout stream, and it contributes much to the trout fishery in the Escanaba at this point. About four stream miles below Sawmill Creek is the Escanaba River State Forest campground near the mouth of Swimming Hole Creek. The deep pool at the creek's mouth where the Escanaba rests before entering the series of rapids below gives this stream its name. This is a popular spot with trout anglers.

The stream bends sharply to the east at the base of a high bluff four miles below the campground; then three miles farther it swings back again to the south and flows a mile or two farther before entering the Boney Falls Basin. Trout continue to dominate the fish populations into the upper part of the impoundment waters, but below this section warmwater species enter the fishing picture.

The Boney Falls Dam has a head of 48.5 feet and impounds about 200 acres.

From here downstream to Dam #3, the Escanaba retains its characteristic features of long pools separated by runs of rapid water over a rocky bottom. Volume of flow fluctuates with the operation of the power plant at the dam.

This is a very productive stretch of stream having an abundance of fish food organisms in the form of insect larvae, minnows, and crayfish. It is a favorite among fly fishermen of the area who often make catches of trout in the 16- to 20-inch range. Trout reproduction is not adequate here, so populations are maintained by annual plantings of brooks, browns, and rainbows which grow rapidly. Trout tend to concentrate in the deeper pools and in cracks and fissures in the stream bottom. Many of these lies have acquired names over the years such as the Orchard, Shays Hole, Gravel Pit, Burnt Camp, the Island, etc.

The five miles of river from the impoundment behind Dam #3 to the mouth is nontrout water.

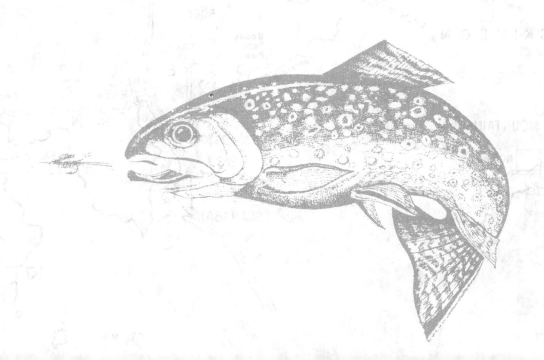

THE TWO HEARTED RIVER

By LELAND ANDERSON
Fisheries Biologist

The mighty Two Hearted River, where the native red men camped and fished at its mouth, where loggers floated their "sticks" to Gitche Gumee, where Hemingway wished he was, and where fishermen today battle the mosquitoes and blackflies in quest of hidden "specks" and rambunctious rainbows, still flows in all its northwoods splendor. It was designated as a Michigan Natural River in 1973. No motors are allowed above the walk bridge near the mouth of the river.

This northern Luce County river is bridged by a logging road near the Antlers and Hemlock Dam, by County Road 407 at the High Bridge, by County Road 410 at the Reed and Green Bridge, and by "Little Mac" footbridge near its mouth. There are several private hunting and fishing camps from its source to the confluence of the East Branch, and state forest campgrounds at the High Bridge, Reed and Green Bridge, and at the mouth. There is also a canoeing campground near the Lone Pine and Highbanks area.

The river system is made up of the mainstream and five major tributaries—the South, West, North and East branches, and Dawson Creek.

The South Branch of the Two Hearted is the best brook trout water in the Two Hearted drainage and is one of the finest in the state. The source of the South Branch (Whorls, Camp One, Beaver Lake, Jack, and Dairy creeks) flows from a rolling ridge of Au Train sandy loam covered with mixed northern hardwood. The river is clear and spring-fed. It flows through open beaver meadows and tag alder fringe to Hemlock Dam and thence through marginal cedar, spruce swamp, and northern hardwoods to its confluence with the West Branch. It lends itself nicely to fly fishing.

Besides brook trout, this section contains some suckers and muddlers. Trout reproduce naturally in a number of small spring-fed tributaries and brook trout up to 12 inches are most commonly taken by anglers; the occasional larger fish is taken from beaver ponds, Whorl, Little Whorl, and Jack lakes. Fingerling brook trout have been stocked at Antlers and Hemlock Dam to supplement the area of heavy fishing pressure. Some rainbow find their way up as far as Camp One Creek during the spring run.

Prior to 1915, the South Branch was used for log drives. There was a water-storage dam at the headwaters (Whorl Club), which was used as a source of water power until about 1955 when a new dam was constructed. The basin is used now as a private trout pond, which is not stocked but has a workable fish ladder. Another water-control structure is found at the Hemlock Dam site. It is no longer usable, but the original timbers are still in evidence.

The only access to Whorl Lake is by logging road and foot trail. There is a poor but driveable logging road to Jack Lake.

The West Branch of the Two Hearted heads into a terrain of rolling sandy-loam hills covered with northern hardwood and hemlock and meanders north and then eastward through a spruce and tag-alder valley. Much of this portion of the river has been intermittently flooded with beaver dams. The West Branch has a moderate flow of clear water, a sandy bottom, and much natural debris for cover. The considerable eel grass in its bed would lead one to believe that the West Branch is warmer than the South Branch. This stream produces an abundance of small brook trout. Martindary Lake at its headwaters is spring-fed and when flooded by beaver has produced some very nice brookies in the 12- to 16-inch class. There is an access road to Martindary Lake; other access is by logging road or foot trail from the south and an old established sand road to Spile Dam from the east.

The West Branch sustains itself by natural reproduction and has not been stocked with trout in the past 25 years. Most fishing is done with live bait.

The main tributary to the Two Hearted River is its East Branch which flows out of the Sleeper Lake marshes and drains the Chesbrough Lake Highlands. Among the tributaries of the East Branch is Widgeon Creek, a clear-water spring creek drawing from wooded sandy ridges and which winds through a flat valley of cutover black spruce, balsam, and hemlock. This small creek contains small brook trout and is not stocked.

An intermittent feeder stream flows in from bog-fringed Stuart Lake. The lower portion of this tributary and other small tributaries from the Sleeper Lake bog are spring-fed but brown-stained. All these feeders have a population of small brook trout, and lake-run rainbow have been noted to move into them in the spring.

Downstream in the vicinity of Potter's Camp and the East Branch Club is an outcropping of gravel and hard pan for a mile upstream and half-mile downstream of the old Shamrock Bridge. It is used extensively as a spawning ground for steelheads and coho salmon.

A good spring run of steelheads attracts a considerable number of fishermen, especially to the vicinity of the Shamrock Rapids and the more open stretches of river below it. This river is not considered canoeable but, for the most part, is wadable.

From the Shamrock Rapids down to the confluence with the mainstream, the banks of the East Branch are steep and sandy; and the sandy bottom deepens at the bends. There are some minor runs of gravelly sand. The East Branch is light brown in color, and its water is soft. Biologically, it is only moderately productive of fish.

The principal game species found in the feeder streams and the East Branch stream is brook trout. Natural reproduction is not considered high.

The mainstream from the confluence of the South and West branches meanders through a sandy valley bordered with tag alder, spruce, balsam, white pine, and marginal hardwood and features many pools four to six feet deep.

This is principally brook-trout water, but a fair number of rainbow work up into this area in the spring. Though tag-alder fringed, this area can be fly-fished with little difficulty. Johns Creek, a small brook-trout feeder, joins the Two Hearted from the south just above the mouth of the North Branch.

Fishing pressure is light to medium with fair access a short distance west of the Ohio Camp. In dry weather the sandy hills are impassable except by four-wheel drive. Fish populations are supplemented by annual stocking of fingerling brook and rainbow trout.

The mainstream between the mouth of the North Branch and the mouth of Dawson Creek begins in a series of moderately deep pools bordered by steep banks of sandy soil. It then builds up momentum over the shallow sandstone ledges with intermittent deep pockets. The river is very rapid for a half-mile upstream and quarter-mile downstream of the High Bridge. The banks are high and steep along the rapids; and the narrow valley is covered by tag alder, jack pine, spruce, balsam, aspen, and red oak.

Fishing is good for brookies and small rainbow trout, especially above and below the rapids. The rapids is a vital steelhead spawning area, and sea lamprey also use them extensively for reproduction. The fish population is supplemented by stocking of fingerling brook and rainbow trout.

Dawson Creek comes in from the south out of a vast flat black-spruce bog interlaced with low ridges of balsam, spruce, jack, red, and white pine. This brown-stained creek is fringed with tag alder.

The terrain along the Dawson is rolling and the soil sandy from the Little Dawson on down; and from the mouth of Whiskey Creek to the mainstream, the valley narrows and the flow quickens over a gravel and a sandstone bottom.

Small brook trout dominate the headwaters and tributaries of the Dawson. Small rainbows are also found in the lower Dawson and the lower portion of the Whiskey, which indicates these to be steelhead spawning areas.

Fishing pressure for brook trout is light to moderate, and natural reproduction is adequate to keep the stream well stocked. Beaver ponds in the headwaters occasionally produce some nice catches of brook trout.

The mainstream of the Big Two Hearted River from the mouth of the Dawson to the mouth of the East Branch flows over a sandy bottom in a predominately northeasterly course, weaving in a narrow valley through rolling terrain of hardwood and evergreen. The stream banks are fringed

with alder, spruce, balsam, and cedar, and stream cover includes deep pools, overhanging trees, undercut banks, and log jams. This portion of the river can be fished from the bank, waded, or is easily canoeable.

Brook trout, rainbows, and menominees await the angler. There is road access to only six places along this eight or nine miles of stream. Spring and summer fishing pressure is medium to heavy and is heaviest during the spring rainbow run in the vicinity of the High and Reed and Green bridges.

Feeder streams along this stretch contribute little to the production of trout, and this portion of the river is stocked annually with rainbow trout, some of which grow to the legal size of 10 inches. Others head to Lake Superior to return a year or two later as full-fledged tackle busters.

The mainstream from the mouth of the East Branch to Lake Superior ranges from 40 to 60 feet wide and varies from one to seven feet in depth. It flows with a moderate current in a narrow valley through slightly rolling jack-pine country. The bottom lands are covered with tag alder, cherry, jack pine, and white birch. There are 25 short rapids on the Two Hearted between the mouth of the East Branch and Lake Superior, but the entire stretch of river is canoeable.

County Road 423 and several fire lanes that branch off County Roads 412, 414, and 423 provide access to the mainstream.

The river flows wide and straight from Little Mac Footbridge to the mouth over a bottom of shifting sand and patches of gravel until its final rush into Lake Superior over a short rapids of agate and other beach stone. The mouth changes its position after each "big blow" from the north. Trout species found in the lower Two Hearted include steelheads, rainbow, brookies, and a few browns.

This portion of river sustains a very good run of steelheads each spring and fall which attracts thousands of ardent anglers, many of whom spend days and weeks at the large, well-kept state forest campground. Coho and pink salmon have found this stream to their liking too, and though none have been stocked here, an ample number of stragglers from points up the lake run this stream each fall.

Though the river sustains a very good run of steelheads, natural reproduction is supplemented by annual stocking. These young steelheads work out into the lake, wax fat, and return in a year or two as three- to eight-pound battlers.

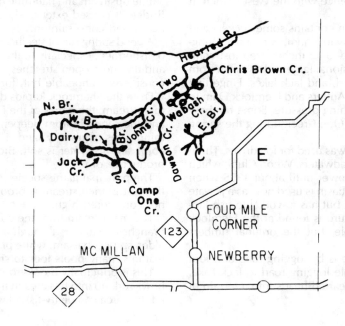

THE SUCKER AND BLIND SUCKER RIVERS

By WILLIAM J. GRUHN
Fisheries Biologist

The Sucker River winds its way northward through the flat to gently rolling pine plains of eastern Alger County before abruptly swinging west and emptying into Lake Superior near the village of Grand Marais. It did not always follow this route. Its natural mouth lies 11 miles east.

The Sucker River was widely used to transport logs in the late 19th century. Difficulty in moving the logs through the Sucker Marsh, even in spring high water, and a long, dangerous trip to Grand Marais via Lake Superior forced the loggers to reroute the river so it would run to East Bay at Grand Marais.

The Sucker river watershed drains about eight square miles. Twenty percent of the watershed is under public ownership and this includes roughly 40 percent of the river's banks.

The water is light brown in color, and water temperatures rarely exceed 70°F. The stream is considered good brook trout habitat and supports a solid spring steelhead run.

While there are no established campgrounds on the river, the lower half is nearly all within the Lake Superior State Forest. Camping is permitted on these lands with a camp registration card, and most of this is high, dry hardwood forest or pine plain.

Accessibility along the entire stream is good. The mainstream can be reached from (1) Segan's Camp Road just one-half mile east of M-77, (2) logging road north from Segan's Camp Road a mile-and-a-half east of M-77, (3) at the confluence of Blood Creek in Section 33, (4) the Old Grand Marais-Seney Road (County Road 709), (5) along the Whitewash Road running south from County Road 700, (6) along the road running north from County Road 700 on the Alger County School Forest about four and a half miles east of Grand Marais, (7) County Road 700 about five and three quarter miles east of Grand Marais, and (8) on a logging road running south from County Road 700 about six miles east of Grand Marais.

The West Branch of the Sucker River has its headwaters at McKay Lake and a tributary from two small lakes just north of McKay Lake. It flows northeast through flat sand plains covered with northern hardwoods and hemlock to its confluence with the Sucker River. There are also scattered stands of jack pine and grassy openings. The stream bank is densely lined here with tag alder, making fishing difficult.

The stream at the M-77 Bridge is 10-15 feet wide, up to 40 inches deep over a sandy bottom, and light brown in color. This area has a good brook-trout population up to 12 inches in length. Many small beaver dams scattered along the West Branch provide good fishing for brookies.

The mainstream of the Sucker River has its headwaters in Nawakwa (Sucker) Lake and flows north to the West Branch junction. The surrounding land and stream banks are similar to the West Branch.

The stream is about 10-20 feet wide, up to five feet deep, is light brown in color, and is clear. The bottom is sand and silty sand with some gravel riffles. The stream is densely shaded by alders and a few instream logs provide cover. The banks are relatively low with little evidence of beaver. Brookies, with a few rainbows, inhabit the stream. Natural foods include minnows, caddis fly, diptera and mayfly larvae, plus leeches. To this point, all adjacent lands are private.

From its confluence with its West Branch, the river flows through the same poor sand, but varies from flat to gently rolling. The land is covered with northern hardwoods and hemlock with scattered jack-pine stands and grassy openings progressing to large grassy open areas in the vicinity of the Old Grand Marais-Seney Road. The dense tag-alder growth thins out as it progresses downstream. A few state-owned 40s flank the stream.

The stream nearly doubles in size at this point and continues to grow as it picks up several fair-sized tributaries through this area. In width it runs from 20 to 30 feet and varies from one to six feet in depth. The bottom changes from shifting sand to gravel and rock rubble and velocity is increased slightly. Rainbow- and salmon-spawning habitat becomes abundant in the lower portion of this segment.

Brook trout also predominate the stream here. The colorful fish seem to be well distributed in the spring but become more difficult to locate as the summer proceeds, suggesting they may be seeking the cooler spring areas. Numerous juvenile cohos and rainbows were collected in this area, indicating good reproductive habitat for these species. Food organisms are caddis, stone fly, mayfly, diptera and mosquito larvae, crayfish, snails, and minnows.

A number of good tributary streams in this area contribute to the Sucker River. Spring Creek, Haverstock Creek, Blood Creek, Klondike Creek, Porter Creek, and Harvey Creek are all small, clear, coldwater brook-trout streams with sufficient spawning habitat to provide ample reproduction to sustain themselves. All but Harvey Creek are of spring origin. Harvey Creek flows out of Harvey Lake; thus, the upper portion of this creek is too warm and sandy to be good trout habitat. All have abundant populations of aquatic insects, plenty of cover, inflowing springs, and all provide homes for beaver. There are nine other small unnamed tributary creeks shown on the map with no data available.

The river downstream from Porter Creek is up to 30 feet wide, features holes to five feet, and has a rapid velocity. The bottom is largely gravel with sand or silty sand shoals and has very little vegetation providing good spawning sites. Cover is made up of log jams, logs, holes, and undercut banks.

Brook trout are abundant in sizes up to 12 inches. Juvenile coho salmon and rainbow trout have been found here as well. There are no tributary streams in this segment; however, there are sufficient springs in the bottom and along the banks to keep the waters cold.

Good fishing for rainbows and brook trout exists in the lower section from County Road 700 to East Bay. This area is a series of sand ridges and loamy sand bottoms covered with jack pine, red pine, and red oak on the ridges and northern hardwoods in the bottoms. The stream bank has scattered clumps of lowland brush made up of willow, alder, dogwood, and huckleberry. The river is from 30 to 80 feet wide and has holes up to six feet deep.

There are two tributaries in this stretch, Grand Marais Creek and Baker Creek. Grand Marais Creek is a moderate to sluggish, clear-water brook-trout stream flowing from Grand Marais Lake. Baker Creek is a small, rapid, light brown, cold, brook-trout stream. The bottom is largely rock and gravel and food is abundant. The banks along this little stream are steep, high, and in some areas raw. Both creeks and the lake have good brook-trout fishing. In addition, Baker Creek is utilized heavily by spawning rainbows from Lake Superior.

The Blind Sucker River lies in the northwest corner of Luce County between Grand Marais (eight miles to the west) and Deer Park Settlement (three miles to the east). It flows from a swampy environment in a northeasterly direction to Lake Superior, draining an area of approximately 18 square miles.

Historically, the Blind Sucker River was a part of the lower portion of the Sucker River which now flows into East Bay at Grand Marais. In the 1870s, by a stroke of engineering genius and lots of hard work, the Sucker River channel was pinched off at Cable Hill and diverted across and between the dunes to Grand Marais Creek and thus into East Bay at Grand Marais 13 miles west of the original river mouth. The remaining portion of the old Sucker River now consisted of a board expanse of swamp, escarpment springs, and the Dead Sucker River and is now called the Blind Sucker River.

After a new concrete and wood dam was built in 1954, 2,000 fin-clipped brook trout were stocked. Several of these and some native brook trout were caught in 1956, but by 1957 numerous catches of small pike were reported. Pike numbers increased rapidly, resulting in the elimination of the brook trout that were left. Since 1958 pike fishing has

been fair to good, but under rather heavy fishing pressure few big fish (over 10 pounds) are taken. Perch are abundant and rock bass and white suckers are common.

A state forest campground with boat launch is available.

The portion of the river from the dam to Lake Superior is classified as a warmwater stream; however, spring and fall temperatures are cool enough to provide a suitable environment for steelheads during the spring and steelheads, chinook and coho salmon, and some brook trout in the fall. Instream cover is lacking in the area below the Grand Marais Truck Trail. Access to the mouth is not good since the road is rough and often impassable.

This lower portion of stream flows easterly between low sand hills vegetated with white birch, soft maple, poplar, oak, jack and red pine. The stream channel is bordered by tag alder and leatherleaf. The stream varies from 15 to 40 feet wide and from six inches to four feet in depth. The bottom is mostly sand but is interspersed with numerous gravel runs which provide good spawning habitat for migrating trout and salmon. Cover consists mostly of occasional logs, tag alder overhang, and undercut banks.

Fishing for steelheads is considered fair to good during the month of May, and for steelheads and salmon during October and November. Access is good (except at the mouth), and the stream is easy to fish. Areas of heavy use are very sandy and some erosion is occurring. The sucker run is heavy in the spring and smelt occasionally ascend the lower portion. Menominee fishing has been good to excellent over the rocky Lake Superior bottom at the mouth of the Blind Sucker. Lake trout, salmon, and steelheads are also taken at the mouth in late spring and fall seasons. During the fall of 1975, the river sustained a fall run of pink salmon. These fish migrate during odd years only and should provide a good fishery every other year.

ALGER COUNTY STREAMS

By WILLIAM GRUHN
Fisheries Biologist

The Miners River, Mosquito River, and the Hurricane River are three Alger County streams worthy of the attention of any serious trout fisherman.

The Miners River arises from a pair of small unnamed lakes in north-central Alger County. It flows south and east for about two miles and then turns to flow almost due north to Lake Superior, just east of Grand Island.

The headwaters, which include several small unnamed tributaries pass through flat spruce-balsam swamps with scattered open marshes and hardwood pine ridges. As the river turns north and crosses the Munising-to-Van Meer Road (County Road 637), the land becomes low and rolling with northern hardwood and hemlock ridges and cedar, spruce, and balsam. The river then flows through partially wooded dunes, through the Pictured Rocks, and into Lake Superior. The soils in the area are basically sandy loams.

The area is used primarily for recreational activities: fishing, hunting, hiking, camping, stone hunting, etc. and lies largely within the Pictured Rocks National Lakeshore. Over half of the lands adjacent to the stream are held by the Cleveland-Cliffs Company, while most of the remainder is in public ownership.

Access to this stream is not as restricted as many others in the area. Direct access can be gained from several roads or trails: (1) Munising-Van Meer Road (County Road 637) at five points; (2) Evelyn Truck Trail (USFS Road 2249), running south from County Road 637; (3) the Pictured Rocks Trail near the mouth; and (4) Miners Beach at the mouth. There are also a large number of mapped and unmapped foot trails and two-track trails providing access to the stream. Therefore, this river provides nearly 20 miles of tranquil fishing for the person willing to get off the beaten path.

There are three distinct segments to the Miners. The first section is from the headwaters down to the mouth of the feeder stream. Here the river varies from 10 to 15 feet wide and up to two feet deep. The water color is brown, and the bottom is made up largely of sand or silt. The water temperature rarely exceeds 70°F, and velocity is slow to moderate. Four tributaries enter this area; all are similar to the mainstream.

Trout fishermen will find this area consists of a series of slicks and pools. Cover is only moderately abundant and consists of undercuts, logs, pools, and tag alder. The banks are low and covered with tag alder and other brush. Food organisms include mayflies, caddis flies, dipterans, beetles, crayfish, and forage fish.

There is adequate spawning and nursery habitat to support a brook trout population here and fishing is fair to good for brookies.

The second segment (from the north line of Section 32, down to Miners Falls) averages 10 to 20 feet wide, up to 30 inches in depth, is brown in color, and has a bottom composed of about 80 percent sand and silt and 20 percent rubble and gravel. Cover is moderate and made up of logs, holes, undercuts, and brush

overhang. Three small tributaries enter this section and help provide adequate brook trout habitat.

Fishermen will find this area to be a series of slicks and riffles with banks up to 20 feet high and covered with cedar, balsam, tag alder, and brush. Fishing is good for brook trout.

The third segment is that area from the Miners Fall down to its mouth. Shortly below the falls the river flows through Miners Lake. The stream in this segment is up to 30 feet wide, four feet deep, and has a rapid velocity. The water is brown and cool, rarely exceeding 70°F. The bottom is roughly 85 percent sand, 10 percent gravel and rock, and five percent hardpan or bedrock. Two small tributaries enter this segment.

This portion of the stream is a series of rapids and riffles with abundant cover (logs, undercuts, brush, and pools). Aquatic vegetation is rare, and banks are high and covered with cedar, spruce, balsam, tag alder, and associated brush. Steelheads and brook trout spawn here.

Miners Lake is a 30-acre lake containing warmwater species. There is no direct access to the lake, but those fishermen willing to canoe or wade upriver, or walk in from the road, might hook a good-size brook trout or rainbow.

The Mosquito River is a small trout stream tributary to Lake Superior in central Alger County. It too lies largely within the Pictured Rocks National Lakeshore and drains about 12 square miles. The Mosquito arises from a small semiopen marsh and flows generally northward—emptying into Lake Superior about four miles east of Munising. In its course of travel, it flows through beautiful rolling hills, covered with a mixture of white birch, maple, and hemlock.

The river, which lies at the bottom of a steep gully, has very limited road access but provides about 7.5 miles of out-of-the-way brook and rainbow trout fishing. Two roads cross the stream: County Road 639, north of Melstrand, off the Adams Truck Trail, and a poor dirt road running south from County Road 639, at the site of the old Cleveland-Cliffs Iron Company Camp 15. All other access is either from foot trails or unmapped dirt roads. Although the Mosquito lies within the Pictured Rocks National Lakeshore, about 40 percent of the adjacent land is under private ownership.

The upper Mosquito, from its headwaters down to Mosquito Falls, varies from four to 15 feet wide and from three to 12 inches deep. The water is dark brown and only moderately clear. The bottom consists mostly of black organic material. Beyond the confluence of the Noble Lake outlet, the water is clearer, and the bottom changes to gravel and rock with just a trace of sand.

This section is characterized by a series of riffles and slicks, with large rocks, pools, a few logs, and undercut banks for fish cover. The stream here is fishable, but success is usually considered poor above Noble Lake outlet. Fishing pressure is light. The principal game species above the falls is brook trout; however, legal-sized fish are not too abundant. Mosquito Falls, with its six- to seven-foot vertical drop, is a barrier to both rainbow trout and sea lamprey. Natural foods in this area include caddisflies, mayflies, stoneflies, mottled sculpin, and dace.

There are several small tributaries in this segment of stream and all are similar physically to the mainstream. None of them provide a fishery; however, the spawning and nursery habitat is available.

The mainstream from Mosquito Falls to the mouth provides the best trout fishing. This portion of the river ranges from 16 to 30 feet wide, up to 26 inches deep, and has moderate to rapid velocity. The bottom varies from mixed gravel and rock to a solid sandstone and hardpan.

The water is clear, light brown, and cold. Although anglers will find this area easy to fish, wading may be difficult in some places because of the rapid stream flow and rocky bottom. There are a series of rapids and slicks, but there is ample cover—mostly logs, boulders, undercut banks, pools, and hardpan shelves. Fishing success is usually good for rainbow and brook trout, and fishing pressure is moderately heavy early in the season.

The West Branch Mosquito River (also called the Little Mosquito River), is the only tributary below the falls. It is a small, clear, shallow-water stream which flows over a rocky bottom through a sharp sandstone cut. Some areas of the cut have near vertical banks from 25 to 40 feet high. The West Branch originates from several springs, which have been dammed by beavers, and is characterized by a series of riffles and rapids. Cover is poor and consists mostly of large rocks and an occasional log. Like the mainstream, it also has a formidable waterfall near the mouth and receives fair numbers of spring-run rainbows.

The Hurricane River is a scenic little stream arising from several beaver-dammed springs about nine miles west of Grand Marais in northeastern Alger County. It drains about 10 square miles and flows generally northward through picturesque rolling sand and sandstone hills. The area is covered with a thin mantle of sandy loam inland, and sandy dunes near Lake Superior. It is vegetated with a mixture of red maple, white birch, beech, and hemlock on the hills, and cedar and tag alder in the low areas. The Hurricane reaches Lake Superior by slicing through Pictured Rocks National Lakeshore dunes near Au Sable Point.

Of the roughly nine miles of stream, only 25 percent of the adjacent lands are under public ownership. However, 33 percent of the private ownership is Cleveland-Cliffs Iron Company land. Since this too is available for recreational activities, a little over half the adjacent lands are open to the public.

Road access to this stream is very limited, however. Direct access may be had from the Hurricane Truck Trail (County Road 14), County Road 700, and from an old logging road off County Road 700. There is reasonble access from numerous foot trails and unmapped dirt roads. Because of the seclusion, this little stream provides nine miles of reasonably remote fishing for brook trout and steelheads.

The river can be divided into three segments: (1) headwaters to the Hurricane River Truck Trail; (2) truck trail to the bridge in Section 14; and (3) from the bridge down to the mouth. The river in the headwaters segment is up to six feet wide, one foot deep, and the water is clear and light brown. The flow is very slow (slicks and pools) due to the flatness of the land and many beaver ponds. The bottom is largely silt over gravel and sand, but spawning habitat is ample to support a good brook trout population. The three major tributaries in this area are very similar to the mainstream.

Food organisms include mayflies, caddisflies, stoneflies,

dragonflies, dipteran larvae, beetle larvae, and worms. Fishing for brookies in this segment is mostly limited to the beaver ponds and is best when the ponds are active.

The river in the middle section (from the Hurricane Truck Trail down to the bridge in Section 14) ranges up to 40 feet wide, 30 inches deep, and is dotted with several small islands. The water is clear and medium brown. The bottom is made up of about 60 percent sand, 25 percent gravel, and 15 percent rock rubble, and velocity is rapid due to a series of riffles and slicks.

There are no tributaries in this segment. The stream is well shaded with an overgrowth of alder, cedar, and balsam fir and abundant instream cover consists of logs, undercuts, rocks, pools, overhanging brush, and vegetation.

Fishermen will find this middle segment of stream readily fishable and moderately productive for spring steelheads and brook trout. Spawning habitat is abundant in this area and so is nursery habitat.

The third segment extends from the road bridge in Section 14 to the mouth and ranges from 19 to 35 feet in width and from 15 to 30 inches in depth. The water is clear, cold (rarely exceeding 65°F), light brown, and flows along rapidly. The bottom is composed of 30 percent sand, 30 percent gravel, 20 percent rock and rubble, and 20 percent bedrock.

Swift slicks and rapids dominate this area, and wading can be treacherous because of the bedrock or rock rubble and the swift current. However, deep holes are nearly nonexistent. Cover is more than adequate for both juvenile and adult trout and is made up of logs, cut banks, pools, boulders, and vegetation. Food is abundant and includes mayflies, caddisflies, stoneflies, dragonflies, dipteran larvae, beetle larvae, and muddlers.

The principal fishery is for the spring-run rainbow, although natural reproduction does sustain a small brook trout population.

Many of the rainbows caught in the river are taken from a pool at the base of a small falls about 400 feet above the mouth. Here, the fish pause for rest after negotiating a 200- to 300-foot long sandstone incline.

(See map on Pages 46-47)

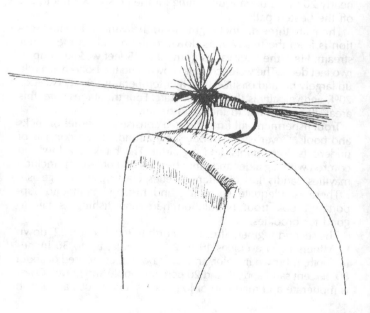

MORE ALGER COUNTY STREAMS

By LELAND ANDERSON
Fisheries Biologist

Other Alger County streams include Beaver, Sable, Carpenter, and Sullivan creeks and are discussed together in this chapter.

Beaver Creek and its tributaries (Lowney, Arsenault, Bill's, and Little Beaver creeks) are located within the Pictured Rocks National Lakeshore in northern Alger County. They originate from springs and seepage (from a ridge and small cedar swamps) and flow northward through the sand dunes into Lake Superior between Grand Portal and AuSable points, draining about 12 square miles. This system is the main drainage of the eastern portion of the Beaver Basin and lies about eight miles northeast of Melstrand and 18 miles west of Grand Marais. Access to the watershed is via the Beaver Basin Road to the Little Beaver Lake public access site.

Arsenault, Little Beaver, and Bill's creeks all flow into Little Beaver Lake which then empties into the west end of Beaver Lake. The channel between the two lakes is short but boatable. It has a sand and silt bottom and varies from 15 to 30 feet in width.

Lowney Creek and its tributaries empty directly into the south end of Beaver Lake. Beaver Creek provides the short (about one mile long) connection between Beaver Lake and Lake Superior.

Arsenault Creek is three to 10 feet wide and has a maximum depth of three feet with beaver ponds that may be somewhat deeper. The surrounding vegetative cover is white birch, oak, and spruce in the upland with balsam and tag alder in the bottom lands.

The stream bottom is composed mostly of sand and silt with sparse vegetation, and the water is brown. Arsenault Creek produces small brookies.

Little Beaver Creek originates from springs and has a moderately steep gradient. The bottom is composed mostly of sand and gravel, except near the mouth where it is sand and silt. This creek is about two miles long, varies in width from two to 10 feet, and is up to two feet deep. Vegetative cover is mixed hardwood in the upland and spruce, balsam, and alder in the lowland. The stream is well shaded and littered with logs and debris so cover is considered good for the small brook trout that live here.

Bill's Creek is a small, spring-fed stream originating from the foot of the ridge. It has clear water with a maximum depth of 18 inches, varies from two to six feet wide, and is about half a mile long. A few small brook trout reside in the stream.

Lowney Creek is formed from the East and West branches and Hemlock and Spring Pond creeks. They originate from springs in marshy lowland and small cedar swamps at the base of the ridge. These creeks have flows which vary from sluggish to moderately rapid and a substrate composed mostly of sand, silt, and egg-size gravel.

Lowney Creek supports a dense stand of northern hardwoods, cedar, and hemlock; however, the lower portion has been heavily logged. The gradient of the stream system is quite high (the East

and West branches having an average gradient of 50 feet per mile).

The water of the Lowney Creek system is generally clear and colorless with the exception of a few brown-stained ponds in the extreme headwaters of the West and Hemlock branches. It is uniformly quite hard and, other things being equal, is relatively productive. Beaver ponds and artificially created ponds throughout the watershed have added to the overall productivity of the stream. Water temperatures get progressively colder downstream due to the addition of spring seepage.

In the East and West branches, where the gradient is steep, the fish population consists mostly of small brook and rainbow trout. From the confluence of these two branches down to Beaver Lake, the stream loses much of its gradient and flows over the bottom of sterile, moving sand. Some brook and rainbow trout are still found, however.

Beaver Creek is the stream that takes the accumulated flow of all the tributaries and Beaver Lake to Lake Superior. This stream varies from 15 to 50 feet in width and ranges up to two feet in depth. It flows through a sand dune topography, but the banks are vegetated with white birch, oak, poplar, and white pine on the high ground and tag alder on the water fringe. The bottom is entirely sand except where it flows across gravelly rubble on the Lake Superior beach. Most of the year this portion of stream has no fish due to its shallowness and lack of cover, but steelheads and salmon use it in their migratory approach to the more productive tributaries.

Beaver Lake has an area of 765 acres, a maximum depth of 39 feet, and contains both warmwater species and brook and rainbow trout and splake.

Sable Creek lies about two miles west of the picturesque little village of Grand Marais in eastern Alger County. It flows from the 628-acre Grand Sable Lake into Lake Superior and drains about 10 square miles.

Sable Creek has a moderate flow, sand bottom, and banks that are well vegetated with tag alder, maple, beech, and mountain ash. About a quarter mile from Lake Superior it plunges for about 50 feet in a series of steep steps and then flows to Lake Superior over a sandstone, rubble, and sandy bottom in rapid fashion. The stream width varies from 15 to 30 feet and in depth from six inches to three feet.

The water is light brown, and temperature changes radically with the season and the influence of surface water from Grand Sable Lake. In dry seasons the flow deteriorates to a "mere trickle," but during the spring runoff, the stream is a veritable torrent. Stream banks are well stabilized so there is not an erosion problem.

The principal fishery occurs from the foot of the falls to the mouth. The stream decline is moderately rapid so pools are long and shallow. Stream cover consists of a few undercut banks, accumulated debris, logs, and overhanging vegetation. There is a formidable jam of driftwood near the mouth which changes with the northerly winds.

A midsummer inventory of species present indicated mostly warmwater fish that undoubtedly came down from Grand Sable Lake. Spring flows pull in good runs of smelt, white and longnose suckers, and steelheads. In the fall of 1975 about 200 to 300 pink salmon were noted below the falls.

Since the stream has become a part of the Pictured Rocks National Lakeshore an access site and improved steps and path have been provided to the falls and down the ridge. Hiking trails branch off up and down the creek and to the adjacent dunes.

Carpenter Creek lies almost entirely within the outskirts of the village of Grand Marais in eastern Alger County. This small, picturesque, but obscure, brown-stained creek originates from springs and seeps atop the Lake Superior escarpment and flows into West Bay. The surrounding hills are vegetated with northern hardwoods, cedar, spruce, and balsam. Tag alders fringe the stream bed.

The stream varies in width from a few feet near its source to about 30 feet as it approaches West Bay. Water depth varies from about four inches to three feet. The gradient is relatively steep, and the spring water flow can be considered torrential. However, erosion is not a problem due to the heavy bank cover.

The bottom is composed principally of gravel, sandstone outcrop, and sand and as such it provides excellent spawning habitat for trout and salmon. Stream cover is also very good, consisting of sandstone boulders, undercut banks, logs, debris, and holes. Vegetation is sparse, but food organisms are moderately abundant and include caddisflies, mayflies, stoneflies, sculpins, and longnose dace.

Stream temperatures rarely exceed 70°F, so brook trout and rainbow trout are present throughout the watershed. Although fish are small, some angling pressure for resident fish (mostly brookies) does occur in the headwaters.

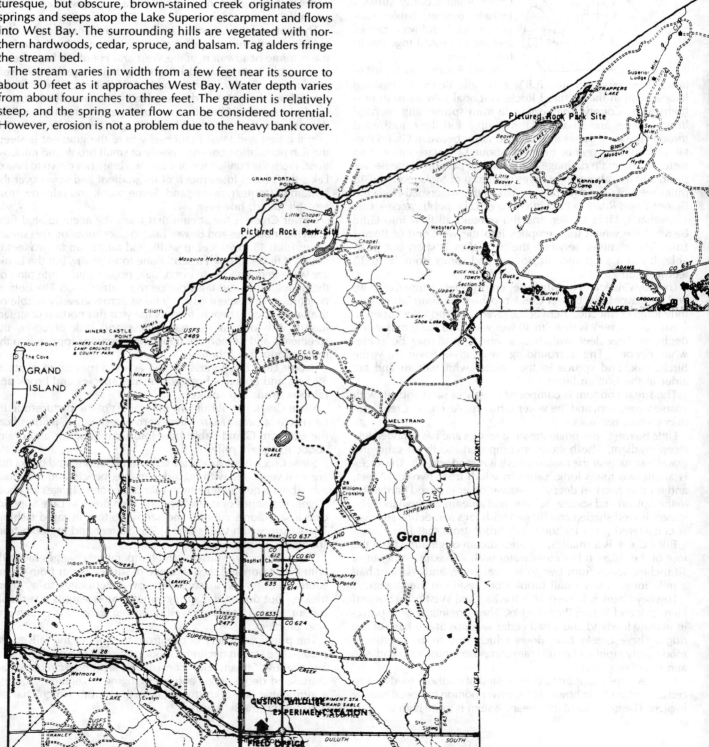

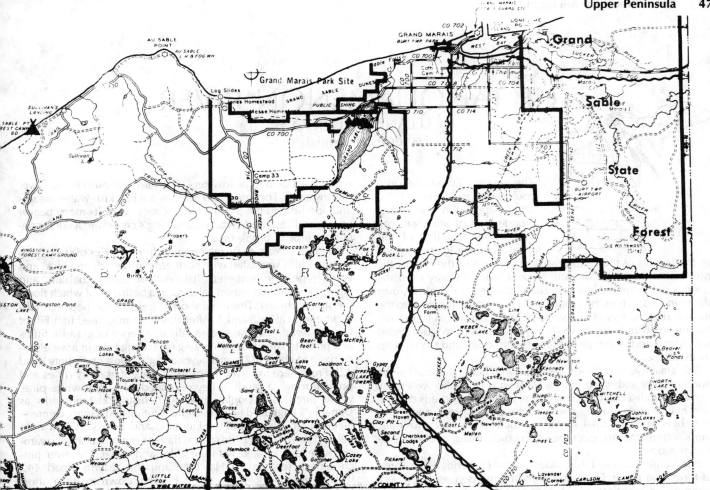

Since growth of resident fish is poor and natural reproduction is abundant, stocking is not necessary. Carpenter Creek receives a spring steelhead and fall coho salmon run, thus providing some fishing in West Bay near the mouth. Both species reproduce naturally here and probably make a substantial contribution to the lucrative fishery in Grand Marais Harbor.

Sullivan Creek is a small stream located in northeastern Alger County. It drains about one-and-one-half square miles and empties into Lake Superior about 12 miles west of the town of Grand Marais. Access is by County Road 700.

It is small (five to 15 feet wide, four inches to three feet deep), has a steep gradient, and begins in a series of shallow spring-fed ponds. The pond bottoms are sand and silt and vegetated with bulrushes and tag alders. The stream bottom from the outlets is sand and gravel. Stream banks are steep, but quite well vegetated with northern hardwoods, hemlock, white pine, and cedar. Stream cover is abundant and consists of undercut banks and accumulated debris.

The most common fish species present are brook and rainbow trout. Pink salmon were noted here in the fall of 1975. Food is abundant in the form of caddisflies, mayflies, and stoneflies, chironomids, and freshwater shrimp; the latter are especially abundant in upstream ponds.

Water chemistry indicates medium productivity. Water temperatures rarely get above 65°F. The water is clear except during the spring breakup.

This creek has a history of a late spring steelhead run out of Lake Superior and a fall run of pink salmon in the odd-numbered years. The lower 300 to 400 feet get a good play from the spring steelhead fishermen. Brook trout fishing has been good in headwater ponds in the past, and at one time these ponds were stocked with brook trout on a regular basis. Because public access to these ponds is no longer assured, stocking has been discontinued.

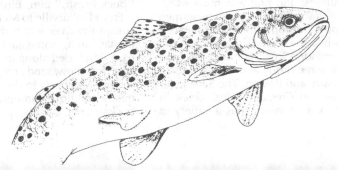

THE TAHQUAMENON RIVER

By LELAND ANDERSON
Fisheries Biologist

The mighty Tahquamenon—you name it, it has it! No other stream in the water wonderland of Michigan can match the versatility of this great and historic river. Famed in the legend of the Chippewa and steeped in the lore of the hob-nailed boot, this aquatic serpent twists its way from the springs of northern Alger and Luce counties at its source, over the twin cataracts of the Upper and Lower falls, and on into the mist-studded waves of Hiawatha's Gitche Gumee at its mouth. Its nursling tributaries drain 790 square miles of wood-studded hills to the northwest, pine plains to the south, and tannic bogs in its valley.

This great river has something for all who have an interest in the north country and much of its watershed is in public ownership.

The naturalist can find a myriad of flowers, hundreds of song and marsh birds, ducks, geese, eagles and ospreys, and many members of the animal kingdom, such as beavers, muskrats, mink, otters, rabbits, deer, bears, coyotes, foxes, and an occasional moose.

The hunter has used this waterway for centuries as a source of travel and game. Duck and coot hunting is considered very good on adjacent Mud Lake near McMillan, the Natalie Marshes inundated by the Dollarville Flooding, and in many bayous and inlets along its entire course.

For the canoeist, there is water to test the expert and satisfy the novice. This stream may be floated from Long Lake above the Eagle's Nest near its source to Whitefish Bay at its mouth. There are many points of access and the principal portages are around the two great falls.

The angler can test his skill along the river's entire course. A great variety of species are found in the river. An electroshocking survey in 1988 showed 11 species to be present from Newberry to the Upper Falls. Among the game species present were walleyes, northern pike, yellow perch, pumpkinseed, sunfish, and rock bass. The river also provides fishing for brook and brown trout. Brook trout dominate the river above the McMillan Bridge and in its tributaries. Between the falls lunker smallmouth and brown trout may be on the angler's menu. Below the lower falls the river again is mostly inhabited by warmwater species: northern pike, walleyes, smallmouth bass, perch, and rock bass. Northerns, muskies, and steelheads are also occasionally taken.

The Tahquamenon River has been stocked in the past with brook trout, brown trout, walleyes, and northern muskies.

Many of the tributaries above the falls also furnish fishermen with imposing targets. The upper portion of the East Branch is well known for brook trout while the lower stretches abound with pike and walleyes. The Hendrie River is noted for good pike fishing, but does produce some brook and brown trout at its headwaters near Fibron Quarry and Rexton. The Sage River is a brown trout stream. Teaspoon Creek, the first creek in Michigan to be set aside for "kid's fishing," has a variety of

species—trout in its headwaters and warmwater fish in the lower marshy areas. The Auger and Murphy are brackish-water streams and add little to the fishery. Silver Creek, with its many beaver ponds, and East, Red, Syphon, and King's creeks are feeders containing mostly brook trout.

The mainstream drainage emerges from a series of steep, rolling sand hills vegetated with northern hardwood, hemlock, and white pine, and scattered "islands" of spruce, balsam, and cherry. The Tahquamenon Lakes form a basin out of which flows the stream thread. There is a short gravelly rapids between Tahquamenon Lakes 2 and 3. After flowing under the High Fill of County Road 422, the stream falls in a series of gravelly riffles and pools to Long Lake, emerging from Long Lake in a wide sandy basin to about 200 yards beyond Eagle's Nest on County Road 421. From here the river drops in a series of gravelly riffles and pools through a sandy valley vegetated with lofty white pine, white birch, and poplar, past such historical landmarks as Danaher's High Bridge and several hunting and fishing camps—Steelbinder, Thompson's, Skinner's, and Ross's. A half mile beyond Ross's Camp, the stream flattens out into a small swampy "spreads" fringed with tag alder and cedar. The river pinches back together at Hatch's Camp on County Road 442 (East Creek Truck Trail). From Hatch's downstream a short distance, the stream winds through a flat, marshy area and then spreads again over a flat swamp of conifers and tag alder. Although it is hard to follow in this area, the mainstream follows the low sandy hills along County Road 442 for a half mile and then swings southward to its confluence with King's Creek. The bottom in the spreads area is sand and silt and littered with windfalls of cedar and spruce. From King's Creek downstream, the river is considered canoeable to the confluence with Syphon Creek, where the river picks up more depth and width, allowing for use of outboard motors from here to its mouth. From Syphon Creek to the mouth of the Hendrie, the river is slow and meandering through bog and low swamp. There are relatively few high spots along this stretch of the river and these are occupied by road crossings, camps, and cabin sites. The McMillan (steel) Bridge spans the river at County Road 415. At Natalie is a public access site and a state forest campground. This popular landing was once the site of Underwood's muskrat farm.

From Dollarville to M-123 about three miles downstream the river winds through several grass and bushy bayous. The banks vary up to 15 feet in height and are vegetated with grass, willow, "buck brush," elm, birch, maple, and tag alder.

From Dollarville to McPhee's Landing about six miles downstream the river winds through low sand hills vegetated with poplar, birch, maple, jack pine, and thornapple. Marshy bayous have developed along its course over the years. The river is relatively shallow, sand and silt bottomed, and littered with debris.

From McPhee's to the mouth of the Hendrie River the Tahquamenon flows through low marshland vegetated with alder, buck brush, cattails, and sedges. Low sandy hills emerge

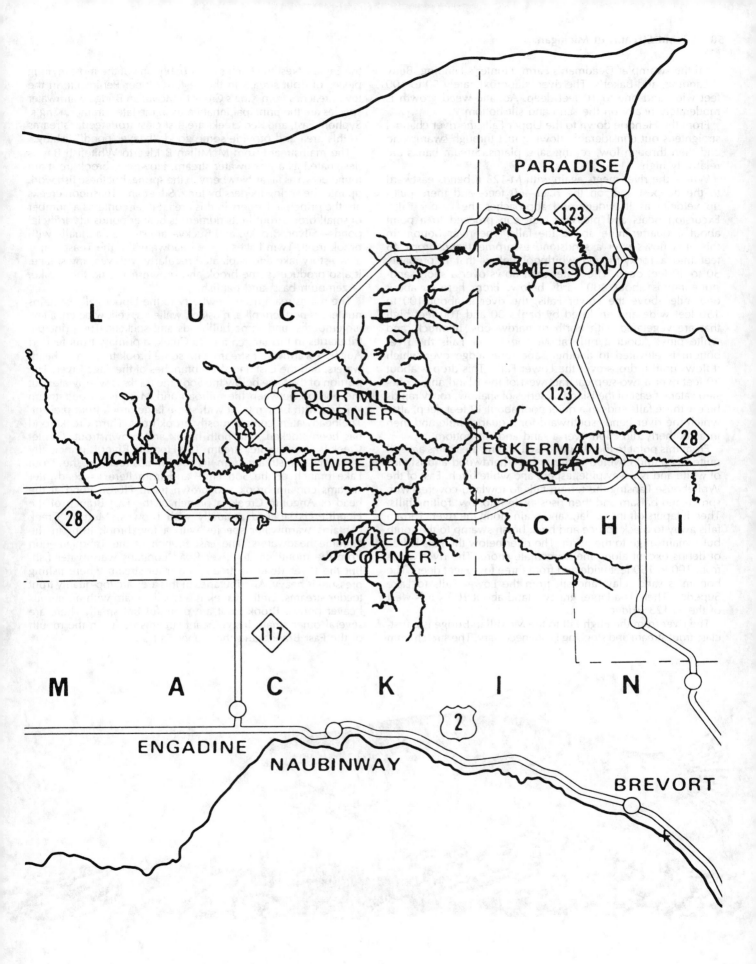

from the swamp at Deadman's Farm, Hunter's Landing, Betty B Landing, and Baker's. The river is approximately 50 to 100 feet wide and one to 10 feet deep. Aquatic weed growth is moderately heavy on the sand and silt bottom.

From the Hendrie down to the Upper Falls the river channel straightens out considerably flowing first through swampland and then through low, rolling sand plains. Stream banks are relatively high.

Where the river meets again with M-123 it bends eastward to the deepest spot on the river—60 feet—and there picks up velocity as it widens and approaches the Upper Falls. Excursion boats and pleasure craft can proceed to a point about a quarter mile above the falls. The river bottom in this area flows over a sandstone escarpment and drops 48 feet into a rocky-fringed whirlpool below that is probably 30 to 40 feet deep. The water then flows over a short sandstone rapids about 400 yards below. From here to about one mile above the Lower Falls, the river is about 100 to 150 feet wide and enclosed by banks 80 and 100 feet high that are vegetated with northern hardwoods, hemlock, and white pine. About a mile above the Lower Falls the river bottom is elevated to another sandstone ledge over which it flows until it drops over the Lower Falls. This drop is about 20 feet over a two-step cataract west of the island and a one-step cataract east of the island. A series of shallow, rocky rapids below these falls ends in a quiet pool about 12 feet deep, after which the river bends southward for a quarter mile and then in a southerly direction over a sand and silt bottom.

From this point to the Whitehouse Landing the banks are still quite steep and covered with northern hardwood and islands of white and Norway pine, aspen, and white birch. East of the Whitehouse Lansing the terrain falls to lowland covered with spruce and balsam and then rises again into low, rolling hills. Then it tapers off into a flat, sand plain along the river. Terrain falls away to black spruce and buck brush swamp to the south but remains high to the north. The river below the falls is free of debris except along the immediate shore. The river varies from 100 to 150 feet wide and from three to 20 feet deep. The bottom is sand, clay, and silt from the Lower Falls to Lake Superior. There is a large, grassy island about 100 yards west of the M-123 Bridge.

The river from the High Fill to the McMillan Bridge is a first-class trout stream and stocking is not necessary. The stretch from the Eagle's Nest to Hatch's is probably one of the most inviting pieces of trout stream in the eastern Upper Peninsula. In the lower reaches from King's Creek to McMillan Bridge warmwater species are the principal inhabitants in the late summer. King's, Syphon, East, and Red creeks are first-class trout feeder streams in this area and provide some good "beaver pond" fishing.

The mainstream from McMillan Bridge to Whitefish Bay is designated as a warmwater stream. However, brook trout are found down as far as Newberry in the spring, but these fish work up into the spring feeders by June. Silver and Teaspoon creeks are the principal feeders in this area. Silver contains a number of small brook trout in its numerous beaver ponds. Its artificial ponds—Silver, Brocky, and Bucky—are stocked annually with brook trout. Twin Lakes at the headwaters of the Teaspoon is a two-story lake and is planted regularly with yearling splake. It also produces some brook and brown trout, northern pike, largemouth bass, and panfish.

The mainstream from Newberry to the Upper Falls contains numerous northern pike, muskies, walleyes, yellow perch, a few largemouths, and some bullheads and suckers. The principal tributaries in this stretch are 39 Creek, a primary trout feeder; Auger, a warmwater stream with some brook trout in its headwaters; and the East and West branches of the Sage River. The portion of the Sage below the Soo Line tracks is warmwater but the portion between the railroad and M-28 is a trout stream stocked with brown trout with some large brook trout present. The headwaters contain mostly brook trout. Third Creek Pond has been stocked with both brook and brown trout. Gimlet Creek is a warmwater stream. The Hendrie River is principally a warmwater stream from its mouth upstream to the Trout Lake branch of the Soo Line, and from here its headwater streams contain brook and brown trout. Fibron Pond at the head of Anguilm Creek, a branch of the East Branch of the Hendrie, is stocked annually with browns. Murphy Creek contains warmwater species with a few brook trout in the extreme headwaters. The East Branch of the Tahquamenon from the mouth up to River Road contains warmwater fish, but the River Road upstream is a trout stream where fishing pressure is heavy. All tributaries in this area are top-quality trout feeder streams. Linton Creek is a small stream with numerous beaver ponds. Brook trout are plentiful but small. There are several other small, insignificant streams between the mouth of the East Branch and the Upper Falls.

THE INDIAN RIVER
By JOHN D. SCHROUDER
Fisheries Biologist

The Indian River watershed contains 108 linear miles of mainstream and tributaries and drains 126,080 acres. The river flows southeasterly through Alger, Delta, and Schoolcraft counties before joining the Manistique River near Manistique. Most of the 41-mile mainstream is composed of marginal or second-quality trout water, but it does grow trophy-size brook and brown trout. Top-quality trout water is found in many tributaries and the upper mainstream. The Indian River is unusual among Upper Peninsula streams in that it: supports a self-sustaining population of lake sturgeon, a threatened species, and produces exceptional mayfly (**Hexagenia limbata**) hatches that stimulate feeding of trophy browns during early summer evenings. It flows through 8,400-acre Indian Lake.

The mainstream is a popular canoeing route from the "Widewaters" U.S. Forest Service Campground located above Federal Highway (FH) 13, down to FH-2212, the last take-out above the "spreads." The river is bridged by FH-13, FH-2258, County Road 437, FH-2213 at Steuben, County Road P441, and M-94. Ninety percent of the watershed is in public ownership under the U.S. Forest Service (USFS) and managed as the Hiawatha National Forest. Only about 15,000 acres are privately owned, most of which is part of the Little Indian Hunt and Fish Club. Four USFS campgrounds are located near the river. Residential development is concentrated only at Steuben.

Forty-three lakes and ponds discharge into the Indian, offering a wide variety of fishing opportunities. They are responsible for summer water temperatures that are marginal for trout. Although 36 lakes empty into the river above M-94, the lower reaches receive enough groundwater to sustain optimal conditions for brown trout. Most of the brook trout in the mainstream seek groundwater springs and seepages during hot weather.

Over 66 miles of tributaries supply water to the Indian, the largest being the Little Indian, which is more than 10 miles long. Other major tributaries include Big Murphy, Little Murphy, Delias Run, Deer, Bear, Kilpecker, Carr, Big Ditch, and Iron creeks.

The Indian River mainstream originates in eastern Alger County and flows through a series of lakes (Doe-Hartney chain) in its upper length. In spite of the lake influence, an excellent native brook trout fishery exists below Hovey and Hartney lakes. Although summer water temperatures approach marginal ranges for brook trout, adequate groundwater and cool tributaries provide good trout survival. Between Crow Lake and FH-13 a warmwater fishery exists due to the influence of the Fish-Barr lake chain. Temperatures begin lowering below FH-13 and optimum feeding levels for brown trout develop between County Road 449 and FH-2213. Below FH-2258 temperatures remain well within the tolerance levels of brook and brown trout.

The Department of Natural Resources stocks the mainstreams in Schoolcraft County with brook, brown, and rainbow trout annually. About 5,500 yearling (five- to seven-inch) brown trout are released at seven sites below FF-2258. Past surveys by the U.S. Forest Service and Michigan Department of Natural Resources show good water temperatures and good survival and some natural reproduction of brook and brown trout. In most of the river brook and brown trout coexist, with brown trout being more numerous. However, surveys of 1988 and 1989 showed a shift from brown to brook trout upstream from Thunderlake Road. This area is more rocky. In addition to trout, a 1979 survey also documented a sizable spawning run (50 to 75) of lake sturgeon upstream to the Steuben area from Indian Lake and the upper river. These three- to five-foot-long fish use the rocky cobble and riffles in the vicinity of the USFS campground. Sturgeon begin moving upstream about mid-May and reach spawning areas by late May or early June.

From its origin in Hovey Lake to FH-13 the mainstram contains excellent brook trout water downstream to Crow Lake. Channel width varies from 15 to 35 feet. The bottom is primarily sand with small areas of gravel and cobble.

Below Crow Lake the river flows through the Fish-Barr lake chain and its fishery reflects the warmwater species which reside in these lakes.

Ninety-five percent of the river between FH-13 and FH-2258 is wadable. Gravel riffles are present at the upper and lower ends of this stretch. Although water temperatures in the main channel become marginal for brown trout and too high for brook trout, groundwater springs along many stream banks provide trout refuge during summer months.

Water temperatures improve below the mouth of the Little Indian, remaining optimum for brown trout all summer. Rock and riffle areas become more common and 85 percent of the stretch between the Little Indian and County Road 437 is wadable. Catches of 10- to 18-inch browns are fairly common and a few large brook trout are also taken above County Road 437 early in the season.

The stretch from County Road 437 to Delias Run is considered very good trout water. Water temperatures are optimum for browns and, at worst, marginal for brook trout during the hottest months. Several unnamed tributaries in this section provide cool water refuge for brooks as needed. Nearly 75 percent of this section is wadable and the entire reach is composed of swift, gravel-bottomed riffles. Adequate cover is provided by boulders, logs, and, in some areas, by overhanging tag alders.

From Delias Run to the Indian River picnic grounds is ranked as fair to good trout water. Numerous log jams in this stretch make canoeing hazardous for inexperienced canoeists.

The USFS maintains a modest-sized picnic and camping area off M-94 along the east bank of the river. A stairway and canoe skid over and down the 40-foot bank to the river is available plus a small dock and landing on the riverbank.

Downstream from the picnic grounds FF-2212 is the last convenient canoe take-out point above Indian Lake. The bridge is no longer present. Between the picnic grounds and FH-2212 the river separates into many small, braided channels— "spreads."

Native brook trout and stocked and wild brown trout are found along undercut banks in the spreads. Excellent mayfly hatches occur just above and below the picnic area in late June-early July that entice lunker (16- to 28-inch) browns to feed on warm, humid, early summer nights. Submerged logs make wading after dark hazardous. Near FH-2212, warmwater fish become more prevalent and mark the end of the better trout water on the Indian system. A very few large brown trout are taken between FH-2212 and Indian Lake, but walleyes, pike, and some smallmouth bass dominate. After flowing through Indian Lake the river flows another three to four miles before joining the Manistique River opposite the Jamestown Slough.

The Little Indian River is the largest and most productive brook trout water in the Indian drainage. Arising from a group of small springs in eastern Alger County, it flows southeast into the Indian. About 85 percent of the frontage is owned by the USFS. The lower reaches of this stream are darkly stained due to leaching organic soils and swamp conifer, tannic acid input. About FH-13 in Alger County the Little Indian is crystal clear. Fish production capability is quite low by statewide standards but average for streams in the eastern Upper Peninsula.

In the headwaters area above FH-13, the Little Indian has a slow to moderate current and a sand and silt bottom. Downstream from FH-13 several small lakes and ponds on the stream are interspersed with swift, gravel-bottomed areas. The channel ranges from 25 to 35 feet wide and one to three feet deep. Cover consists of undercut banks and submerged logs and brush. Below FH-13 natural reproduction of brooks is excellent and fish up to 13 inches are common. Fishing pressure is light in the stretch between FH-13 and FH-2173 due to limited access.

From FH-2173 to the Little Indian Club property (north line of Section 15) the Little Indian is of pool-riffle character. Stream bottom is mostly sand with some gravel areas. The channel is from 25 to 35 feet wide and one to four feet deep. Brook and brown trout spawning is limited in this stretch. Fishing pressure is moderate to heavy in this reach during spring and early summer. Brook trout comprise most of the catch and creeled trout range from eight to 16 inches.

The portion of the Little Indian between Section 15 and the mouth is owned by the Little Indian Club and therefore inaccessible to the public.

Murphy Creek, considered marginal trout water, arises from Thunder Lakes in western Schoolcraft County. It ranges from 20 to 40 feet wide and one to three feet deep. It is primarily sand with clear to light brown-colored water. Much of the creek is overgrown with tag alders which limit its fishing potential. It does grow a few trophy brook and brown trout in its lower reaches but also contains warmwater fish.

Little Murphy Creek contains better trout water than Big Murphy Creek but requires stocking to sustain a fishery. It is clear, from 20 to 40 feet wide, one to two feet deep, and originates in wetlands north of Leg Lake in Schoolcraft County. It flows southeast about five miles to its confluence with the Indian River. From its source to Big Murphy Lake the slow-flowing Little Murphy Creek contains few trout. Below Big Murphy Lake some brook and brown trout spawning occurs in the limited gravel areas, but trout numbers

are low. The trout population increases near the mouth. Log jams are widely scattered through the section.

Delias Run Creek starts in the Big Island chain of lakes in western Schoolcraft County and flows southeasterly to the Indian River. The stream is generally slow, wide, and marshy in the headwaters. Beaver impoundments and natural lakes result in marginal or excessive summer water temperatures for brook trout. There is an area about two miles above County Road 437 suitable for trout spawning where the stream current increases and the bottom is mostly gravel. Cover is also very good and trout are taken here in the spring.

Downstream to County Road 437 the stream bottom is mostly sand with some gravel areas near bridge crossings on the Haywire Trail. Spring seepage is common, providing a better summer habitat for brook trout than in the area above. There is beaver activity near Jar Lake, where soft muck impedes wading. Tag alder is very dense above County Road 437 and cover is good.

The best brook trout population in Delias Run Creek is found between County Road 437 and the mouth, providing good early-season fishing. Gravel spawning areas are found just below County Road 437 and near the mouth.

Deer Creek is a small, second-quality warmwater tributary originating from McKeever Lake. Except for an occasional brook trout taken from beaver ponds below McKeever Lake, the fishery is dominated by warmwater species.

Bear Creek flows through a warmwater lake and several beaver ponds, arising from wetlands in eastern Delta County which give it its dark brown color. An occasional native brook trout is taken above Bear Lake and a few large browns are caught above Bear Creek's confluence with Big Murphy Creek.

Although the Little Indian River is the best brook trout water in the Indian River system, Kilpecker and Carr creeks probably rank second and third. Kilpecker Creek arises from cold springs in northeastern Delta County and flows southeasterly to Thunder Lake. Tag alder and brush border its banks for most of its length.

Carr Creek is classified as a top-quality coldwater tributary where natural reproduction of both brook and brown trout occurs. It arises from springs in northeastern Delta County. This 10- to 15-foot-wide stream flows through four ponds, all of which provide excellent trout fishing for wading and canoe fishermen.

To enhance the natural reproduction of trout above Carr Lake, the DNR constructed three spawning riffles between Carr Lake and Zigmaul Pond. A rough-fish barrier was also installed about 100 yards below Carr Lake to keep out suckers and northern pike.

Big Ditch Creek was dredged in the early 1900s to drain an area on which mint was grown. The former mint field sites and ditches became state and federal property in tax reversion sales during the 1930s. Today the "mint farm" area above M-94 through which Big Ditch flows is a state wildlife management area which harbors sharptail grouse. Wild brook and brown trout spawn in Big Ditch below M-94, but populations are sparse.

Iron Creek supports only minnows and suckers.

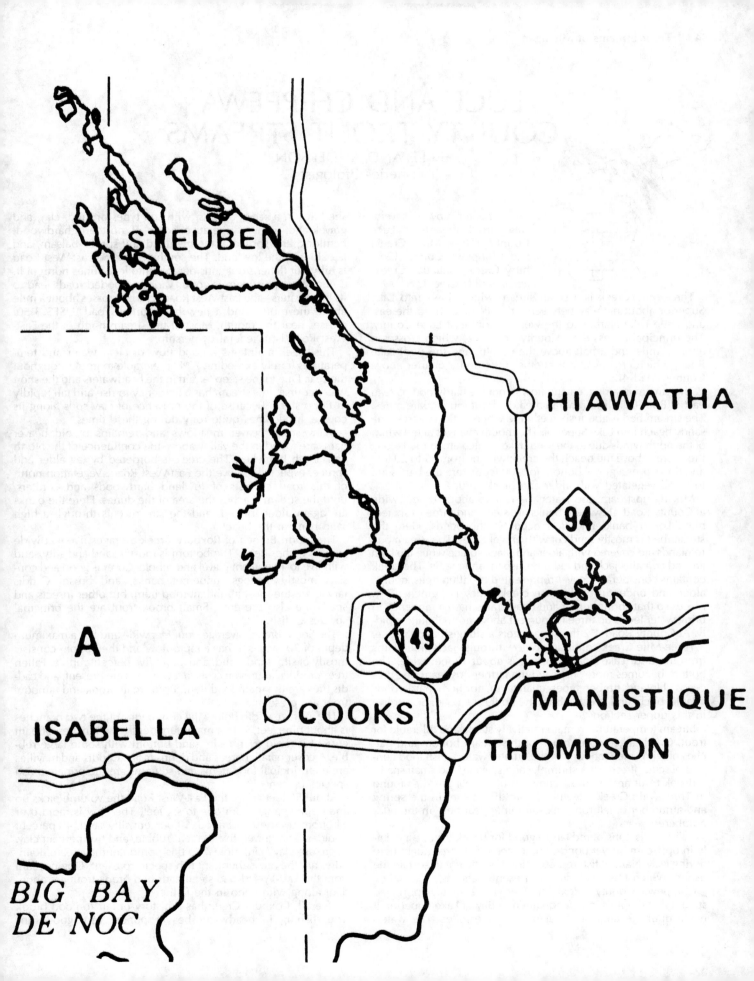

LUCE AND CHIPPEWA COUNTY TROUT STREAMS

By LELAND ANDERSON
Fisheries Biologist

This chapter covers several small trout streams in Luce County (Three-Mile Creek) and Chippewa County (Roxbury Creek, Halfaday Creek, and Pendills Creek).

Three-Mile Creek is a small stream which flows into Lake Superior about halfway between Crisp Point Light to the east and Little Lake Harbor to the west in northeast Luce County. The principal access is by County Road 412, which crosses it about a mile and a half above the mouth, and the Bodi Lake Road, which crosses about another mile and a quarter above County Road 412.

This stream is spring fed and flows from the hardwood plateau east of Bodi Lake, draining an area of about four square miles. The stream bed is about six feet wide where it flows across the sandy beach into Lake Superior. The mouth changes at the whim of the north winds due to the sand dykes which are formed along the shore. Above the beach the creek widens from 15 to 20 feet and flows over a gravel bottom for 200 feet. Here the banks are low and vegetated with alder and black spruce.

Moving upstream, the waters narrow to about 15 feet wide at County Road 412 where banks are steep and three to six feet high. Lower banks and flats occur in the bends. Here the stream bed is mostly sand cut with gravel riffles. The stream bottomlands are covered with alder and black spruce while the high ground contains jack and red pine, aspen, and maple. The creek contains considerable cover represented by fallen trees, debris, alder, and undercut banks. The creek valley is "pinched" in places so that spring runoff and heavy rains have a tendency to bring water levels up three to four feet above normal quite rapidly. At County Road 412 the stream gets a sluggish appearance.

Three-Mile Creek continues to flow through jack-pine plains from the Bodi Lake Road where it is about 10 feet wide. The bottom becomes more silty sand the farther upstream one proceeds. Upland timber types change to northern hardwoods (maple, birch, and beech) above the Bodi Lake Road. Beaver live in this upper section.

Stream temperatures remain relatively stable and tolerable for trout. Green algae cover much of the stream bottom and patches of wild celery abound in the quieter waters. Fish food consists of scuds (freshwater shrimp), caddis larvae, and small snails.

Brook trout are the most common of the game fishes found in Three-Mile Creek. Steelheads run this stream in the spring and a number of fall-run pink salmon appear here in the odd-numbered years.

Fishing is considered fair to good for brook trout, especially in upstream beaver ponds. Some steelheads are caught here during May. Natural fish reproduction is sufficient to sustain the fishery which this small stream presently affords.

Chippewa County's Roxbury Creek is a small, spring-fed stream that empties into Tahquamenon Bay of Lake Superior. It has a drainage area of about nine square miles. The watershed lies in a series of hills, with soil types of sand, clay, and gravel and with a vegetative cover of northern hardwood, hemlock, and spruce in the highland and spruce balsam, and tag alder in the lowland. The southwest of the East-West Road is hilly but flattens out considerably into low dunes north of it.

Access to the stream is good. Various wooded roads lead to its headwaters—the East-West Road (gravel) crosses about a mile above the mouth and a new hard surface road (USFS 3150) crosses near the mouth. Most of the stream north of the East-West Road is in federal ownership.

This creek maintains a good flow of clear water and temperatures (rarely exceeding 70°F) preferable to trout throughout the year. Due to the steep terrain in the headwaters and the short water course, this stream has a tendency to rise and fall rapidly in flood stage. Because of the presence of clay soils along its course, it becomes quite roily during these times.

Many small beaver meadows and remains of old beaver dams are found in the valley above the confluence of the North and South branches. The creek is bordered by tag alder and spruce, especially above the East-West Road. Vegetation north of this road consists of lowland hardwoods and conifers, until the stream reaches the area of the dunes. Here the banks are again alder fringed, and the stream cuts through a high sand bank at the beach.

The North Branch of Roxbury Creek averages five feet wide and six inches deep. The bottom is mostly sand and silty sand with five to 10 percent gravel and rubble. Cover is good and consists mostly of logs, undercut banks, and brush. Caddis larvae are the most abundant food item, but other insects and snails are also present. Small brook trout are the principal species of fish.

The South Branch averages four feet wide and has a maximum depth of 20 inches. It has a rapid flow and the bottom consists mostly of silty sand, sand, and about five percent rubble. Fallen trees produce abundant cover, a few weeds are present, and caddis flies are the main food item. Both small brook and rainbow trout are present.

The average width below the confluence of the two branches is about nine feet, with a maximum depth of 18 inches. Stream current is rapid over a silty sand bottom with some large rubble. A cover of fallen trees and debris is fair. Caddis and mayflies are the principal food items and sculpins are the principal fish species present.

About 50 feet above the East-West Road the volume picks up and depths range from one to six feet. The flow is rapid over a bottom composed of about 50 percent silty sand, 40 percent boulders and gravel, five percent rubble, and five percent clay. There are clay "sink holes" in this portion of the stream. Rainbows are the most abundant fish species present. Downstream from the East-West Road steelheads and brook trout are abundant along with coho in the fall.

Overall, Roxbury Creek has a history of fair to good brook trout fishing in headwater beaver ponds; very good runs of steelheads, suckers, and smelt in the spring; and runs of salmon in the fall. However, the principal fishery is for the spring-run rainbows from Lake Superior. Though stocked at one time with brook and rainbow trout, it was determined that natural reproduction is adequate to sustain the small fishery this stream affords. Rainbows do not grow to legal size within the stream itself.

Two borrow-pit-type ponds near the mouth of the Roxbury (just south of the new Lakeshore Drive) are managed for brook trout and are stocked annually with sublegals.

Halfaday Creek is a small, spring-fed stream in Chippewa County that empties into Lake Superior east of Tahquamenon Bay. It is about 12 miles northeast of the village of Strongs and can be reached via a hard surface road (USFS 3159 and Lakeshore Drive).

This stream has been well known for its spring and fall steelhead runs, fall salmon runs, and a fair population of brook trout in the headwaters. Suckers and smelt run the Halfaday in the spring while menominees and salmon can be caught at its mouth during the spring and fall. The mouth is bordered by U.S. Forest Service lands but much of the lower mainstream and West Branch watersheds are on private property. The headwaters of the mainstream are also on Forest Service lands.

The mainstream heads up at the edge of the Rexton sand plains and flows northward through a relatively steep valley in gentle rolling hills covered with maple, elm, white birch, and aspen. Here the main soil type is sand with some clay outcropping. There is some abandoned farm land on the plateau above Lake Superior. The terrain near the mouth is flat and sandy and is covered with soft maple, oak, aspen, and white birch.

The mainstream varies in width from three feet in the headwaters to 20 feet at the mouth, and the depth ranges from four inches to three feet. The water is clear and colorless but may become turbid after a heavy rain or during the spring runoff. There is evidence of beaver dams in the headwaters. Stream cover is abundant in the form of logs and downed timber, undercut banks and alder overhang, and bottom soil types are mainly sand, silty sand, clay, gravel, and rubble.

Stream pick-up volume indicates numerous spring inlets, a quality indicative of a good trout stream. Spawning grounds are most abundant in the upper middle reaches where gravel and rubble are most prevalent, and many steelheads have been known to spawn here in the spring.

The West Branch begins in sandy plains near USFS 3156 and dips down into an old beaver meadow. The surrounding high ground is vegetated with northern hardwoods, spruce, and balsam. The lower ridges are comprised of birch, poplar, and balsam, and alder fringes the low river banks.

Stream soils are 80 percent silty sand and 20 percent gravel and rubble. The water is clear and colorless and temperatures rarely reach 70°. Stream cover is good, insect life moderately abundant, and small brook trout and slimy muddlers are the predominate fish species present.

The midsection of the West Branch is rapid. The bottom is 85 percent silty sand, with 15 percent gravel and rubble (there are some good gravel runs). Width varies from two to five feet, and depth from two to 15 inches. Cover is fair and consists of fallen brush, logs, and undercut banks. A number of large springs feed this area. Stream banks are steep and covered with spruce, aspen, and white birch, while tag alder is heavy in the bottoms. This section contains small brook, rainbow, and coho fingerlings. Caddisflies, mayflies, and stoneflies are the main form of fish food. Downstream the West Branch widens to 11 feet, with deep spots of two feet or so.

Pendills Creek and its tributaries drain an estimated nine square miles in north-central Chippewa County. The watershed is located within 10 miles of Raco on M-28. It can be reached via the Dollar Settlement Road and Lakeshore Drive or USFS 3157 (Rexford Road), 3156 (Avery Grade), and spur roads and grades.

The mainstream begins in shallow Pendills Lake and flows westward through a cedar swamp to the approximate mouth of the Viddian Creek tributary. It then skirts a high ridge as it flows northwestward into Pendills Bay of Lake Superior. Sand dunes covered with spruce, balsam, aspen, and white birch lie along its northern margin.

Pendills Creek is fed by numerous spring-fed streams that flow from the high ridge whose steep valleys are deeply notched into hills covered with maple, beech, aspen, and white birch until they reach the valley, which is a wet, spring-fed cedar swamp. Tag alders fringe much of the creek edge. Viddian Creek is probably the largest of the main tributaries, and because it has a constant flow of clear, clean water, much of it is diverted into the federal hatchery system located at the mouth of Pendills Creek.

To get a better understanding of stream character and distance, the following description is offered beginning at the mouth and proceeding upstream. Because of a narrow sand beach, the mouth changes from time to time depending on direction and strength of wind off Lake Superior. The West Branch, which receives water from the hatchery, enters the mainstream about 200 feet above here, is about 10 to 15 feet wide, and has a maximum depth of six feet. The banks are steep and alder fringed, while the surrounding terrain is flat and covered with aspen, cherry, white birch, and spruce. The bottom is composed of sand, silty sand, and rubble, and a cover of logs and debris lines the stream. The creek contains lake, brook, rainbow, and brown trout, and coho salmon.

The mainstream of Pendills Creek is sluggish for the first 300 feet above the West Branch, has a width of 20 to 40 feet and a maximum depth of eight feet with a sand and silty bottom. Some eroded sand banks occur in this area. From a point 100 feet below Lakeshore Drive, Pendills Creek narrows down to 30 feet and becomes very rapid-flowing over mostly rock and rubble from the vicinity. Above this point three control structures (dams) inundated Pendills Creek up to the vicinity of Viddian Creek. These serve to provide a portion of the water supply to the hatchery but are fitted with a fish ladder to permit migrating species to ascend to the headwaters. Water is clear and light brown, with water temperatures rarely exceeding 70°F. The bottom is about 70 percent sand and silty sand, and 30 percent gravel and rubble. Stream banks are steep and alder fringed.

The principal modern-day fishery is concentrated from the water-control structures downstream to Lake Superior. This stream has had a history of good brook, brown, and rainbow fishing, both during the spring rainbow, smelt, and sucker runs and the fall salmon and steelhead runs. However, the Indian fishery in Lake Superior has severely reduced the sport fishery for lake trout, salmon, and menominee at the rivermouth and immediately offshore.

From the mouth of the Viddian upstream to Pendills Lake, the stream varies from 20 to 40 feet wide with a maximum depth of four feet. The bottom is mostly sand and silty sand with numerous vegetated sand bars. It flows through a bottom land covered with white cedar, spruce, and balsam, and the creek has a tag alder fringe.

The principal species of fish in this upper stretch are brook trout and some brown and rainbow trout fingerlings as well as occasional warmwater species such as perch, rock bass, bullheads, northern pike, suckers, and minnows that work down from Pendills Lake. The spring-creek habitat type is most conducive to trout production, and good fishing is

provided at times on the beaver ponds in adjoining valleys.

Lake-run browns make Pendills Creek an annual rendezvous, and both rainbows and coho salmon use the gravel riffles below the dam as their spawning grounds in season.

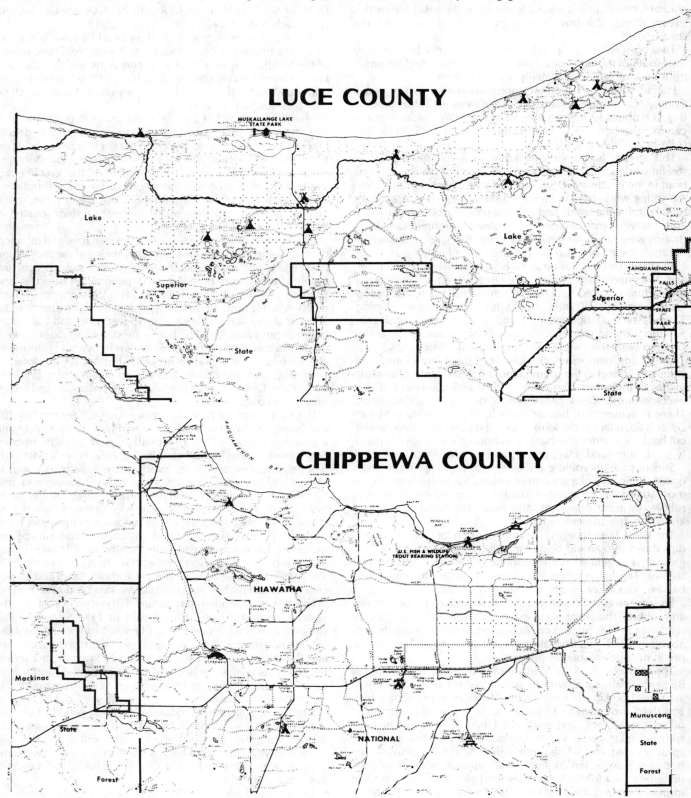

LUCE COUNTY

CHIPPEWA COUNTY

THE BLACK RIVER
By WILLIAM J. GRUHN
Fisheries Biologist

The Black River, flowing south through western Mackinac County to Lake Michigan, once supported a shingle mill, annual log drives, and good rainbow runs. It still flows much as it did when the original surveys were made in 1849. The Black River got its name because its water is darkly stained (black in appearance) from drainage of the surrounding bogs. It drains approximately 42 square miles and water temperatures rarely exceed 68°F, even in the lower end.

It is bridged by the Hiawatha Trail, the Peter's Creek Truck Trail at the Black River Forest Campground, the Black River Truck Trail, the Flowing Well Truck Trail, the Borgstrom Truck Trail, the Strickler Truck Trail, and US-2. The surrounding lands are largely under jurisdiction of the state, with only scattered blocks under private ownership.

The river system is formed by the mainstream and two major tributaries: The East Branch of Black River and Borgstrom Creek. There are several smaller tributaries: Peter's Creek, Silver Creek, Bark Creek, O'Neil Creek, Brennan Lake outlet, and some un-named tributaries which add lesser amounts of water.

One of the major tributaries, Borgstrom Creek, flows through a low, swampy bog containing numerous small knobs and ridges covered by swamp hardwoods and hemlock, black spruce, and balsam fir. It originates from two unnamed lakes southwest of Garnet and one unnamed creek. This creek is clear and spring fed with moderate flow and drains a soil area of loose sand and peat.

The bottom is characterized by sand and limited spawn-ing-quality gravel (below the Flowing Well Truck Trail) plus mud and debris in the deeper holes. There are several active beaver dams and a couple abandoned dams creating pools along its course.

Brook trout, rainbow trout, muddlers, and several species of small minnows are found in this stream. Most of the trout pre-sent are sublegal and don't offer much to the angler. However, this stream is important to the rest of the system as a reproduc-tion and nursery area.

The East Branch, the other major tributary of the Black River, originates just southeast of Garnet. It flows south and then west to join Borgstrom Creek near its mouth. The East Branch flows through a swampy bog dotted with small knobs and ridges covered by swamp hardwoods, hemlock, black spruce, and balsam fir. The soils are the same loose sand and peat found around Borgstrom Creek.

The clear, spring-fed waters of the East Branch run rapid in its headwaters but become sluggish in the lower stretches. The river bed is characterized by stretches of spawning-quality gravel and sand with mud and debris in pools and eddies. There are a few beaver dams along its course.

The East Branch has brook trout and the associated species found in Borgstrom Creek, but it also enjoys yearly runs of

steelheads. The upper end of this stream is principally a nursery area, with few fish of legal size. There is, however, an abundance of food available, namely stoneflies, caddis, and mayflies, which put excellent growth on young fish.

The mainstream of the Black River originates in a blueberry marsh in Section 24 of T43N, R9W and flows south, picking up a small unnamed brook before it is joined by Bark Creek. Bark Creek—flowing from an open blueberry marsh—is a small, shallow, brown-stained creek with a sand, rock, and mud bot-tom. Its fish population includes brook trout, rainbow trout, muddlers, and small minnows. The Black is small and dark in this area and its bottom is soft sand and mud plus some gravel, rock rubble, and an occasional limestone outcropping. The stream is dotted with abandoned beaver dams and log jams. It holds brook trout, muddlers, and small minnows, with a few trout reaching legal size.

The mainstream down from the mouth of Bark Creek varies from 10 to 30 feet in width and flows fairly rapidly. It flows through an area of low swamp bog, loose sands, and peat with swamp hardwood, hemlock, black spruce, and balsam fir cover.

From below the Hiawatha Trail to its confluence with the East Branch it is rimmed by high steep banks. Found here are brook, brown, and rainbow trout and muddlers. While only brook trout reach legal size lake-run rainbows begin adding to the creel in this stretch around old US-2 (Hiawatha Trail).

Below the confluence with Bark Creek, the mainstream picks up three small, clear, spring-fed feeder streams: Silver, Gilchrist, and O'Neill creeks. They provide spawning habitat for brook trout but very little fishing (except when impounded by beaver).

The Black River from Gilchrist Creek to the Black River Forest Campground is 30 to 40 feet wide and up to five feet deep. Its flow is rapid and its bottom is hard sand, gravel with silt, and debris in the deeper holes. Its course is dotted with limestone outcropping, log jams, and old beaver dams.

The river here flows entirely through state-owned land and, consequently, access is good. The two campgrounds and Black River Truck Trail, which follows the river closely, make it a popular fishing and camping area. Two old dam sites here fur-ther enhance its scenic value.

The fish present here are rainbow trout, brown trout, young coho salmon, muddlers, and white suckers. There are also runs for rainbow and brown trout, coho salmon, smelt, and white and longnose suckers. This stream gets light to moderate pressure by fishermen from the Upper Dam at the campground to its mouth.

Peter's Creek flows into the Main Stream of the Black River just north of Peter's Creek Truck Trail. It is a small, clear-water stream dotted by occasional beaver dams containing brook and rainbow trout (including steelheads), sculpins, and small min-nows. The trout are largely small fish, but this stream has a reputation for good fishing behind its beaver dams. It contains good spawning habitat for trout.

The Black River from the forest campground downstream to

its confluence with the East Branch flows through rapids and pools for the first half mile, then slows down to alternating pools and slicks. The bottom is hard sand and gravel with silt and debris in the holes. It is an inviting place to fish. The terrain here is loose, sandy soils covered by lowland hardwoods and some aspen. The rainbow and brown trout, white suckers, and muddlers that inhabit this stretch are seasonally joined by the migrating species mentioned earlier.

The Black River between the East Branch and Lake Michigan is fairly sluggish, flowing over a sandy bottom. It generally does not contain trout.

The Black River has long supported fine runs of steelheads, however. Many of the old-timers in the area can recall dipping these lake-run rainbows by the bushel-basket full, just below the old Shingle Mill, in the early 1900s. Since the destructive sea lamprey has been brought under control in Lake Michigan, the local fishermen will admit that some very nice runs of rainbow trout (both spring and fall runs) are beginning to return, plus some large lake-run browns and coho salmon. These large rainbows begin entering the stream in mid-September and have retreated back to Lake Michigan by the following June.

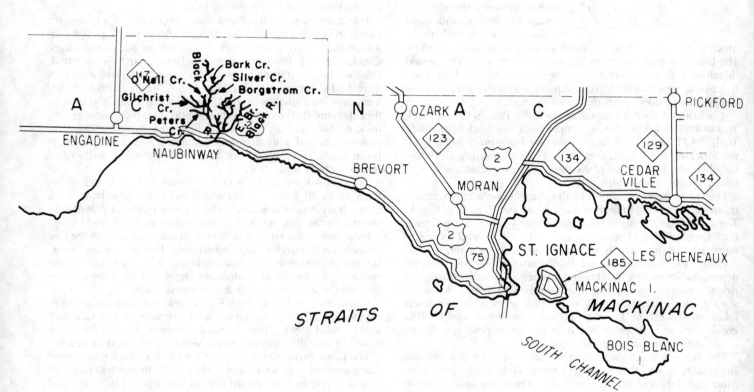

THE JORDAN RIVER
By JACK BOWMAN
Conservation Officer

The Jordan River is located primarily in northeastern Antrim County, and its watershed includes a drainage area of about 127 square miles. Although a relatively short system (only 22 miles long), the Jordan flows through a steep valley and develops rapidly into a sizable river before entering the South Arm of Lake Charlevoix. Originating in upland hardwoods, it flows primarily through spruce and cedar swamp, interspersed with abandoned farms.

The Jordan River has a wealth of history associated with it, dating back to the lumbering era when it was used principally as a log-driving stream. Then, as now, it was an excellent trout stream. Part of its fame today is due to the lack of development along its entire length. This, combined with the abundant spring- and ground-water supply, has given the Jordan the reputation as being the least polluted and having the best water quality of any stream in Lower Michigan.

From the headwaters to its confluence with the Green River, one mile above Graves Crossing, the Jordan River flows for 13 miles exclusively through state land. By the time it reaches the Green River, the Jordan is 40 feet wide and one to three feet deep. It is characterized by its low, brushy, undercut banks and a stream channel with many stumps and cedar slash and tops, all of which provide excellent fish cover but make the upper river virtually uncanoeable. Wading is also difficult.

This area is a bait fisherman's paradise, primarily for brook and brown trout. Access points are numerous, principally off the Pinny Bridge Road which parallels most of this portion of the river.

The upper Jordan, though primarily brook trout water, holds some native browns and rainbows in the transition zone between the mouth of Green River and Graves Crossing. Seven- to 12-inch brookies are the mainstay of the trout fishery, but occasional 14- to 16-inch brookies and some late spawning, lake-run rainbows may be taken in the old beaver ponds. Fair hatches occur from Graves Crossing upstream, and pleasant fly-fishing is available in the old beaver floodings.

The upper Jordan is fed by many small, swift, cold tributaries. A good bait fishery does develop in the spring, but access is difficult. Low water temperatures and few holes combined with light fishing pressure result in poor growth, and most brookies are sublegal.

Green River, the only major tributary to the upper Jordan, arises from a series of springs and private ponds and flows about six and a half miles to its confluence with the Jordan. It is very similar to the upper Jordan, being a generally fast and shallow brook trout stream with occasional holes. Access is limited to the bridges and the fishery is primarily with bait during the summer by locals who fish a few pet spots. As in the smaller tributaries, trout growth is poor, and most brookies are small.

The physical features of the Jordan change drastically below the mouth of the Green River. Many log jams and right-angle turns have created deep holes and undercut banks, and these, together with overhanging brush and sunken logs, provide excellent fish cover. Although floatable from here to the mouth, the many jams and turns, together with the fast current, make canoeing difficult for the novice and wading a challenge to the expert.

Much of the lower Jordan flows through private land; however, the six public sites in this nine miles make access easy. Public ownership is increasing under a vigorous acquisition program. The lower Jordan averages about 60 feet wide and two and a half feet deep, but with many holes four to six feet deep. The bottom is composed mostly of sand and gravel, except in the holes where sand, silt, and mud prevail. Many good gravel riffles provide excellent spawning sites for browns and steelheads. Although the Jordan rarely freezes over, shelf and anchor ice do develop in the lower portion. This ice, together with the swift current, causes some flooding during spring breakup on an otherwise extremely stable stream. The only major tributary to the lower river is Deer Creek, a second-quality trout stream which enters the Jordan a mile and a half above Lake Charlevoix.

Just about its confluence with Deer Creek, the Jordan loses most of its gradient and becomes relatively slow moving, wide (100 to 200 feet), and deep (three to six feet). The river bottom here is heavily silted, but good trout fishing is still available. From Deer Creek to the South Arm of Lake Charlevoix, the Jordan is boatable; however, the use of motors has been prohibited.

Although not well documented, there are indications that there have been major changes in the species composition of the Jordan River since the 1930s. Originally, native rainbow trout were well distributed throughout the river and some large brook trout (up to three or four pounds) were found the whole length. At this time browns were present, but scarce, in the lower portion. Some steelheads ran the river to spawn.

In the early 1940s there was a decline in both native and lake-run rainbows, coincident with the declines of these species in Lake Michigan. During this period, brown trout populations remained relatively low in the Jordan; however, by the late 1940s and early 1950s, good populations existed in Deer Creek. By the late 1950s, browns and brown trout fishing were on the increase. Since 1966 the resident brown trout fishery has apparently stabilized at a somewhat lower level, and a good lake-run fishery has developed. Since 1968 the rainbow and steelhead fishery has expanded somewhat.

The Jordan River fishery begins when the early spring season opens on the lower river. Steelheads, which had begun their spawning run in September, are now spawning and returning to the lake and providing an excellent fishery in April and May, chiefly with spawn sacks, night crawlers, and artificial lures. Many six- to eight-pounders are regularly taken, and 10-pounders are not uncommon. As the steelheads move out, the fishery shifts to native rainbows and browns from late May through June, mostly between Websters and Rodgers bridges. However, some

16- to 18-inchers may be taken as far upstream as Graves Crossing.

With the start of the "Michigan caddisfly" (giant mayfly) hatch (about mid-June), big lake browns begin moving up from Lake Charlevoix. The hatch begins near the mouth and progresses upstream, fading out near Graves Crossing after about six weeks. During the hatch, lake-run browns may be taken either on artificial flies or streamers, lending credence to the theory that this is a food rather than a spawning run. Night fishing between Websters and Rodgers bridges usually produces the best success, with many seven-, occasional 10- to 11-, and a few 13-pounders being caught. The brown trout fishery peaks about the first week of July and ends by August when a bait fishery for natives again predominates.

By early September, steelheads begin to enter the river and by late September they are present in about equal numbers with the lake-run browns which are starting their spawning run. Spawn sacks, worms, and artificial lures are the most effective baits for both species at this time. The extended fall season again permits a fishery on the lower river until the end of December, making the Jordan River one of the Lower Peninsula's top choices.

In recent years spawning chinook and coho salmon have dominated the entire Jordan River in the fall. This has lead to an abusive and often illegal fishery, creating extraordinary law enforcement problems. As a corrective measure, a salmon block-ing weir was constructed at the mouth of the Jordan in 1988. This weir effectively prevents large anadromous fish from entering the Jordan in September and October. This has a minimal effect on fall steelhead runs which peak in late November.

There has been much concern over the effects of fly hatches in the Jordan River by the periodic treatment with the lampricide TFM. In 1988 an electrical lamprey weir was constructed in the Jordan River at the PAS above Rogers Pond. This weir was operated for the first time in the spring of 1989 and appears to be an effective barrier to spawning lampreys. Future studies will be made to determine if the electrical weir is effective and if a positive response in fly hatches occurs.

Heavy bedloads of sand in the upper Jordan have resulted in a reduced standing crop of trout. In 1984 a cooperative stream improvement project was initiated with the Headwaters Chapter of Trout Unlimited with funding from the Harder Foundation, Trout Unlimited, and the Inland Fisheries Cooperative Grant program. To date, extensive soil erosion control on the county road paralleling the Jordan as well as stream bank stabilization has resulted in significant reduction in the amount of erodible material entering the river. Also, three sand traps have been constructed in the mainstream and an additional eight sand traps in the tributary streams. These efforts should result in improved trout fishing in the Jordan River.

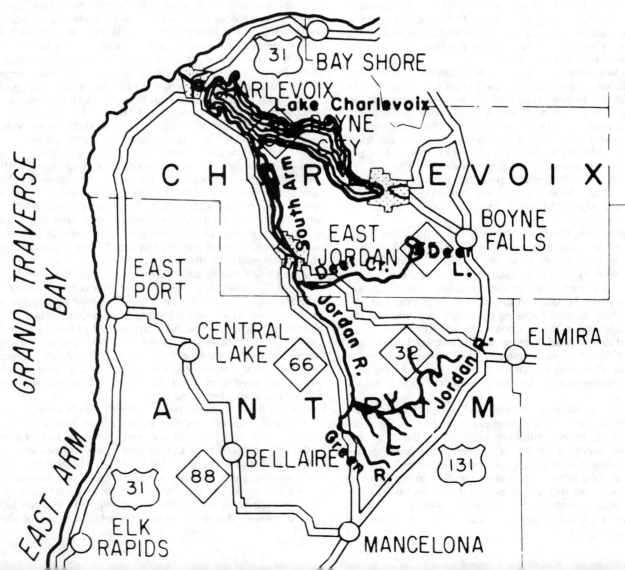

THE STURGEON RIVER

(Otsego and Cheboygan counties)
By JANET D. MEHL

The Sturgeon River between Gaylord and Indian River offers trout enthusiasts some of the most challenging brown trout battles they will ever encounter. Flowing into Burt Lake near Indian River, the Sturgeon is one of the few inland rivers in Michigan to produce steelhead runs. Although it flows generally parallel to I-75 with both I-75 and US-27 providing direct routes to the river from most of southern Michigan, the Sturgeon is not fished as heavily as many of Michigan's other rivers. Access points are limited in number. Downed timber in the upper reaches and very fast, deep water in the lower reaches make the Sturgeon a very difficult river to fish.

Brown trout now predominate throughout the entire mainstream of the Sturgeon River. Brook trout fishing is limited to the headwaters, several small tributary streams, and the West Branch.

Stephen Swan, DNR district fisheries biologist at the Gaylord office, said the Sturgeon, like the Jordan River, is one of the few rivers in Michigan to support runs of anadromous browns during the course of the entire summer. The extremely cold water temperatures, comparable to those of the Jordan, account for the summer runs. Swan said the runs were good, particularly during the **Hexagenia** (giant mayfly, commonly misnamed "caddis") hatch which occurs in July rather than in late June as in most other rivers. The browns are large enough to bring the water to a boil—five to 10 pounds—and are taken on flies, worms, spawn, spinners, and other lures.

The Sturgeon also holds many bragging-size browns year-round, some brook trout in its headwaters and tributaries, and an occasional rainbow in the mainstream. Swan suggested that the best parts of the river to fish might be the middle stretch and the West Branch, which joins the mainstream at Wolverine. He said the river was most heavily fished from Wolverine to the mouth, the portion where extended-season regulations apply.

Fred Snook of Gaylord, a former Trout Unlimited chapter president, fishes the Sturgeon regularly for browns between Vanderbilt and Wolverine, where fallen logs crossing the river make fishing a real test of patience. Snook described the river as "one of the fastest up here, faster than the mainstream Au Sable," which makes wading dangerous. Many portions of the river downstream from Wolverine, where the river rushes through a deep, narrow river channel, are over a person's head.

Samuel Schwartz of Wolverine fishes the Sturgeon nearly every day of the season from about three miles south of Wolverine to White Road. He uses Rapalas to catch browns two to three pounds and larger except during spring and cold weather in the fall, when he uses spawn with hopes of also catching steelheads. His favorite time of the year to fish is during October when the browns are spawning.

Most of the Sturgeon contains good trout cover with some relatively barren areas near Wolverine. The river bottom is mostly sand above Old Vanderbilt Road Bridge and mostly gravel below. Good tree cover is found lining the banks along most of the river's length with some open areas near Wolverine and Indian River. River frontage is largely underdeveloped with some cottages near the Wolverine, Rondo, and Indian River areas. Several miles of the upper river are privately owned by large clubs and are therefore inaccessible. The upper half of the river drains primarily coniferous swamp while the lower half drains hardwood swamp and uplands with banks often 20 feet high or more.

Canoeing is virtually impossible upstream from Trowbridge Road in southern Cheboygan County due to fallen logs, and portages are occasionally necessary from here down to Wolverine. Downstream from Wolverine, where the West Branch doubles the size and speed of the main river, is no place for beginning canoeists. Rapids—likely places to pick up a rainbow—are found about 2.5 miles above Wolverine between Trowbridge and Secord roads, about one mile below Wolverine, and again just below Rondo. From this area down to the mouth the water is so fast and powerful that even boating can be tricky and motoring upstream is practically impossible.

Frank Lasik of Wolverine fishes the river between Wolverine and Indian River, where he said browns weighing seven and eight pounds are taken. He fishes for browns and steelheads with spawn, particularly during spring and fall. Fishing for browns and rainbows tapers off during the summer in this stretch, he said.

From its headwaters to Old Vanderbilt Road, the Sturgeon is too narrow and congested to fly-fish. This stretch produces good-sized brook trout for the bait fisherman who is patient enough to fish them. Brooks and browns are found between Old Vanderbilt and Trowbridge roads, and there is a public fishing site at the Old Vanderbilt Road Bridge. Access to this stretch has been facilitated by the acquisition by the state of the Green Timbers Ranch tract from McLouth Steel Company in 1982.

Club Stream, which arises just west of Vanderbilt and enters the main river near the northern Otsego County line, is privately owned above Fontinalis Road by the Fontinalis Club. Much of the lower Club Stream is included in the Green Timbers property.

The main river between Trowbridge Road and Wolverine receives greater fishing pressure and excellent brown trout fishing is found here. The dam at Wolverine formerly raised the water level to force water into the ponds at the state trout-rearing station until 1971, when the dam was partially removed after the ponds were found to be infected with whirling disease. River-run browns, formerly concentrated in the area below the dam, were allowed to disperse throughout the rest of the river, much to the dismay of some fishermen.

Public access below Wolverine is limited largely to county road sites and two public fishing sites at Scott Road and Haakwood. The Haakwood State Forest Campground, located two miles north of Wolverine, offers 18 campsites on the river.

The West Branch, originating from Hoffman Lake in southeastern Charlevoix County, flows northeast to Wolverine, where it joins the main river. Downstream from the headwaters the first access site is at what is known as Shingle Mill Bridge on Wilderness Road in Cheboygan County. A shingle mill was located here during the lumbering days of the Sturgeon and the foundations are still evident. This is an excellent area for both brook and brown trout and is wide enough to fly-fish. A short distance upstream, however, brush and fallen logs make fishing a real chore. Below the bridge the stream soon becomes criss-crossed by fallen logs again and wading is impossible.

Schwartz said the West Branch was very productive for fishermen who enjoy ''rough fishing,'' particularly later in the summer when fish enter the colder water of the West Branch from the main river.

Near McEachron Bridge the West Branch widens and there is again good fly fishing in excellent trout water. Good-sized browns often move into this area in July and August. Fish seem to move out of the lower reaches of the West Branch during the latter parts of summer even though the water remains cold. Perhaps they prefer the denser cover upstream.

Fly hatches on the Sturgeon are not as good as on some other rivers, but Snook said there are hatches of stoneflies, Hendricksons, White-winged Blacks, Brown Drakes in selected areas, and good hopper fishing near Wolverine. Other hatches on the river include **Hexagenia**, Light and Dark Cahills, Gray Drakes, and Pale Watery Duns.

Steelhead runs usually peak in late October and again in early April. The fish run from three to 10 pounds and are taken on Rapalas, spawn, flies, and streamers.

In 1984 a stream improvement project was initiated on the Sturgeon River. All eroding banks were identified on the mainstream and to date 95 percent of these sites have been stabilized with field stone. In addition, with funding from the Headwaters Chapter of Trout Unlimited, five sand traps have been constructed in the upper 15 miles of mainstream. These traps are cleaned out annually. These efforts should substantially increase trout numbers in the Sturgeon River.

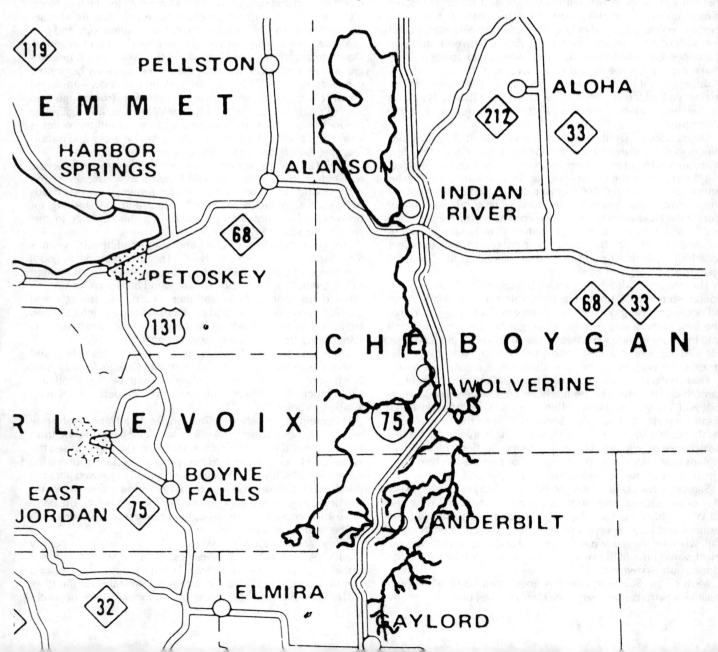

THE TOBACCO RIVER

By DONALD R. PETERSON
Fisheries Biologist

The Tobacco River system is located in the central part of the Lower Peninsula, mainly in Clare and Gladwin counties. Two major highways—US-10 and US-27—intersect and traverse the watershed east-west and north-south, respectively. Because this stream is located within easy driving distance of the heavily populated areas of the south and east, it represents a valuable resource to the weekend trout fisherman.

Originating in southeastern Clare County, the system drains a surface area of about 176,000 acres and includes approximately 207 linear miles of stream. There are also four impoundments and 19 connecting lakes on the system before it eventually drains into the Tittabawassee River flowing to Saginaw Bay on Lake Huron. The stream system is isolated, however, from the Tittabawassee by a dam at Ross Lake near Beaverton. This dam acts as a barrier to the upstream passage of fish. Because of this barrier, the stream can be considered as three separate streams, the North, South, and Middle branches, which all merge at Ross Lake.

The South Branch of the Tobacco arises out of a swampy area surrounding Deadmans Lake near Farwell and flows easterly through farm woodlots and elm flats broken by occasional meadows. The stream is small and brushy above Farwell Mill Pond, but here it picks up water from Elm and Overton creeks and becomes sizable enough (15 to 20 feet wide) to be fished with flies in some areas. Below the mouth of Newton Creek, the South Branch becomes large enough to be fished with flies or spinning tackle for the rest of its length.

There is a fair population of brook trout in the upper reaches of the South Branch above Farwell Pond. Elm and Overton creeks, both small and brushy, contain good populations of brook trout. Between Farwell Pond and the mouth of Newton Creek, the South Branch is marginal and contains few trout.

Between Newton Creek and Shamrock Lake resides a fair population of large brown trout, but temperatures are such that the stream will not support a large population of trout.

Newton Creek, which is almost as large as the South Branch where they join, contains a fair population of brown trout from Surrey Road to the mouth. Above Surrey Road to the junction of Loon Lake Creek, it has a healthy population of brown trout with some brook trout in its upper reaches and in Loon Lake Creek.

Below Lake Shamrock the South Branch carries a heavy silt load from farmland and is marginal for trout. High turbidity caused by runoff from clay soils makes this area unattractive to trout fishermen. There are reports of a few brown trout being taken from the stream immediately below Shamrock Lake.

Five Lakes Creek is the last trout tributary before the stream reaches Ross Lake. This creek enters the South Branch about midway between the mouth of Newton Creek and Clare. It is a small, brushy stream and contains a fair population of brook trout.

The North Branch of the Tobacco, formed by Beaver, Jose, Spikehorn, and Mostellar creeks, is a fine trout stream. Its four headwater creeks arise in swamps and are small and brushy, but they all contain healthy populations of brook and brown trout.

The North Branch of the Tobacco attains fair size by the time it reaches Cornwell Avenue, and there it begins to flow through farmlands and woodlots. Streambank cover consists of tag alder, conifers, and some aspen and elm. The stream can be fly-fished from here to Ross Lake. It contains a good population of brown trout above the Clare-Gladwin county line and a fair population below the county line.

In 1970, to eradicate the whirling disease infecting the trout, the North Branch, including Jose Creek, was treated with chlorine and all its trout killed down to the Gladwin County line. Good fishing has since been restored.

The Middle Branch of the Tobacco, the smallest of the three branches, begins in East Trout Lake, midway between Harrison and Clare. Clear Creek, which drains Beebe Lake, is its only tributary containing trout. Above Rogers Avenue, the Middle Branch flows through rolling country but is bordered by a considerable amount of swamp. This stretch is good brook trout water. Below Rogers Avenue, the stream emerges into farm country, and there is some tag alder along the stream as well as elm flats in woodlot areas.

In the vicinity of Rogers Avenue brook troiut are joined by brown trout and the stream becomes open and large enough to permit fly fishing. The lower reach of the stream is brown trout water.

The Middle Branch is a medium-size stream excellent for the wading trout fisherman.

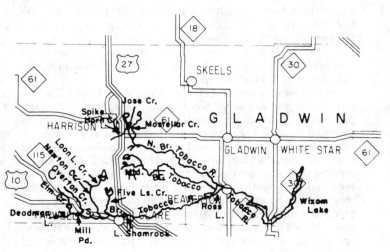

THE BLACK RIVER

(Otsego, Montmorency, and Cheyboygan counties)
By JANET D. MEHL

The Black River in Michigan's northern Lower Peninsula is famed as one of the finest brook trout rivers in the entire Midwest by anglers and biologists alike. Almost entirely undeveloped, this beautiful stream provides excellent fishing all season.

Arising from spring-fed creeks in eastern Otsego County east of Gaylord, the 50-mile Black River mainstream flows through a small pond impounded by Saunders Dam and forms a large "C" through the Pigeon River Country State Forest. It flows through the northwestern corner of Montmorency County where the mainstream is owned by either the Blue Lakes Ranch or the Black River Ranch, both large, private hunting and fishing clubs. The Black River Ranch ownership extends a considerable distance into Cheboygan County. Most of the river north of "the spreads" on the Otsego-Cheboygan county line is too deep to wade and is fished by canoe. Tower Pond marks the end of the trout stream designation for the Black River.

After flowing through two impoundments, Tower and Kleber ponds, the upper Black River hairpins its way north to the western side of Black Lake. It exits the northwestern corner of the lake and flows northwest. After passing over the dam at Alverno, the fourth of the Black River's four major dams, the Black soon joins the Cheboygan River a few miles south of Cheboygan and empties into Lake Huron.

The Black River watershed south of M-68 flows largely through lowland swamps which do not lend themselves to riverside campgrounds. The Town Corner Lake Campground in western Montmorency County, however, offers about 10 remote campsites within ¼ mile of the river and serves as an excellent base for fine fishing. Fishing pressure on the Black is somewhat greater than that on the moderately fished Pigeon River lying just to the west, particularly on the portion of the Black flowing through the Pigeon River Country as access is greater here. The watershed contains several major tributaries, including the East Branch and Canada and Milligan creeks, all of which offer excellent brook trout fishing.

Stephen Swan, district fisheries biologist at the DNR's Gaylord office, said the extensive brook trout management plan implemented on the Black River is the first of its kind. To curb the rapid increase in brown trout populations and maintain the quality brook trout fishery, the Black River was electro-shocked upstream from the Clark Bridge Road in the Black River Ranch holding in 1981 and from 2,000 to 3,000 brown trout were removed and planted in Town Corner Lake. Swan said the shocking and removal efforts over the 20-mile stretch were done twice to ensure that a greater number of the browns were captured. He felt the program was very successful. Without browns competing for choice feeding locations, the growth rates and numbers of brook trout are expected to increase and fishing should improve.

Dave Smethurst of Vanderbilt said much of the Black River's best trout water is also the most accessible. Fishermen can easily fill their creels between McKinnon Bend and Tin Shanty Bridge where 14- to 16-inch brookies are not uncommon. This is also a pleasant stretch to canoe but debris both upstream from McKinnon Bend and downstream from Tin Shanty Bridge require frequent portages. Many fiesty fish are found near Clark Bridge Road, the northern boundary of the Black River Ranch property, but deep areas downstream make wading difficult. The Crockett Rapids area in Cheboygan County is also big trout water and is shallow enough to wade. It is very scenic and accessible and produces many lunker-class brookies up to 18 inches or more. A general rule of thumb is the farther upstream from Tower Pond, the better the fish.

The headwaters join to form the mainstream in the small impoundment formed by Saunders Dam, part of a private hunting and fishing club holding. More than a mile downstream the small, brushy stream becomes fishable, lending itself best to bait fishing. Many sweepers and fallen trees downstream to the public fishing site off the end of Old Vanderbilt Road provide excellent refuge for darting brookies but make wading and fishing difficult.

Downstream about two miles or so from Saunders Dam is what is known as the Pinnacle, another large, private holding on the west bank. It was formerly a cattle ranch before it became the Tyrolean Hills ski area, which is no longer operating. Access to this trickling stream below the Pinnacle is attainable only from the west bank until the river is crossed by Tin Shanty Bridge Road. Dirt roads to the south of Old Vanderbilt Road lead to the first public access point on the river. At the public fishing site off the end of Old Vanderbilt Road the Black has attained a width of only about 15 to 20 feet, hardly wide enough to dab a fly. Just downstream from the fishing site about one-half mile is McKinnon Bend, a very popular access point with room to park several cars.

Below McKinnon Bend, the gliding stream slows and deepens until it reaches Tin Shanty Bridge. The gravel stretches upstream from McKinnon Bend give way to a bottom of sand with some silt areas. Only localized areas of the Black River system contain silt areas suitable for hatches of **Hexagenia limbata** and this stretch contains a number of them. The thigh- to waist-deep waters hover through deep pools and beneath undercut banks and cedar roots which harbor big brookies up to two pounds or more. Although deeper, the stream channel is still narrow—about 20 feet wide—but the cedar-root-stained waters resulting from the surrounding swamp make fish a little less spooky.

Below Tin Shanty Bridge the river widens slightly and resumes its gurgling path between fallen trees, flowing southeasterly until it reaches Montmorency County. Fishing remains good in this stretch, although it may lack the number of large fish. All but a very few areas of the river bottom from Tin Shanty Bridge to Main River Bridge are gravel. Tin Shanty Bridge marks the upper limit of easy fly fishing.

Tubbs Creek enters the mainstream near the county line. It

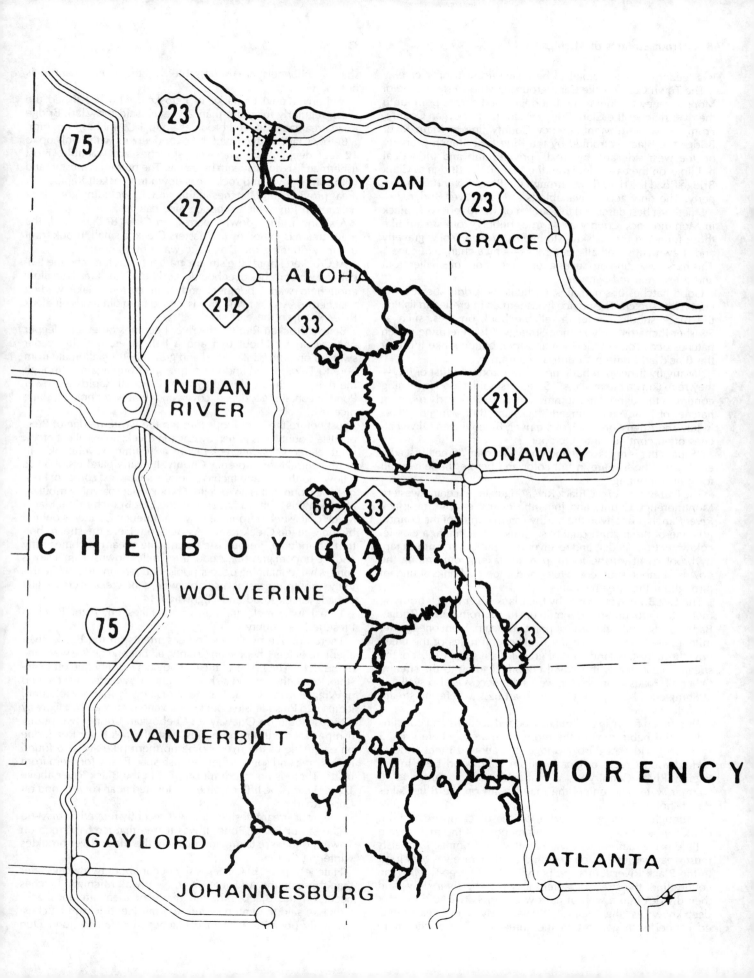

is a feeder creek too small to be a significant fishing creek.

The Town Corner Lake Campground on the western edge of Montmorency County is the last developed access point until the river reaches the Clark Bridge Road in Cheboygan County. From the western Montmorency County line to Main River Bridge the Black is fronted by the Blue Lake Ranch property on the west side and by small, private club and individual holdings on the east side. From the Main River Bridge to Clark Bridge Road the river flows through the Black River Ranch property. The only access available is at Main River Bridge.

Smethurst best described this stretch of the 40-foot-wide Black in Montmorency County as "a true, bubbly trout stream like those found in the Catskill Mountains of New York, gravelly and strewn with football-sized rocks—a nice change of pace." This nursery section produces good populations of smaller trout and a few real rod-benders.

Good hatches of small flies, particularly caddis species, occur on this stretch. The novice fly fisherman interested in fishing the Black should consult a reliable book on flies, such as Swisher-Richards' "Fly-Fishing Strategy," to determine which hatches occur on cobblestone and rock bottoms like those of the Black, and time his outings accordingly.

"Many fly-fishermen hang up their fly rods the first of July—they're making a big mistake," Smethurst said. Good fly-fishing continues throughout the summer, he said, with early morning hatches of Tiny White-winged Blacks and Blue-winged Olives in July and August on much of the river. Blue-winged Olive hatches often continue into October.

"September is my favorite month to fish trout," Smethurst added, "when the fish are in full color and before the leaves fall for grouse hunting."

The East Branch of the Black River originates in central western Montmorency County and joins the mainstream in the Black River Ranch property in the northwestern corner of the county. It is one of the highest quality streams in Michigan, a classic, coldwater trout feeder, and receives little public pressure. Scrappy brookies fit for the frying pan are taken from among the downed timber, submerged logs, and undercut banks abundant throughout the stream's course.

The East Branch is owned by the Black River Ranch from the mouth to about one-quarter mile upstream from Barber Bridge. Barber Bridge is the first access point upstream. From one-quarter mile above Barber Bridge the next several miles of the creek flow through state land. Dirt or gravel roads follow most of the stream's east side with several cut-offs leading to the stream. Other dirt roads approach the west side. Access is also available at Shingle Mill Bridge at County Road 622, where the stream is 10 to 15 feet wide.

The stream flows in and out of wooded sections and contains some fly-fishable runs in the more open areas where it is 25 to 30 feet wide. At Barber Bridge it is about 25 feet wide.

Hardwood Creek, originating from Hardwood Lake in the Pigeon River Country, is a marginal trout stream due to warmer water and enters the mainstream on the Blue Lakes Ranch holding.

Although canoeing is possible on the Black upstream from Clark Bridge Road, it is not recommended as the mainstream is little more than 40 feet wide at its widest points. Canoeists must weave around fallen trees and push themselves over logs. In the Black River Ranch property on the Otsego-Cheboygan county line, the stream gradient lessens. The river slows and then divides into a web of narrow channels two to three feet deep known as "the spreads." It is very easy for even experienced canoeists to get lost in the spreads. Some of the more shallow channels are impassable yet the main channel is not the widest.

Anthony (Tony) Dunaske of Petoskey, who has fished the Black regularly for more than 20 years, said the Clark Bridge Road area has produced brookies up to 17½ inches from him.

Below Clark Bridge Road the river deepens with pools up to 12 feet deep. Although select stretches are wadable, most fishermen fish downstream by canoe. The bottom is mostly sand with some gravel and rock areas down to Crockett Rapids. Silt areas provide good hatches in this stretch, including good **Hex** hatches in July which produce nice catches.

A short distance downstream from Clark Bridge Road, the mainstream is joined by McMasters Creek, a small, brook trout tributary draining the Dog Lake waterfowl flooding.

At Crockett Rapids the stream gradient increases and the tea-colored water rushes over boulders. Although the area is shallow enough to wade, boulders and swift current make wading treacherous. Access to the area is gained from dirt roads off Black River Road on the east side.

Below Crockett Rapids, the river becomes quiet and deeper once again for about two and a half miles, draining cedar swamps on both banks. Sand and gravel bottom alternate from here to Tower Pond and the current picks up again. Although the river is fished only lightly from Crockett Rapids to Tower Pond, it contains good feed, cover, and trout water holding some nice fish.

Just before the river loops through the western edge of Presque Isle County, it is joined by Canada Creek, an excellent brook trout feeder. Canada Creek begins as it drains several lakes in north-central Montmorency County. It nearly parallels M-33 as it flows northward and then crosses the southwest corner of Presque Isle County. It is an excellent brook trout spawning tributary although it is a little smaller than the East Branch of the Black. Much of its stream frontage in Montmorency County is owned by the Canada Creek Ranch Association. Here the stream bottom is sandy. In Presque Isle County the stream becomes riffly and the bottom gravelly. About three miles downstream it slows somewhat, containing deeper pools, and remains much like this to the mouth. Access is available where the creek is crossed by Canada Creek Road and Highway 634.

Tomahawk Creek, draining several lakes, enters the Black in Presque Isle County.

There are five public fishing easements on the Black River after it re-enters Cheboygan County, all but one on the west side of the river. The first is at the Cheboygan County line off Comstock Road, the second a short distance downstream at the end of Wigglesworth Road. The stream is largely inaccessible until it dips into Presque Isle County again and is crossed by Highway 638 just south on Onaway. In Cheboygan County two public fishing easements are found just east of Black River Road, one on each side of the river. Some northern pike are also found in this area and some fishermen fish specifically for them from boats. There is no size limit on pike in the Black River above Tower Dam. The fifth easement is located near Tower Pond off Cope Road.

The trout stream designation was recently moved from M-68 to the tail of Tower Pond. It was feared that ice fishermen on Tower Pond were taking too many of the Black River brookies wintering there.

Hatches on the Black generally occur about two weeks later than those on the Au Sable River. Nearly all Michigan hatches occur on the Black although many of them are localized. Dunaske said the entire system has fair Hendrickson hatches, generally poor Brown Drake hatches, and fair to good Dun hatches. A variety of caddis hatches are excellent.

Both Tower and Kleber dams are hydroelectric dams owned by the Northeast Michigan Electric Co-op. Both impoundments contain warmwater fish. There is a popular sucker fishery in Tower Pond each spring.

Just below Kleber Dam the Upper Black River is joined by Milligan Creek, an excellent brook trout spawning tributary. Milligan Creek arises from Duby Lake and flows northward, fed by many small feeder creeks along its course. It is accessible from dirt roads leading to the east bank from Tucker Road, from M-68, and from the public fishing easement on Brady Road near the mouth.

The Black River from Red Bridge to Kleber Dam has recently been designated as trout water and therefore is open to fishing only during the statutory trout season, except for the special April and May closure to protect spawning sturgeon. This reach warms in the summer and the trout migrate into the colder water of Milligan Creek.

In recent years extensive beaver dams in the headwaters of the Black River have resulted in significant warming of stream temperatures. This in turn has resulted in reduced numbers of brook trout in this reach of the Black during the summer. In 1989, with funding from the Headwaters Chapter of Trout Unlimited, a beaver-harvest and dam-removal project was initiated in the upper 15 miles of the Black. It is hoped that this will restore cool water to this reach of the Black and in turn restore the excellent brook trout fishery experienced in the past.

Erosion control projects have been carried out in the East Branch of the Black and Canada Creek. In addition, three sand traps were constructed on Canada Creek in 1984 and have been cleared out annually. These efforts should improve trout fishing in these streams.

Most of the 80- to 100-foot-wide river can be waded with caution. The river consists of a continuous series of wide, hairpin bends all the way to Black Lake.

Biologist Swan said Black Lake is one of the best fishing lakes in the Lower Peninsula, offering sturgeon, Great Lakes muskies, walleyes, smallmouth bass, and perch. Good walleye runs as far downstream as Alverno Dam occur.

Below Black Lake the Black River contains warmwater fish.

Small steelheads migrate up the Cheboygan River as far as the Cheboygan Dam, attracting local fishermen.

THE PIGEON RIVER
By JANET D. MEHL

Nestled between the Black and Sturgeon rivers of Michigan's northern Lower Peninsula, the Pigeon River arises from a web of spring-fed creeks just east of Gaylord in Otsego County. It flows northerly through rolling, wooded hills for about 43 stream miles and empties into Mullet Lake in Cheboygan County, fed by many small tributaries.

Several years ago the Pigeon was known as a brook trout stream. While brook trout still prevail in the headwaters above the Song of the Morning Ranch Pond (still known locally as the Lansing Club Pond), thousands of trout were lost when tons of silt were flushed into the river from the pond in the summer of 1984 when operators of the ranch drew down water to repair a dam.

The Pigeon River's excellent accessibility and water quality throughout its entire length make it a favorite stream among many trout fisherman and canoeists. More than one-third of the river flows through state-owned land, including part of the famous Pigeon River Country State Forest, home to Michigan's elk herd. Vast stretches of the river banks are undeveloped. In addition to several campgrounds and public access points found on the river, numerous county roads and trails approach or parallel the river, many leading from nearby I-75.

Most of the Pigeon River is wide enough to fly-fish and deep enough to canoe. Its width ranges from about 25 feet above the Song of the Morning Ranch Pond to more than 100 feet near the mouth. The midsection between the pond and M-68 averages 50 to 75 feet wide. The current velocity is moderate and the entire river is generally wadable.

Although the Pigeon is easy to fish and canoe, pressure is generally light. Few trout fishermen and canoeists heading north can bypass Michigan's more publicized rivers, such as the Au Sable, Pine, and Big Manistee. Pressure on the Pigeon increases during the summer, particularly near the campgrounds and on weekends. But during the week or early and late in the fishing season a fisherman may have his favorite stretch all to himself. The solitude found on the Pigeon may be worth a few extra miles.

The Pigeon River contains only one major dam—that owned by the Song of the Morning Ranch, which impounds about 50 acres of water. It was known as the Lansing Club Dam, privately owned by a hunting and fishing club until the late 1960s. The club's holdings then changed ownership and became the Song of the Morning Ranch, a private meditation retreat facility which allows river access to the public.

Anthony (Tony) Dunaske of Petoskey has fished the Pigeon regularly for more than 20 years from five miles above the Song of the Morning Ranch Pond to the mouth of the Little Pigeon River near McIntosh Landing. He said huge browns used to be taken from the dam to about a mile-and-a-half above Red Bridge before the 1984 silt spill and below Red Bridge where the river contains deeper holes and good gravel runs. He has taken many

16- to 20-inchers on flies in these areas and fishermen accompanying him have twice taken 25-inchers from the Pigeon.

John Palmer of Gaylord, a Trout Unlimited member, fly-fishes the Pigeon from Old Vanderbilt Road upstream, where most fish average 10 to 12 inches. Palmer said he caught many 14-inchers and a three-pounder in 1981 alone and lost much larger fish. He said the best holding water above the dam is in the bridge area which is accessible by dirt roads paralleling both sides of the river.

Upstream from the dam the river averages about a foot-and-a-half deep with pools up to six feet. The banks are lined with tag alder and cedar swamps. Some gravel-riffle areas are found in the tag alder stretches. Cover is provided by overhanging alder and cedar roots, undercut banks, pools, and log jams. Stephen Swan, district fisheries biologist at Gaylord, said that while brook trout are still dominant above the dam, brown trout numbers are steadily increasing.

The many creeks which join to form the Pigeon River headwaters are inaccessible due to a large private holding. The Panorama Ranch owns the area surrounding Wing Dam and it too is inaccessible. Access below the dam is provided by the public fishing site at the Old Vanderbilt Road Bridge, at the county parking lot a few miles upstream, and from two-tracks leading from Whitehouse Trail and Old Vanderbilt Road. Dirt roads parallel the river from the county parking lot to Sturgeon Valley Road. About midway between the public fishing site and the Song of the Morning Ranch Pond, the river enters the Pigeon River Country State Forest. The remainder of the river flows through the Pigeon River Country.

Downstream from the dam the river is somewhat slower, lacking in riffles, with pools up to seven feet deep. Extensive river studies and stream improvement and management practices had resulted in improved fishing. Between the pond and Tin Bridge the river is 30 to 40 feet wide and the bottom is all gravel with rocky areas about one mile below the Pigeon Bridge Forest Campground and above Tin Bridge. Several meadow areas between the pond and Tin Bridge provide excellent terrestrial fishing all summer.

The Pigeon Bridge Forest Campground, 11 miles east of Vanderbilt on Sturgeon Valley Road, offers 10 campsites on the river. Ned Caveney of Vanderbilt, forester in residence on the Pigeon River Country State Forest, said the Round Lake Forest Campground just east of the pond on Road Lake Road, was abandoned in 1983 due to budget cuts. The Pine Grove Campground, offering eight secluded sites on the river east of Wolverine via Webb and Campsite roads, was also abandoned in 1983, he said. The Pigeon River Forest Campground, offering 19 campsites on the river 14 miles east of Vanderbilt via Sturgeon Valley and Osmund roads, is the finest campground in the forest, Caveney said.

Caveney said the best fishing stretches of the river were above Old Vanderbilt Road for the fisherman interested in brook trout and greater numbers of fish and below Sturgeon Valley Road for fishermen seeking big trout.

Dave Smethurst of Vanderbilt said he needed to go no further than the Pigeon and Black rivers to find excellent fishing. He said some of the more accessible areas of the Pigeon have the best trout populations. Super fishing is found between the Pigeon Bridge and Pigeon River forest campgrounds, he said, with DNR shocking efforts in recent years producing a 20-inch

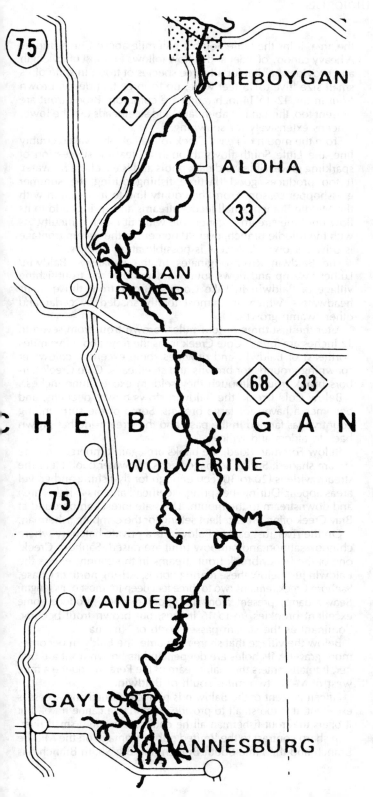

fish in literally every hole. He recommended a stretch downstream from Tin Bridge as another convenient area to fish with good trout populations. While the habitat is not quite as good as that upstream from the Pigeon River Forest Campground, fishing success is good.

Smethurst said when he began fishing the Pigeon in 1969, the trout population was about 80 percent brook trout and 20 percent browns. Now these figures are nearly reversed in some stretches, he said. Browns and brookies comprise the population above Tin Bridge and a few rainbows are added to the catch below the bridge.

Below the Pigeon River Forest Campground the stream narrows to about 30 feet and the current velocity increases considerably, doubling between Old Vanderbilt Road and the Pigeon River Bridge. Measurements recorded by the U.S Geological Survey show that at Tin Bridge the midstream flows at a rate of four feet per second. The river's narrow channel and numerous sweepers make it a tricky stream to canoe. Slightly wider stretches downstream still require portages around fallen trees.

The Elk Hill Campground, especially designed for horseback riders wanting to camp on the river, is located on Osmund Road about one mile north of Hardwood Lake Road. Hopper fishing is excellent along the large grassy area bordering the river.

Below Tin Bridge the river slows and widens with stretches from three to six feet deep. The bottom contains many sandy areas for the next few miles. About one mile above Red Bridge at Webb Road the stream becomes flat and riffly with the small pockets providing less holding water. The bottom becomes gravelly again with rocky areas both above and below the bridge. The adjoining banks, fringed with tag alders, drain hardwood lowlands all the way to M-68. Below Red Bridge the river contains deep pools again. Nelson and McIntosh creeks enter at McIntosh Landing, another access point about one mile below Red Bridge, between McIntosh Landing and the Pigeon River Road Bridge (not to be confused with the Pigeon River Bridge near the Pigeon River Forest Campground) much of the river is from three to six feet deep and the bottom contains many sandy areas.

Below M-68 much of the river is too deep to wade and is seldom fished for brookies or resident browns. It is fished for lake-run browns and five- to 10-pound steelheads, although runs are small. The stretch from M-68 to the mouth is open for the extended season, April 1 to December 31, and attracts local fishermen.

The Pigeon also receives a spring sucker run and the M-68 to Mullett Lake stretch is a popular spot for both hook and line and spear fishermen. Mullett Lake provides some of Michigan's finest fishing for a variety of fish, including sturgeon.

The river is fly-fishable below the Song of the Morning Ranch Pond and offers all common hatches. Hatches on the Pigeon, like those on the Sturgeon and Black rivers, generally occur about two weeks later than those on the Au Sable and most other Michigan streams. Hendrickson hatches in May are fair. Brown Drake hatches are good in localized areas. The **Hexagenia limbata** (giant burrowing mayfly) hatch in mid-July is also good but sporadic, occurring only where silt edges are found along the river, such as below Tin Bridge and in many areas below McIntosh Landing. Fair Sulfur hatches overlap **Hex** hatches in the latter part of July. Hatches of a variety of true caddis are rich. Blue-winged Olive hatches are good until September.

Two Little Pigeon rivers enter the mainstream, one just below McIntosh Lansing and the other near Mullett Lake. Both contain brook and brown trout, but access is very restricted.

THE PERE MARQUETTE RIVER

By DAVID P. BORGESON and WILLIAM H. BULLEN
Fisheries Biologists

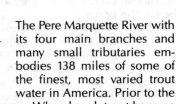

The Pere Marquette River with its four main branches and many small tributaries embodies 138 miles of some of the finest, most varied trout water in America. Prior to the 1880s it was a fine grayling stream. When brook trout became established, they too provided excellent fishing. Michigan's first brown trout were planted in the Pere Marquette in 1883 and rainbows came shortly thereafter. These two species have dominated the river and have been the mainstay of its legendary fishing ever since.

Numerous small intermittent creeks and springs in the Chase area give birth to the Middle Branch which flows west for 17 miles before it merges with the Little South Branch to form the mainstream of the Pere Marquette River. The Baldwin River is another tributary to the mainstream. Through heavy spring seepage, the Middle Branch quickly gains fishable size within two or three miles southwest of Chase. The bottom is gravelly, and brown trout are abundant. The Middle Branch is one of the few good grasshopper streams in Michigan, which means good midday fishing for sizable brown trout in late summer—a rare combination for Michigan fly-fishermen (the grasshoppers, however, are the rare green oak variety).

Steelheads set up housekeeping from March through May and provide many hours of frustration for the angler trying to outwit a trophy in a small, clear stream. Most of the riverfront property along the Middle Branch is privately owned but several good sites accommodate fishermen.

As the stream passes out of the maple- and oak-covered headwaters into the typical oak, pine, and sand country south of Idlewild, the gradient lessens, gravel loses ground to sand, and the holes deepen. Tag alders and willow form a dense bank cover and provide conditions more suited for the bait fisherman. Log jams, undercut banks, and clay ledges become common. Added cover is provided by the extensive stream-improvement structures which were completed in the early 1960s.

Beginning in the Oxford Swamp in north-central Newaygo County, the Little South Branch flows almost straight north to meet the Middle Branch.

Due to the river's low gradient and silt-covered bottom in the headwaters, brown trout are not abundant above Jackson Bridge. The stream is already sizable at Jackson Bridge, and here it begins to increase in velocity with shallow gravel areas appearing. Steelhead production is good here, and deep holes and log-brush jams provide excellent cover for brown trout.

Ten-feet-wide McDuffee Creek flows through private farmland, but it is lined with a dense cover of elms, alders, and willows. It is good to excellent brown trout water and also produces some respectable brook trout. Below the mouth of the McDuffee, the Little South Branch improves in size and quality noticeably with some good open water available to the fly-fisherman.

Pease Creek, one of the finest coldwater trout tributaries in

the area, joins the Little South a half mile above Curtis Bridge. A heavy canopy of alder and willow follows for most of its length and provides habitat for all three species of trout. In spite of its small size (five to 15 feet wide, up to three feet deep), brown trout in the 12- to 14-inch range are common. Brook trout are present too, though not abundant, and steelheads use the lower reaches extensively for spawning.

From the mouth of Pease Creek to the Lake-Newaygo county line, the Little South flows through a pleasant succession of sparkling gravel riffles and dark pools and is excellent fly water. It too produces good daytime fishing during the summer grasshopper season. From the county line to its junction with the Middle Branch, small feeder streams and springs add to its flow until the stream is canoeable without much difficulty. As with the Middle Branch, over 90 percent of the stream frontage is privately owned. Access is possible at all bridges.

The Baldwin River originates in the expansive Baldwin/Luther Swamp and flows southward through the trout-fishing village of Baldwin in Lake County. Brook trout thrive in its headwaters, which are almost totally shaded by cedar and other swamp growth.

After the first three or four miles, brown trout from seven to 12 inches are found. Cole Creek joins the flow about five miles northeast of Baldwin and provides some excellent coldwater spawning grounds for browns and steelheads. Cole Creek harbors brook trout, although they seldom exceed nine inches.

Below Cole Creek, the Baldwin slows down, deepens, and becomes a haven for large browns. Some of the surrounding country was farmed in the past, and the streamside has grown back to alders and willow.

Below Foreman Road, the banks are again timbered and the stream shaded. Spring seepage keeps the water cool. Here the stream widens (20 to 30 feet) enough for fly-fishing and gravel areas appear. During the spring, steelhead anglers fish this area and downstream to the mouth. The state forest campground at Bray Creek offers an excellent setting for the camping fisherman.

On the river just east of Baldwin is a private hatchery where chinook salmon and rainbow trout are raised. Sanborn Creek, one of the better brook trout streams in the county, enters the Baldwin just below these rearing ponds. Arising north of Chase, Sanborn Creek remains two to three feet deep for most of its length. Beaver dams, present along its upper reaches, produce some excellent brookies up to 16 inches, but brown trout become dominant as the stream passes north of Nirvana.

Below the village that shares its name, the Baldwin becomes more gravelly, its holes are deeper, and its brown trout are bigger. It finally enters the mainstream of the Pere Marquette a mile west of M-37, two miles south of Baldwin.

Fifteen percent of the Baldwin is publicly owned and access is excellent. It is too small to provide comfortable canoe travel, but it offers the trout fisherman all he could ask for in a small river.

In sharp contrast to the limited public frontage on the Middle Branch and the Little South Branch, the Big South Branch has over 30 percent of its banks in public ownership. It is a large stream, quickly becoming wadable with care below its origin at the junction of Beaver and Winnepesaug creeks in northwestern Newaygo County. It is canoeable, although the log jams and overhanging brush make this mode of travel challenging.

Beaver Creek holds a few pike in its lower reaches but offers little for the trout fisherman. The Winnepesaug is brushy and dark colored, as is Beaver Creek, and supports some brown trout and brookies.

As the Big South continues toward the northwest corner of Newaygo County, it is joined by Freeman and Allen creeks. Freeman is a small stream (five to 10 feet wide) which flows through pine plantations and elm swamps. Brown trout are scattered throughout, and brookies are found in its headwaters. Allen Creek has a fine population of brook trout.

In addition, steelheads are common in this section of the Big South and provide excellent angling challenges. The water itself has a strong tea color most of the year which is caused by its drainage from oak-pine uplands and the surrounding cedar swamps.

While passing through northeastern Oceana County, Ruby Creek, an excellent nursery stream, enters the Big South Branch. Brookies are common in this five- to 15-foot-wide stream, flowing almost entirely through a narrow cedar swamp which is publicly owned. Large brown trout spawners from the Big South run Ruby Creek in the fall and big steelheads take over in the spring.

The Big South, only a fair trout stream, is at its best at Ruby Creek. Gravelly riffles, bend holes, log jams, and smooth runs make for fine, good-looking fly water. Most of the river in Mason County flows through public land. This section is readily canoeable although frequent log jams make short portages a necessity. Wading is possible, but use caution.

During late fall and spring months, many good steelhead and brown trout are taken. Summer temperatures are sometimes a shade warm for trout, causing them to concentrate in spring holes. This section also provides excellent fall coho and chinook salmon opportunities from strays finding their way into the system.

Once the Big South reaches the floodplain of the mainstream, it slows down and spreads out. Many bayous provide excellent northern pike fishing. This water is best fished from a boat or canoe.

The Pere Marquette River mainstream begins at "the Forks" of the Middle and Little South branches, one-half mile east of M-37. The first eight to 10 miles consist mostly of large riffle areas in the straight sections broken by deep, slow-water holes on the many sinuous bends. This is the heart of the Pere Marquette. The riffles are literally covered with spawning steelheads during the early spring months and spawning chinook salmon during September and October. Ideal water temperature, cover, and bottom type make it a haven for lunker brown trout.

Fly hatches of all descriptions occur almost continuously from mid-April through October. Fly-fishing only, year-round regulations apply to the river from M-37 downstream to Gleason's Landing, a distance of about eight river miles.

The first two to three miles of stream are dotted with quality cottages and homes along with a handful of the old traditional fishing camps. Tall white pine, red pine, oak, and elm line the high banks and provide an ideal setting for the trout fisherman. Areas such as the Whirlpool, Birch Hole, Grayling Hole, Claybanks, and First Rollway and the famous fishing camps

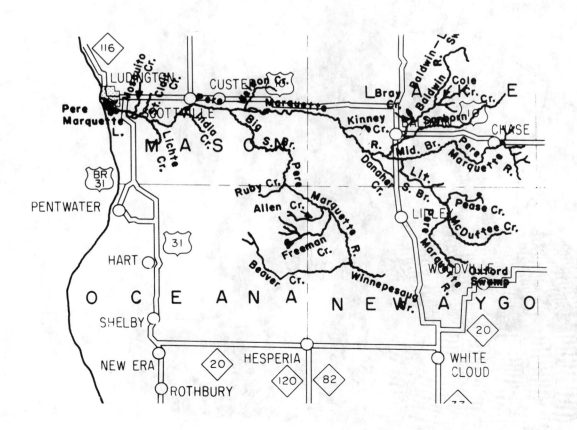

add historical interest for the fisherman or canoeist.

Upon reaching Danaher Creek, the river slows somewhat and deepens. The surrounding lands vary more from elm lowlands to high oak banks. Near Bowman Bridge the water is not easily wadable and is best fished by canoe or boat. Big brown trout, reaching well into the 20-inch size range, are here for the taking.

Downstream from Bowman Bridge, the current quickens again, and a few gravel riffles reappear with many good bend holes. Kinney Creek, a fine trout tributary, enters from the northeast. This is the beginning of truly big brown trout waters and is also excellent steelhead water. Since most of the streamside property is privately owned, a river boat or canoe is the best means of fishing. Some sections are wadable but only with caution. Rainbow Rapids is a fine public take-out point after a day's fishing down from Bowman Bridge.

As the river nears the Mason-Lake county line, it becomes strictly boat and canoe country. The fly-fisherman has plenty of room and the "garden hackle" man can find more brushy holes and log jams than he can use.

The area around Upper and Lower Branch bridges and Walhalla Bridge is known for big brown trout, sometimes reaching the eight- to 10-pound class. These heavy brown trout feed on gray drakes and *Hexagenia* (mayflies) in May and June and shatter the composure of the most calloused veteran fly-fisherman.

Weldon Creek enters above Indian Bridge between Walhalla and Custer in an area of broad marshland. It provides additional

spawning grounds for both browns and steelheads and holds a good resident brown trout population of its own (one of the best small streams in Mason County in this respect).

At Custer, the scene of a big Indian war, the Big South Branch enters, and the river is best fished from a boat. Lunker pike frequent the many bayous in this section. This area yields chinook salmon during August and September.

Downstream from Scottville, the river breaks up into several channels as it meanders through marshland. The river banks are often separated by dense cattail marshes, and a canoeist or boater can easily become stranded. The river water generally has a murky brown color by now due to drainage from the agricultural lands of western Mason County.

India, Litchie, Swan, St. Clair, and Mosquito creeks all enter the mainstream between Scottville and Ludington. None are good trout producers, primarily due to the open farmland drainage and lack of spawning areas. This particular section of the Pere Marquette is one of the wildest to be found on the entire system. The floodplain is wide and undeveloped and for about 13 miles only one building is visible from the stream. Trout numbers are low compared to upstream waters but during the steelhead and chinook runs many fish are taken here.

At US-31, the river branches just prior to its entrance to Pere Marquette Lake. Warmwater fishes are common here with pike, bass, and suckers taking the place of trout, except during steelhead season.

THE OCQUEOC RIVER

By JANET D. MEHL

The entire Ocqueoc River is contained in western Presque Isle County with a mainstream approximately 40 miles long. Although it contains small-mouth bass, northern pike, walleyes, and other warmwater fish, it is designated as a trout stream from its mouth at Lake Huron to Barnhart Lake, the first of a chain of many lakes located south of the valley of Millersburg. This chain of lakes, from which the river arises, keeps water temperatures above the optimum for trout until it is fed by groundwater seepage and spring-fed creeks as it flows northward.

The river sustains populations of brook, brown, and rainbow trout as well as coho and chinook salmon and steelheads during spring and fall spawning runs. Some brown trout are found in the main river all year, but during the summer they are restricted to areas where cool water can be found—near springs and the mouths of feeder creeks. During this time fishing pressure is nearly nonexistent with only a few local fishermen who know the river well fishing the above-mentioned areas. Stretches of the river downstream from the falls contain cold spring areas.

Mason Shouder, fisheries biologist for the Department of Natural Resources at Indian River, said runs of pink salmon have developed in recent years. These occur only during odd-numbered years. The runs begin in late summer and last until early fall.

A few miles north of Millersburg the river begins supporting trout where overhanging brush and undercut banks provide limited cover for small browns. The river is about 30 feet wide and from one to two feet deep, and the banks are lined with willow and tag alders, which give way to wooded uplands. It contains many gravel areas but warm water temperatures allow little natural spawning. As the river approaches the falls, depth increases up to four feet and logs, brush, and undercut banks provide fair cover for eight- to 10-inch browns.

About midway between Barnhart Lake and the river's mouth are the scenic Ocqueoc Falls. The area immediately around the falls is rocky and wooded uplands of jack pine, oak, birch, cedar, balsam, and aspen—a beautiful setting for the 14-site Ocqueoc Falls Forest Campground, located 10 miles northeast of Onaway via M-68 and Millersburg Road. Canoe and boat landings are located above and below the falls.

Just below the falls the river is joined by the Little Ocqueoc River, one of the Ocqueoc's two main tributaries. It contains good populations of brook trout running eight to 10 inches as well as a few browns and rainbows. The Little Ocqueoc and its tributary, Fox Creek, are swift, spring-fed, and contain some gravel areas which provide good spawning grounds. Some natural reproduction of salmon and steelheads also occurs in the Little Ocqueoc. It is accessible primarily from its south side and is best suited to bait fishing. Just below the mouth are four

high clay banks which have presented some erosion problems.

DNR plantings supplement brown trout populations in this stretch of the mainstream for several miles below. Cover provided by old saw logs, overhanging brush, deep pools, and undercut banks is abundant. Joined by three unnamed feeder creeks, the river increases to about 40 feet in width and many pools exceed four feet in depth. Just below the mouths of these creeks the wooded country along the river is interspersed with some pasture land which also presents some erosion problems.

About a mile below these creeks the river is joined by Silver Creek, the river's second main tributary which is also the last to contain trout before reaching the river's mouth. Some natural reproduction of cohos and chinooks takes place here. The creek also supports brook trout and a few rainbows. Most of the creek, which is about 18 feet wide at its mouth, drains low swampland.

As the river approaches Ocqueoc Lake, it increases to about 50 feet in width and from two to five feet in depth, with some deeper pools. Some large browns and warmwater fish coexist in this stretch until the river reaches Ocqueoc Lake.

Ocqueoc Lake provides good fishing for warmwater species and a few fishermen fish the lake for steelheads and salmon during runs. Most of the west shore is state-owned and remains in its natural wooded state. Of the 21 miles of river between Ocqueoc Lake and Millersburg, about eight miles of river and five sections of land are state-owned, including Ocqueoc Falls.

Between Ocqueoc Lake and Lake Huron, the river receives the greatest pressure from steelhead and salmon fishermen, particularly near US-23. Although steelheads were not planted in 1978 or 1979, annual stocking was resumed in 1980 with 10,000 yearlings planted, which should provide good runs in subsequent years. Spawn bags, Little Cleos, and Mepps spinners bring the best results, with the vast majority of fishermen using spawn bags. Runs usually peak in early May. Runs have improved somewhat over the past few years as some natural reproduction occurs in the river. Lamprey control and stocking efforts in Lake Huron have also increased the numbers of lake-run browns in the river in the fall.

Chinook salmon were first planted in the river in 1968 and again in 1969—200,000 yearlings each year—to provide a back-up source of eggs from Lake Huron. These fish began returning in 1969 and, unfortunately, access sites were lacking and fishermen wrought havoc to the river banks and private-property owners. The first half of the river between Ocqueoc Lake and Lake Huron is relatively straight and stream banks do not exceed 10 feet in most places. But the lower portion of the river consists of sharp, winding bends with sand banks often exceeding 25 feet. Hundreds of square feet of sand were pushed into the river, particularly in the spring when the ground was often wet, as fishermen made their way to the water. With no public facilities, litter and fish entrails discarded along the river became a serious problem. Trespassing and noise became major concerns for private-property owners, particularly during night hours when runs are heaviest. On September 13, 1969, the river was closed to fishing for the remainder of the season from the outlet at Ocqueoc Lake to Lake Huron to eliminate such problems.

The Ocqueoc has since been opened to year-around fishing, including the reach from the US-23 bridge to Lake Huron. A Soil Conservation District stream improvement project using Resource Conservation and Development funds was undertaken around 1985. It involved bank stabilization from Ocqueoc Falls to Lake Huron. Fishing berms were installed below the US-23 bridge to reduce erosion of sand banks caused by fishermen. Property above the US-23 bridge was purchased for fishing access and installation of an electrical lamprey weir.

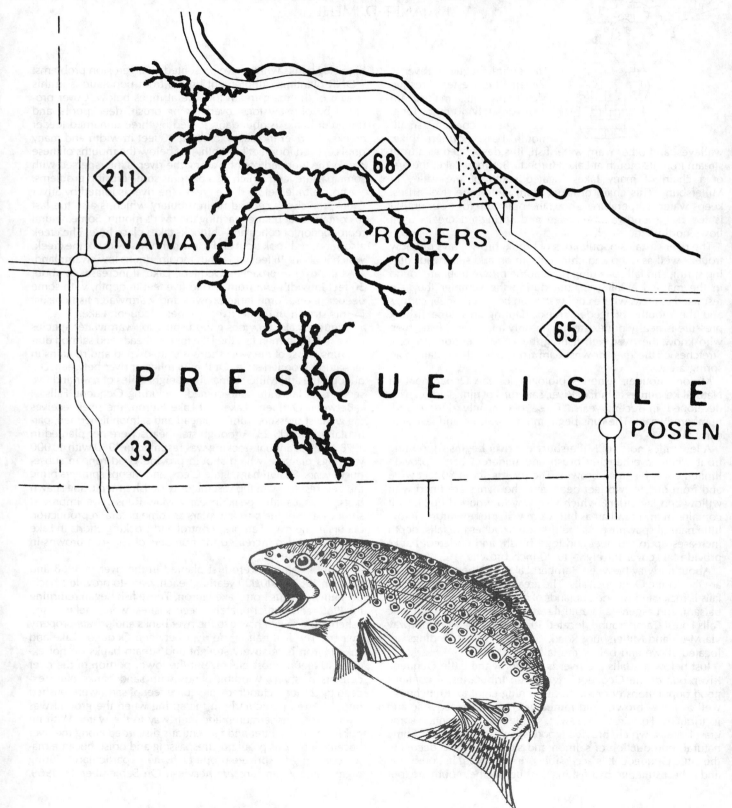

THE MAINSTREAM OF
THE AU SABLE RIVER
By JANET D. MEHL and DAVID W. SMITH,
District Fisheries Biologist

Ask 100 trout fishermen to name the finest trout stream east of the Rocky Mountains and 99 will say the Au Sable River in northeastern Michigan. Only a handful of rivers in the entire world can match the superb trout fishing, vivid history, aesthetic beauty, and variety of fantastic fly hatches found on this outstanding river system. It has remained world-famous ever since the 1800s when the once-bountiful grayling was exploited from its waters and towering white pines were plundered from its banks. Today thousands of canoeists, campers, hikers, photographers, hunters, and fishermen flock to the river each year from all over the eastern United States.

The excellent water quality of the Au Sable makes it most highly acclaimed for its trout fishing opportunities: from enticing a scrappy brookie from beneath the banks of a gurgling brush-choked creek, to netting a lunging eight-pound brown that inhaled an Adams pattern, to battling a mighty steelhead in the roaring water below Foote Dam. Phenomenal fly hatches and 59 miles of quality-fishing (flies-only) water make it a mecca for fly-casters. Excellent accessibility and camping facilities, generally swift current, crystal-clear water, and scenic terrain also make it a haven for canoeists, however, who descend the river in droves from Grayling to Mio Pond and often restrict weekend and summer fishing to morning and evening hours. Although the Au Sable is fished and canoed more heavily than any other river in Michigan, excellent natural reproduction and very limited DNR plantings sustain fine fishing.

Only 110 miles of the 148-mile mainstream are free-flowing due to the six hydroelectric dams found on the lower river from Mio to Oscoda. Mio, Alcona (Bamfield), Loud, Five Channels, Cooke, and Foote dams were built by Consumers Power Company between 1913 and 1924 and all continue to produce power. Salmon and steelhead runs—Michigan's best on the Lake Huron side of the state—are restricted to the lower 10 miles of river between Foote Dam and Oscoda.

Numerous tributaries join the mainstream along its entire course, draining 1,932 square miles. Many are of excellent trout quality, particularly the North, South, and East branches, which are discussed in separate chapters.

The Au Sable has been the center of trout research ever since it received Michigan's first "California" (rainbow) trout in 1876. It is **the** stream where present trout-fishing and trout-management philosophy have been developed, setting regulation precedents.

Most of the people who enjoy the many recreational opportunities offered by the Au Sable River watershed are from southern metropolitan areas. The river is crossed by several major highways, including I-75, M-52, M-33, M-65, and US-23. County roads and trails, public fishing sites, and campgrounds provide good access to most of the system.

Kolka and Bradford creeks, draining several lakes in south-western Otsego County, join to form the mainstream three miles north of Frederic. The narrow, winding channel flows south 12 miles through low cedar swamp and open tag-alder marsh areas to the Old Power Pond two miles west of Grayling. It contains almost entirely brook trout and receives only light fishing pressure. Fishing is very good from Cameron Bridge Road just above Frederic to about one mile below Batterson Road, where the water ripples over gravel bottom, receives cold groundwater inflow, and contains good cover with many log jams and under-cut banks.

Above Cameron Bridge Road, beaver dams, very shallow depths, and lack of bank cover and groundwater inflow make water temperatures marginal for trout. Fishing is fair below Twin Peaks Road, a county road crossing Kolka and Bradford creeks, and the creeks and mainstream flow almost entirely through state land to Cameron Bridge Road. The 10- to 25-foot-wide river contains four-foot pools to one mile below Batterson Road. The next five miles of stream hold low numbers of trout as the current becomes sluggish, the stream averages less than 18 inches deep and is braided in places, and both bank and in-stream cover are lacking, making temperatures too warm for good trout habitat. The bottom is sand and silt to one mile above Pollack Bridge, where the stream character changes abruptly. The current becomes swift, creating many riffle areas, the bottom is primarily gravel, and the stream contains pools holding fair numbers of brook trout although cover remains poor. Just below Pollack Bridge is the Old Power Pond.

Below Cameron Bridge Road access is limited to county road crossings. Cabins are scattered along the stream from Cameron Bridge Road to the Old Power Pond with concentrations near Frederic and Pollack Bridge.

Below the Old Power Pond the river flows east until it enters Alcona County. The first few miles contain warm water and are heavily developed, flowing through Grayling, where there are at least six canoe liveries. The stretch of river between Grayling and Wakeley Bridge is one of the two most heavily canoed lengths of the river, the other being the South Branch from Roscommon to Smith Bridge. The first mile of the river below Grayling is 30 to 40 feet wide, flowing swiftly from pool to pool, and holds fair numbers of brook and brown trout. The East Branch enters the mainstream three-quarters of a mile below Grayling, increasing the width of the mainstream to about 50 feet and cooling its temperatures. About one-quarter mile downstream the gradient decreases, the current slows, and the bottom becomes sandy for the next few miles. Many minnows provide an excellent food supply and growth rates are excellent in this stretch, producing some hefty trout.

The river winds past Beaver Island and into the Shellenbarger Marsh about one mile below I-75, commonly called "the Swamp" by local residents. It splits into several channels which flow like molasses through two miles of semiopen marsh. The water is generally too warm for trout but does hold a few browns in the spring. The Au Sable River Canoe Forest Campground is located just downstream from the Swamp on the north bank west of Headquarters Road, offering 15 campsites and an additional 20 sites for camping canoeists.

At Headquarters Road four miles east of I-75, the river changes rather abruptly again. Just off Headquarters Road on the south bank is Burton's Landing, the beginning of what is aptly named the "Holy Waters," truly the heart of the Au Sable River trout fishing. Gary Schnicke, former district fisheries biologist at the DNR's Mio office, said the stretch is unique from any other portion of the mainstream, containing the finest trout nursery section in Michigan. It extends to Wakeley Bridge at Wakeley Bridge Road, containing more than eight-and-a-half miles of quality-fishing (flies-only) water held in highest esteem in the hearts of fly-fishermen. Fly hatches are fantastic and the Au Sable offers a greater variety than any other river in Michigan.

At Headquarters Road the stream bottom becomes primarily gravel, the gradient becomes steeper, the current increases to two to three miles per hour, and the 40- to 50-foot-wide river begins receiving an excellent groundwater supply. The riffle-pool ratio is top quality, and cover provided by log jams, deep pools, and sweepers is excellent—all conducive to superb natural spawning conditions. All trout caught in the Burton-to-Wakeley stretch are wild as it has not been planted since the 1950s. It is the most productive stretch of river stream for trout in Michigan despite being part of the section extending to McMasters Bridge, which is the most heavily fished in the state. It contains all three species of trout, with rainbows concentrated

near Stephan's Bridge. Browns are the predominant and the most highly sought after, partly because anglers not wanting to dodge canoes must fish in the early morning or late evening when browns are actively feeding. The relatively even bottom beneath the calf- to waist-deep waters makes night wading safe, but an angler may still take a swim if caught off guard by the swift current.

Banks in the stretch are generally two to 20 feet high and forested with jack pine, red and white pine, cedar, aspen, birch, and oak. There is less brush along the banks below Burton's Landing, making the river more open than many. Cottages are quite dense along the Holy Waters, particularly between Stephan's and Wakeley bridges, which is more heavily developed than any other part of the river. Some are very large and elaborate with terraced lawns, seawalls, bridges, and/or docks.

Because the Holy Waters is a nursery stretch, it contains many small fish and the growth rate is slow as competition for food is keen. Few fish grow to exceed 16 inches. Long-time anglers claim the fishing has steadily declined over the past several years due to tremendous public pressure. A variety of special size regulations have been practiced on the 8.7-mile length to help alleviate the small average size and decreasing number of its trout although it has been a flies-only stretch for decades.

After six years (1973-78) with a 12-inch, three-fish limit and 10 years (1978-88) with a "slotted size" (12- to 16-inch keeping size), five-fish limit, a catch-and-release or "no-kill" limit has been implemented on this stretch.

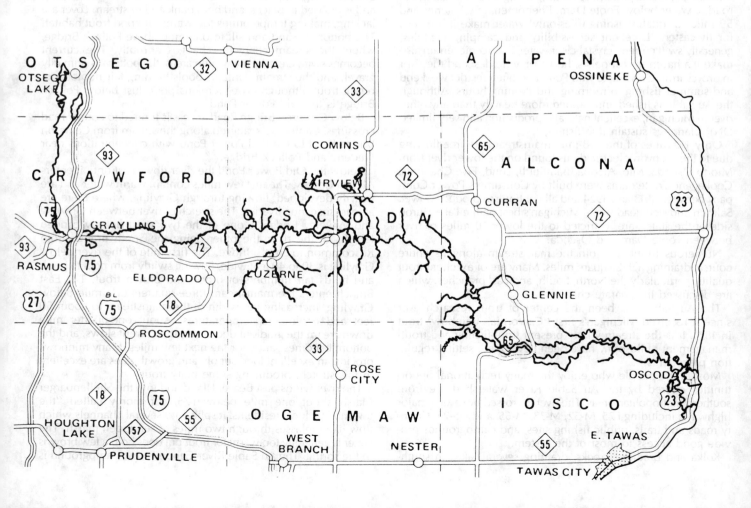

Access to the Holy Waters is particularly good. The Burton's Landing Forest Campground just off M-72 on Burton's Landing Road offers access to anglers and canoeists as well as 12 riverside campsites. Louie's Landing Road, the next road approaching the river from the south, also provides access. Keystone Landing Road, the first road east of Louie's Landing Road approaching the river from M-72, leads to Keystone Landing Forest Campground, which offers access to anglers and canoeists and 18 campsites to campers. The next road leading to the river from M-72 is Thendara Road, at the end of which is an undeveloped access site heavily used by anglers. It also leads to Camp WaWaSum, which serves as a meeting place for outdoor organizations. The lodge buildings are visible from the river about two miles above Stephan's Bridge. Near Camp WaWaSum the river becomes the northern boundary of the Huron National Forest until it reaches Mio, where the boundary extends north and the rest of the river flows through the national forest. There is a public fishing site and canoe launch at Stephan's Bridge, one of, if not the, most heavily-used sites in the system. Another undeveloped site is found off the corner of Pine Road just below the bridge. The Wakeley Bridge public access site has a boat ramp.

There are three fishing resorts on the river offering lodging and fishing guide services. Gates Au Sable Lodge & Pro Shop at Stephan's Bridge has served fishermen for several decades and offers dining, canoe rental, and an excellent fly-fishing tackle shop. The Edgewater on the Au Sable resort, operating since 1946, is located about one-eighth mile above Stephan's Bridge, accessible on Edgewater Lane about 200 yards south of the bridge. The Henderson Lodge is found on the river about one-half mile below Wakeley Bridge and can be reached via Henderson Lodge (Wilderness) Road on the south side of the river. For more information, call Gates Au Sable Lodge at (517) 348-8462, the Edgewater resort at (517) 348-8466, or the Henderson Lodge at (517) 348-9208.

Concentrations of each trout species vary greatly within the Holy Waters, although browns generally make up at least 50 percent of the total trout population. The greatest numbers of brook trout are found between Louie's Landing and Camp WaWaSum. Near Camp WaWaSum the river spreads to a width of nearly 100 feet, consisting of long, swift, shallow riffles with only an occasional deep pool. This wide flat stretch extends to Stephan's Bridge. Near Camp WaWasum a few rainbows enter the catch, increasing in number to Stephan's Bridge where they make up about 25 percent of the trout population. Below the bridge their numbers decline again until about two miles downstream there are very few, although an occasional rainbow can be caught all the way to Wakeley Bridge. Why these rainbows remain concentrated in this relatively small area is not entirely understood as they reproduce naturally. The swift riffles and gravel bottom—conditions favored by rainbows—extend to Wakeley Bridge, but the rainbow concentrations do not.

The river nearly doubles in volume from Stephan's Bridge to Wakeley Bridge, where it is from 80 to 110 feet wide. It becomes increasingly deeper between the two bridges and the trout habitat becomes better and better to Wakeley Bridge. The crystal-clear water tumbles beneath many sweepers and undercut banks, through deep pools, and over log jams, hiding many rambunctious browns and some brookies. Barker Creek, a small coldwater tributary, trickles into the mainstream from the north about one mile above Wakeley Bridge. Wakeley Creek draining Wakeley Lake enters just above the bridge.

There are several named reference points within the Holy Waters among avid anglers, such as the Whirlpool about one-

half mile above Thendara Road, and the Whippoorwill area located midway between Stephan's and Wakeley bridges. The Au Sable has long been known as a favorite among Trout Unlimited members and the organization owns two tracts of Holy Waters frontage: the Stranahan Tract above and across from the Edgewater resort and the Knight or Thunderbird Tract above Wakeley Bridge.

Fly hatches on the Holy Waters are fabulous. Bruce Dalrymple, a Trout Unlimited member of Saginaw, said the Thendara Road to Pine Road section is his favorite on the mainstream. He said Hendrickson hatches in late April and early May are very good, followed by excellent hatches of Little Black Caddis. Yellow Mayfly hatches from Memorial Day to mid-June provide superb evening fishing. They begin about 5 and a size 16 usually produces the best action. Among June's exceptional hatches are Sulfur and Brown Drake hatches, which usually occur about the same time. Late July and early August bring excellent hatches of Tiny White-Winged Blacks from Thendara Road to Wakeley Bridge. Different species of little Blue-winged Olives provide good fishing all season long, some in August, which occur about 10 a.m., and others in September, which occur in the afternoon.

Dr. William Priest of Hemlock said Hendrickson hatches on the Stephan-to-Wakeley stretch are unsurpassed, the best hatch of the season, although most of the others already mentioned are also exceptional. Although there are hatches of **Hexagenia limbata** on the Holy Waters, they are not as good as on the other portions of the river due to the lack of silt beds.

Below Wakeley Bridge the river changes rather abruptly again. The current slows, the bottom contains greater amounts of sand, and the river becomes much larger. Most of the pools below the bridge are too deep to wade, particularly those found in the series of winding bends from the Henderson Lodge to the White Pine Canoe Campground. Canoes can be rented at Wakeley and McMasters bridges, however, for anglers who prefer to float this area. Although brown trout are not as numerous in this stretch as they are in the Holy Waters, they are larger.

The section from the White Pine Canoe Campground to Conners Flat a few miles downstream is known as "the Stillwaters," a very wide, slow stretch noted for big brown trout. Historically, it was a very deep area but is now shallow, having filled with sand, and contains many weed beds. The South Branch of the Au Sable joins the mainstream just below the White Pine Canoe Campground. Below the mouth of the South Branch, the mainstream is from 110 to 150 feet wide, nearly 200 feet in spots. Access to the Stillwaters can be obtained on the north side of the river from the public fishing sites at the White Pine Canoe Campground east of Wakeley Bridge Road or at Conners Flat just off Conners Flat Road. The White Pine Canoe Campground offers 25 campsites and an additional 25 sites for camping canoeists.

Below Conners Flat, the river contains swift riffles once again, becoming narrower and therefore deeper. The Rainbow Bend Forest Campground, located about one-half mile east of Conners Flat, offers access to anglers but only five campsites and five additional campsites for groups of camping canoeists. Access is also available at McMasters Bridge. The remainder of the river is brown trout water except for the impoundments and the lower 10 miles.

Below McMasters Bridge access is more limited, but the river offers some lunker browns for the angler willing to fish big water. The North Branch of the Au Sable joins the main river about one mile below the bridge, increasing the width of the mainstream to about 200 feet. Silt-bed areas along portions of the river from McMaster's Bridge to Mio Pond produce clouds of **Hexagenia limbata** around July 1. Good brown trout water is found until the river spreads to form the seven-mile-long Mio Dam Pond just above the town of Mio in central Oscoda County. Access is available at Parmalee Bridge and the Parmalee Bridge Forest Campground (offering seven campsites) at County Road 489, at the Luzerne County Park on the south bank about one-and-a-half miles downstream, and at the public fishing site where the river approaches County Road 606 (Old River Road).

Several tributaries enter the river between McMasters Bridge and the Mio Dam Pond. Sohn and Beaver creeks west of Parmalee Bridge are poor trout streams due to beaver activity. Lost Creek, located west of the Mio Dam Pond, usually dries up in the jack pine plains during the summer. But biologist Schnicke said Big Creek, a sizable tributary entering the mainstream from the south, is perhaps the finest quality trout water in the entire Au Sable River system. It is a very picturesque stream consisting of an East and a West branch. It contains good trout populations, primarily browns with brookies in the headwaters, but is so clear that it is difficult to fish. The West Branch arises in northern Ogemaw County and flows through largely forested land. It is accessible from United States Forest Service trail roads, a roadside park where it is crossed by County Road 4890, and at county road crossings. Most of the smaller East Branch is privately owned and contains a small impoundment at Luzerne. Where the two branches join, the creek is 30 to 40 feet wide, swift, and the bottom is gravel to the mouth.

The 14-mile stretch of the river between Mio and McKinley Bridge is a quality fishing area with special regulations. Only artificial flies and lures may be used. Brown trout, the dominant species, must be 15 inches long and other trout must be 12 inches long with a limit of only two trout per day. Although trout populations are generally low, the growth rate is tremendous so the trout are large. The river is fast and big, averaging three to six feet deep with 10- to 12-foot pools. Fishing pressure is generally light except during the good **Hexagenia** hatches.

The river bottom is gravel and rock and the river can only be fished from boats. It flows through a narrow floodplain, often close to the valley walls which are up to 50 feet high. Access is available at Mio (M-72) and at the public fishing site at County Roads 600 and 601.

Several good trout tributaries enter this section, including Cherry, Perry, and Comins creeks.

If you are after lunker browns, try the main river below McKinley Bridge. Fishing pressure is limited because there is little access. But local anglers catch some huge browns on flies and small spoons, Rapalas, and spinners during the first half of the summer.

The river enters Alcona County several miles east of McKinley Bridge and swings south to Bamfield (Alcona) Pond. Schnicke said the river below Bamfield Pond is the least fished stretch of all but the best in which to get a 24-inch-plus brown trout. A word of caution, however; water is released from the dam in the evening, raising the water level three feet or more and making fishing nearly impossible. The river flows south from the pond several miles, enters Iosco County and eventually the chain of impoundments.

The 10 to 12 miles of river below Foote Dam host massive runs of salmon and steelheads. Hardy boat fishermen can catch steelies in the river throughout most of the winter and the mainstream is open to fishing all year long. Most of the river bottom is sandy—poor spawning habitat—but heavy plantings each year maintain the heavy runs. The river flows through Oscoda and into Lake Huron.

Additional fly hatches on the mainstream of the Au Sable are too numerous to list, as several often occur at the same time and on nearly every day of the year. But some of the more significant hatches include the March Brown from mid-May to mid-June; a variety of duns, including the Iron, Sulfur, Dark Sulfur, Pale Evening, and Mahogany, with hatches ranging from April to mid-September; Gray, Yellow, and Brown drakes, ranging from late May to late July; the Light Cahill from mid-June to late August; and the White Miller in late August.

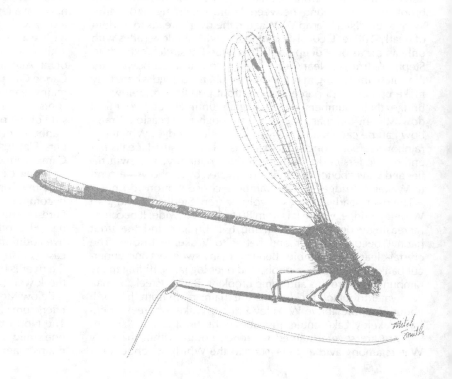

THE NORTH BRANCH OF
THE AU SABLE RIVER
By JANET D. MEHL

The North Branch of the Au Sable River is a favorite stream among anglers wishing to escape the tremendous pressure on the South Branch and mainstream. Limited access, shallow water, and numerous sweepers and small islands restrict most canoeing to below Kellogg's Bridge. The North Branch contains excellent trout populations, offering some of the finest brook trout fishing in the Au Sable system. Although it does not produce as many trophy-sized browns as the South Branch, it is known for good numbers of jumbo browns up to eight pounds. Its big brown trout fishing is rated superior to that of the mainstream, and considerably less competition for river space adds to fishing enjoyment.

The North Branch is a fly-fisherman's paradise, hosting fantastic hatches all season long. Nearly the entire length of the wide, flat stream can easily be fly-fished as it averages 96 feet wide. The lower 21 miles of the 36-mile river is a Quality Fishing (flies-only) Area open until October 31. Five fish may be taken per day, no more than three of which may be over 16 inches. Minimum sizes remain the same at eight inches for brook trout and 10 inches for other trout.

John Palmer, an ardent fly-fisherman from Gaylord, said the North Branch offers excellent hatches of "every mayfly in the book" with exceptional Hendrickson and Brown Drake hatches. Unlike early season fishing on many Michigan streams when fish cannot see dry flies due to high, riley water, the clear shallow North Branch offers good fly-fishing at the onset of the season when Hendricksons dot its rippling surface.

DNR electro-shocking surveys have been concluded on the North Branch for more than 20 years. Gary Schnicke, former district fisheries biologist at the DNR's Mio office, said the North Branch is resuming its 60 percent brook trout/40 percent brown trout ratio of the 1950s and '60s. In the early 1970s brown trout took over and became the dominant species, a natural trend which is not usually reversed, he said. But surveys in recent years show brook trout to be regaining their former abundance. The reason is not totally understood, but Schnicke attributes the reversal to a combination of factors specifically favorable to brook trout reproduction. Brook trout do not need as much gravel to spawn as browns or rainbows do, he said, but need more well-oxygenated groundwater inflow of slightly colder temperatures. Winter and spring weather conditions in recent years have favored this requirement, resulting in better brook trout reproduction, he said.

Schnicke said the stretch of the North Branch between Twin Bridges and Lovells contains higher concentrations of brook trout than any other part of the Au Sable system. The wide, flat nature of the stream makes it an excellent stretch to introduce youngsters to the world of trout fishing. Schnicke said the number of 15- to 20-inch browns is surprising despite the flat water, but most browns average eight to 12 inches. Portions of

the North Branch offer some of the Au Sable's finest trophy brown trout fishing, he said.

The North Branch originates as a man-made channel exiting the east side of Otsego Lake just south of Gaylord. It flows southeasterly through the Pigeon River Country State Forest, draining several small lakes. It is soon joined by Turtle Creek from the north and Club Creek draining a chain of lakes from the south. The confluence of these three streams marks the beginning of fly-fishing water as well as the upper limit of brook trout water. Bordered by tag alder swamps, the stream is quite open, wide, and shallow and is easily fly-fished throughout the remainder of the mainstream. From Chub Creek downstream several miles the North Branch is bordered by a National Guard artillery range on the south side. As the stream swings south, the range borders it on the west. The bottom is sand and gravel down to Lovells, where it becomes primarily gravel all the way to the mouth.

The Chub Creek Forest Campground offers six campsites at Lower Chub Lake near the mouth of the creek. Nearly three miles of North Branch frontage above Dam 2 is privately owned.

The dilapidated Dam 2 is a remnant of the lumbering days. It once served as a holding area to collect logs and increase water flow. When the dam was released the surging water sent hundreds of logs plunging downstream to mills. The dam no longer restricts water flow.

Below Dam 2 the stream is 70 to 80 feet wide, shallow, quite straight, and open, dotted with many small islands. Large semiopen areas of grass and sedge provide nesting sites for many upland sandpipers and are also used extensively by woodcock. Cover and water temperatures are only considered fair for trout. Crapo Creek, draining a chain of lakes, enters the North Branch four miles below Dam 2 but is too warm for trout. Although most of the river frontage is privately owned north of Crawford County, development is limited. Most of the river frontage is privately owned from Twin Bridges to the mouth, but development is limited except for heavy residential areas for a mile-and-a-half below Lovells and on the lower six miles of the river below Kellogg's Bridge.

The river flows through state land as it enters Crawford County. Trout habitat improves considerably and three public fishing sites within a short distance, located just off Twin Bridge Road (F97), provide access to fine fishing downstream. The first two sites are undeveloped but are commonly used by anglers and campers. The third site is a developed site although not for campers, who frequent the area located about one-half mile above Twin Bridges. It is known as the Sheep Ranch site and is the upper limit of the flies-only water extending all the way to the mouth. The river is also accessible at Twin Bridges, the two bridges carrying Twin Bridge Road across the river.

Biologist Schnicke said the 100- to 150-foot-wide stretch of the river from about four miles above Lovells to about one mile below Lovells is one of the finest nursery sections in the Au Sable system. Concentrations of brook trout in the knee- to thigh-deep water are higher than in any other part of the Au Sable and 15- to 20-inch browns are not uncommon.

County Road 612 crosses the river at Lovells. The bridge site provides an undeveloped access point for anglers.

About one mile below Lovells the stream channel narrows to about 60 feet and the gradient increases so the current is swift. The next three miles contain excellent holding water but are largely inaccessible as the Marianne and High Banks lodges own the frontage to Dam 4. Brook trout numbers are lower, but more big browns are found in this stretch and trout production remains excellent to Kellogg's Bridge.

Although Dam 4 is privately owned, public access has been allowed there. Several rows of pilings with a small gap in the middle are all that remain of this lumbering dam, but they do restrict water flow below. They mark the beginning of another nursery section, a wide, shallow stretch containing excellent brook trout populations and some dandy browns. The remainder of the river is of a pool-riffle character except for only very short nursery sections. The current is so swift that it makes wading difficult.

Just above the Sheep Pasture Access Site located about three miles above Kellogg's Bridge is another deep pool area formed as the river swings back and forth. It ends at the Sheep Pasture site, another camping spot located just off Lovells Road (F97).

One of the last access points on the North Branch is at Kellogg's Bridge at North Down River Road. From the Crawford

County line to Kellogg's Bridge the river doubles in size, being more than 150 feet wide at the bridge. Below the bridge a wading angler may float his hat if he is not careful. The river continues to contain good cover and offers big browns. It is almost 200 feet wide in places downstream from the confluence of Big Creek, a good coldwater trout tributary joining the North Branch about a mile below Kellogg's Bridge.

BIG CREEK

Big Creek consists of a West, Middle, and East branch and contains more than 66 stream miles, including its few small tributaries. The creek is about 40 feet wide near the mouth and portions offer good hatches of **Hexagenia**.

The West Branch is the largest and longest branch. It is the

site of beaver activity in the headwaters and there are few trout. But below County Road 612 (Lewiston Road) there are good groundwater inflow and good brook trout populations. A short distance downstream brown trout become dominant and offer good fishing. Most of the creek offers good hatches of **Hexagenia**. Most of the stream bottom is sand near County Road 612, but gravel patches increase near the mouth.

The West Branch is largely undeveloped, but access is limited to the upper part of the stream. It begins as it drains several lakes in northeastern Otsego County and flows south almost to the North Branch before it is joined by the East Branch of Big Creek just above Blonde Dam Bridge at North Down River Road. The stream is accessible from trail roads leading north from County Road 612 and from the Big Creek Forest Campground at County Road 612, which offers 10 campsites. Most of the first three miles of the creek below County Road 612 flows through state land.

Although most of the Middle Branch of Big Creek flows through the eastern edge of Crawford County, it originates from West Twin Lake in southwestern Montmorency County. Nearly all of the creek above Town Line Road flows through state land and parallels Walsh Road. About four miles above its confluence with the East Branch is a 94-acre wildlife flooding impounded in 1964. There are only poor to fair numbers of brook trout above the flooding, but below the flooding the Middle Branch contains the best quality trout water in the Big Creek system. Cold groundwater keeps water temperatures in the 60s. Both bank cover and in-stream cover are good, supporting an excellent brook and brown trout population.

The East Branch of Big Creek flows through Oscoda County, originating as it drains Little Bear, Snyder, and Tea lakes. Much of the midstream flows through state land. There is another Big Creek Forest Campground on County Road 489 (Big Lake Road) offering six campsites.

The East Branch contains the poorest quality trout water in Big Creek, holding only modest numbers of brook trout above the confluence with Wright Creek. The lower portion of the East Branch has a good gravel bottom, colder water temperatures, and good trout populations, but its frontage is almost entirely private property.

The short mainstream of Big Creek produces some big browns. It contains good gravel runs, good cover, and cold water temperatures which help cool the North Branch of the Au Sable.

The North Branch flows into the mainstream a short distance below McMasters Bridge.

The North Branch is noted for phenomenal fly hatches. Win Case of Saginaw, a national Trout Unlimited director and riverfront property owner, said three very prolific hatches occurring throughout the North Branch were mayfly hatches of Hendricksons, Sulfur Duns (**Ephemerella dorothea**), and Brown Drakes. Other prolonged hatches of **Ischonichya** (Maroon Drake) and **Tricorythodes** (tiny White-winged Blacks) also occur throughout much of the river, he said. Most **Hexagenia** hatches on the North Branch occur near the mouth.

Bruce Richards of Midland, a Trout Unlimited chapter official and production supervisor for Scientific Anglers 3M Company, has fished the Lovells area for several years. His favorite hatches occur in May with very consistent hatches of sulfurs and little black caddis and what are locally named "popcorn" caddis, which look like popcorn when they fly. Richards said the little black caddis hatch is often excellent but difficult to fish. They hatch very fast and emerging patterns often work best. Although fish are rising, they are chasing these emerging larvae.

THE EAST BRANCH OF THE AU SABLE RIVER

By JANET D. MEHL

The East Branch of the Au Sable River flows southwest 16 miles from its source in north-central Crawford County to the mainstream three quarters of a mile east of Grayling. It ripples through the Hartwick Pines State Park east of M-93. Unlike most of the Au Sable system, the East Branch is small—too small to canoe—and receives only light pressure from local fishermen. This coldwater tributary is an excellent brook trout stream and contains chunky browns up to six pounds. It is often overlooked for the hundreds of miles of bigger water found in the Au Sable system. Many anglers do not realize that much of the stream can be fly-fished by a skillful angler. Terrestrial fishing is excellent in the open meadow areas below the park. The East Branch should also be considered by spin and bait fishermen seeking small-stream solitude.

Robert Smock, Sr., of Grayling has fly-fished the stream extensively for many years from the Wilcox Road Bridge, the first bridge east of I-75, upstream to Hartwick Pines. He said it is not difficult to catch 40 to 50 browns in an evening, many 10 to 14 inches long. A considerable number of 18- to 20-inch browns are caught below "the Pines" during the **Hex** hatch, Smock said. **Hex** hatches occur slightly later than those on the mainstream, continuing through the first week in July, he added.

Much of the 15- to 20-foot-wide stream would not typically be considered fly-fishing water, but local anglers fly-fish meadow areas near bridges with six- or seven-foot fly rods, often casting only six to 12 feet of line.

The stream is largely undeveloped as most of it flows through a National Guard artillery range. Only the extreme headwaters draining several small lakes are too warm for trout. Cold groundwater inflow soon cools the stream and excellent brook trout fishing is found below County Road 612. From its source to what is known locally as the "Army Tank Bridge" about one land mile below Hartwick Pines, nearly the entire stream flows through state land. Most of the stream down to I-75 can be fished with hip boots as pools seldom exceed four feet. It is 30 to 35 feet wide at the mouth.

The East Branch is primarily a brook trout stream, containing brookies all the way to the mouth. Big browns are found below Hartwick Pines. Smock said many big browns begin entering the East Branch from the mainstream Au Sable in July for fall spawning, attracted by its colder water temperatures as they travel upstream. The stream offers a number of late-season drake and caddis hatches, Smock said, and the greater number of big browns in the East Branch at this time provide exciting fishing.

The Jones Lake Forest Campground, nine miles east of Frederic on County Road 612, offers 42 campsites near the stream.

The East Branch becomes especially picturesque in Hartwick Pines, its crystal-clear water gurgling over many gravel stretches and fallen trees and swirling beneath brush-choked undercut banks. Brook trout populations are excellent as are a variety of

other wildlife species in the area. Numerous trail roads approach or cross the stream, most of which are not named on county maps. The first bridge one meets in the Pines is called Friday's Cabin Bridge by local old-timers, although the cabin has been gone for years. The next bridge a few miles downstream is the Scenic Trail Bridge. The road is labeled the Lewiston Grade on county maps but becomes part of the Scenic Trail when it enters the park. The bridge on Old Pine Road running east and west between Lewiston Grade and Jones Lake Truck Trail along

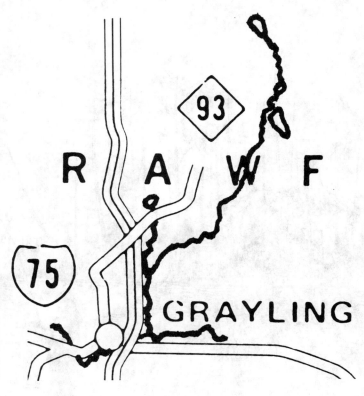

the southern boundary of the park is known as the Pines Bridge. Here the stream is about 15 feet wide.

Fred Blaauw of Grayling lives on the banks of the East Branch at the Pines Bridge and has fly-fished the stream below the Army Tank Bridge for many years. He took a whopping six-pound, 24-inch brown during one of the East Branch's fine **Hex** hatches in the late 1970s. Above the Army Tank Bridge the stream slows and contains deeper pools holding big browns, Blaauw said. It flows through a sandy, grassy area commonly known as "the Meadows." Gravel stretches become less frequent and grassy areas more numerous below the bridge.

The road supported by the Army Tank Bridge just off Jones Lake Truck Trail about one mile below the Pines does not appear to cross the river on most county maps. The bridge got its nickname because the National Guard hauls army tanks over it to northern parts of the artillery range. The Wilcox Road Bridge east of I-75 provides access. Milliken Road leading north from Grayling along I-75 also provides access. The river is accessible just above the mouth near the old trout hatchery rearing ponds.

The stream current picks up again below the Army Tank Bridge. Below Wilcox Road the river contains deeper pools and is considered more typical fly water. It has carved excellent holding areas beneath the banks and overhanging tag alders provide additional cover down to I-75. Blaauw said good holding is found in the rather lengthy stretch of knee-deep water between the north- and southbound lanes of the expressway. The bottom is gravel between the two but below the southbound highway the bottom is sandy to the mouth. When I-75 was

built in 1965, tons of sand and silt were washed into the river. Trout populations are lower below I-75 due to the sand, but good fly hatches attract fishermen.

Blaauw said shifting sand and sedimentation was a serious problem throughout the East Branch, decreasing the quality of this "very productive little river" year by year.

The lower quarter of the river below the old trout hatchery rearing ponds has been maintained as a youngster's fishing section. At the time of this writing, Grayling residents were making plans to resume hatchery production and create a local tourist attraction.

The East Branch hosts many of the same fly hatches that the mainstream Au Sable does, including very good hatches of **Hexagenia** from the Meadows downstream. Excellent hopper fishing in the afternoons during July and August also produce good catches in this stretch.

THE SOUTH BRANCH OF THE AU SABLE RIVER

By JANET D. MEHL

The South Branch of the world-famous Au Sable River contains some of the finest big trout water in the Au Sable system—in the entire Midwest, for that matter. It plays a major part in distinguishing the Au Sable River as one of the—if not the—very best trout streams east of the Rocky Mountains. Thousands of fishermen from all over the Midwest flock to the South Branch each year to wet their flies on Michigan's finest fly-fishing waters. Tackle-breaking browns up to eight pounds are taken at night when clouds of **Hexagenia limbata** dapple the riffling waters, each insect gliding but a short distance downstream before another ''slurp'' devours it. The action peaks in the state-owned Mason Tract for which the South Branch earns its fame, extending from Chase Bridge, truly the heart of the South Branch, to Smith Bridge at M-72.

Bob Julius of Lansing, a Trout Unlimited fly-fishing instructor, said the excellent fishing on the South Branch has not declined since he began actively fishing the stream in 1969. Both DNR surveys and U.S. Forest Service studies show the excellent populations of trout of a large average size have remained as good as those of 10 years ago.

The South Branch is also known for its super hatches of Brown Drakes and a variety of other flies. Julius said the hundreds of fishermen who flock to the South Branch for the **hex** hatch have just missed Brown Drakes that hatch in clouds and offer comparable fishing. During the **Hexagenia** hatch in late June, fishermen are lined elbow-to-elbow for miles, particularly in the Mason Tract. There is a 16-mile quality-fishing (flies-only) stretch from Chase Bridge to the mouth open until October 31 where five fish per day may be kept. Beginning in 1983 no-kill catch and release regulations went into effect on a four-and-a-half-mile stretch from Chase Bridge to the High Banks. Creel limits are five fish per day, no more than three of which may be over 16 inches in length.

The relatively even bottom of the stream makes night fishing easy, although wading fishermen can drink without bending in early season high water levels and near the mouth. The current is moderately swift below Roscommon. The South Branch fluctuates from a torrent in early spring to a riffling stream in summer after water levels drop as much as three feet. In addition to difficult wading, Gary Schnicke, former district fisheries biologist at the DNR's Mio office, said the dramatic change presents some trout-managing problems. High water levels occasionally move cover and low water levels expose cover along the banks. It is relatively consistent from year to year, however.

Canoeing pressure is extremely heavy on the South Branch below Roscommon and may restrict daytime fishing during the summer months.

The South Branch is quite accessible below Roscommon. Both I-75 and US-27 lead very near to the river from all of southern Michigan, with M-72 leading to prime fishing from the east and

west. M-144, which swings northeast from Roscommon, parallels the river on the south and intersects several roads leading to its banks. Dirt roads follow much of the river's edge. More than 10 miles of river flow through the Mason Tract, donated to the state of Michigan by George W. Mason in 1954 so that future generations could enjoy its quality fishing and primitive environment. Public fishing sites are located just over the Crawford County line and at Steckert, Chase, and Smith bridges. The Canoe Harbor Campground on the river just south of M-72 offers 45 sites to campers, anglers, and canoeists.

From its source at Lake St. Helen to Roscommon, the South Branch is primarily a warmwater stream lacking cold groundwater seepage. Its slow, meandering channel drains large cedar swamps, elm flats, and open tag alder marshes for more than 15 miles, flowing first northward and then straight west to Roscommon. These vast cedar swamps serve as crucial wintering yards for deer and are heavily hunted in November. The stream does contain some big browns in the spring above Roscommon. Below Sherman Bridge at County Road 602 the stream is a continuous series of winding bends clogged with log jams.

Some tributaries of the South Branch above Roscommon contain brook trout. In the St. Helen oil fields South Creek enters the mainstream, a fair brook trout tributary with gravel bottom and cedar-lined banks. East Creek, a sandy, fair brook trout stream, joins the South Branch near Sherman Bridge. Hudson Creek, draining the big Hudson Creek Swamp, is only a marginal trout stream.

Robinson Creek drains the Robinson Creek Waterfowl Flooding near I-75 and flows north to join the mainstream in Roscommon. Biologist Schnicke said it is noted for its trophy-sized brookies up to two pounds. It also contains browns near the mouth. Portions of the creek are fly-fishable. Access is gained from dirt roads which parallel much of the creek.

From Roscommon down to Steckert Bridge, the sand-bottomed South Branch offers good early season fishing for browns and some brook trout. It is accessible from the public fishing site near the Crawford County line. In late June, warm water temperatures urge these fish to seek colder water in Robinson Creek and Beaver Creek, a sizable tributary entering the South Branch near the public fishing site. It is an excellent coldwater feeder draining cedar and tag alder swamps. Cover-choked areas flooded by beaver activity offer fine brook trout fishing and hefty browns enter the catch near the mouth.

Steckert Bridge marks the upper limit of good trout-holding water and excellent hatches, offering good fishing all season. The stream begins receiving excellent groundwater inflow and takes on the riffle-pool character conducive to quality trout habitat. The bottom is primarily gravel from here to the mouth. From Roscommon to Chase Bridge, the narrow stream channel continues to drain tag alder to cedar swamps with two- to four-foot banks. Cabins dot much of the shoreline. Midway between Steckert and Chase bridges, Deerheart Valley Road dead-ends at the south bank and provides access.

The essence of the South Branch begins at Chase Bridge six miles below Roscommon as the stream enters the pristine Mason Tract, now formally named the George Mason River Retreat. The waist-deep waters, 40 to 50 feet in width, offer chunky browns to the night fisherman and some brookies. The gravel bottom contains some rocky areas. Wide, winding bends create deep pools. The banks rise up to 20 feet in many places, as high as 50 feet toward Smith Bridge, draining forests of jack pine, red and white pine, balsam, cedar, birch, and aspen. Numerous small, coldwater feeders enter the Mason Tract, including Hickey, Douglas, Thayer, and Sauger creeks.

Access is available where Leline Road dead-ends at the south bank one mile below Chase Bridge. About two miles below Chase Bridge the river straightens for about two miles, lacking deep holes but producing bigger brook trout. There are no **Hex** hatches in this area as the stream bottom and edges are rock and gravel, but there are excellent true caddis hatches.

"Marlabar" or Daisy Bend as it is known locally, an old canoe take-out point at the end of Peterson Road, begins a five-mile stretch of even bigger trout water. Large pools harbor jumbo browns up to two feet long and some brook trout. The river resumes its winding bends where log jams, undercut banks, sweepers, and bank cover provide excellent shelter. Brown Drake and **Hexagenia** hatches are superb in this section. Near the end of Peterson Road are the foundations of three buildings set back from the river's edge, all that remains of Durant's Castle. Built in the 1920s, Durant's Castle was a popular meeting place for sportsmen and politicians until it was destroyed by fire.

The current in this stretch is comparable to that of the upper mainstream Au Sable, although the channel is narrower and deeper, averaging 50 feet wide but reaching 80 feet in spots. The deep pools connected by riffles continue to the Mason Chapel, built by the DNR to commemorate George Mason's contribution. Rounding a wide bend in the river, one can see the chapel on the east bank 50 feet above the water.

Below the Mason Chapel the gradient increases and the current picks up. When the river reaches Smith Bridge it is about 65 to 70 feet wide with pools well over a person's head. It no longer drains any lowlands but high terraces with some banks exceeding 50 feet. The six miles of river below Smith Bridge are largely inaccessible due to large private ownerships by the Oxbow Club and Consumers Power Company. Homes and cabins scattered along the banks below Smith Bridge and near the mouth are built on land leased from Consumers Power.

From Chase Bridge to the mouth, the South Branch doubles in size and is 80 to 100 feet wide at the mouth. Portions of the river below Smith Bridge are too deep to wade. The big water contains big trout, however, and a few pike. Halfway to the mouth the river gets slower, deeper, and sandier and produces super **Hexagenia** hatches. The last mile of the river drains a low, old river floodplain before entering the main Au Sable River.

Not only do trout, anglers, canoeists, campers, photographers, and snowmobilers find the South Branch a favorite environment, a variety of species flourish in the watershed's prime wildlife habitat. In addition to containing priority deer-wintering range, the swamps and stream above Roscommon host plenty of beaver, otter, mink, and muskrats. Local trappers seek these fur-bearing animals although most people pursuing the recreational activities offered by the South Branch and mainstream Au Sable are from southern Michigan. Bald eagles have been nesting near Lake St. Helen. The endangered Kirtland's warbler, unique to the jack pine stands of the Au Sable watershed, nests between the South Branch and Mio. Black bear are plentiful enough to support a hunting season in eastern Roscommon County.

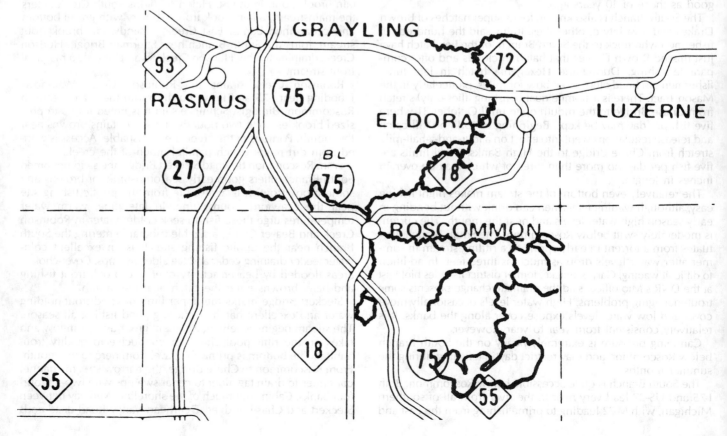

THE MANISTEE RIVER
By JANET D. MEHL

The Big Manistee River can be reached from most points in northern Michigan in an hour's time. Its numerous campgrounds and access sites, limited development, fine canoe waters, and variety of fishing opportunities make it one of Michigan's most popular rivers. The upper Manistee contains quality trout and canoeing water, yet does not get the pressure that the neighboring Au Sable River receives. The lower portion of the river offers some of Michigan's most famous steelhead, coho and chinook salmon, and lake-run brown trout fishing, as well as walleye, pike, and smallmouth bass fishing.

The Big Manistee originates as a group of small, spring-fed tributaries in southeastern Antrim County and the southwestern tip of Otsego County. It then flows southwesterly through Crawford, Kalkaska, Missaukee, Wexford, and Manistee counties and into Manistee Lake before emptying into Lake Michigan at Manistee. More than 100 feeder streams of trout quality flow into the river, draining some 2,000 square miles. The mainstream is about 170 miles long.

The Manistee receives most of its water from groundwater sources and is influenced little by run-off, making it one of the most stable rivers in Lower Michigan. Its size and rate of flow remain fairly uniform throughout the year and temperature fluctuation is at a minimum.

The upper portion of the Manistee located west of Grayling in Crawford and Kalkaska counties offers fine fishing for brook and brown trout. Most trout fishermen fish above the town of Sharon in south central Kalkaska County, as below this point the river becomes too warm to be ideal trout habitat. Rough fish (suckers, redhorse, creek chubs) and warmwater predators (pike and walleyes) predominate. Above Sharon water temperatures exceed the 70° maximum tolerated by trout only a few days of each year.

Below Sharon the river is large enough to travel with boat and outboard motor. Canoes and light craft are used from the ghost town of Deward in northern Crawford County down to M-66 at Smithville near the southern Kalkaska County line. Development is limited with concentrations near Sharon and M-72, which canoeists, campers, and anglers all find very appealing. Turbidity is low due to the absence of clay and water is generally clear. Many hard-surfaced roads and dirt trails follow much of the river's length, providing excellent access.

The best trout fishing is found above M-72 where cover and natural food supplies are excellent. This is also the most natural and scenic portion of the river, frequented by ducks, deer, and other wildlife. Most of the few homes and cottages along this stretch are not visible from the river. This stretch is easily waded as the current velocity is slow to medium and water depth seldom exceeds three feet, although pools are often three to six feet deep.

Natural reproduction sustains excellent populations of browns and

brook trout above Cameron Bridge. The trout fisherman can usually leave this portion of the river with a full creel, even if fishing during midday. Eight- to 10-inch brookies are caught, with browns running eight to 12 inches common. Large browns, some reaching 20 inches with an occasional four- to five-pounder, are taken from these waters at night on flies. Log jams, stumps, undercut banks, overhanging trees, and shaded pools provide excellent cover.

A few rainbows are added to the catch a few miles above M-72. Some natural reproduction of browns occurs in the gravel areas near M-72 but not enough to sustain populations. The DNR plants several thousand brown trout in Crawford, Kalkaska, and Missaukee counties annually. Ben Butts of Grayling, board member of the Upper Manistee River Association, said the association plants from 1,500 to 2,000 trout from County Road 612 to Sharon each year, most of which run between eight and 10 inches with some as long as 16 and 18 inches. Butts said the association is hoping to plant browns in the future because planted rainbows tend to move downstream if not caught. He said the Manistee River Association below Sharon also planted brook trout in 1981.

Only the headwaters above Mancelona Road are too narrow and brushy to fly-fish and are best suited to bait fishing. Below Mancelona Road the stream drains low, flat terrain covered by tag alder, willow, and hardwood swamp. Banks are less than three feet high and much of the stream bottom is sand with some gravel areas. The river averages 30 to 40 feet wide so streamside vegetation shades much of the water, which, along with spring seepage, keeps water temperatures especially cold and more suitable for active trout.

Harry (Art) Weideman of Grayling fishes the Manistee regularly in the Deward area, where he said most of the water is about knee-deep and nine out of 10 fish he catches are browns.

Above Cameron Bridge, which is located about three miles south of Deward, the river is designated as first-class quality trout water by the DNR, while that below is rated as good. The river above Cameron Bridge is also considered the most scenic portion. Gravel areas between Deward and Cameron Bridge provide suitable spawning areas. Brown trout comprise most of the fish population with increasing numbers of brook trout found downstream to Long's Canoe Rental.

Below Cameron Bridge the streamside vegetation changes to that of coniferous swamp containing red and white pine, cedar, balsam, tamarack, and spruce. The average width of the river has increased from 40 to 50 feet until just below the bridge it divides into several braided channels less than three feet deep. These join again before reaching Red Bridge at County Road 612.

Robert Andrus of Grayling manages the Watershed Club located about one mile north of Long's. He said bigger fish were found above and around Red and Cameron bridges.

Below Red Bridge brook trout are predominate, the stream bottom is sandy, and stream vegetation is sparse. The sandy, three- to 20-foot banks, covered with pine forests, provide excellent sites for the two Manistee River Forest Campgrounds. About two miles downstream the river again splits into several good brook-trout-producing channels, draining aspen and cedar swamps. Long's Canoe Rental, three land miles north of M-72, is located within these spreads and provides good fishing for brooks and browns. Down to this point much of the river frontage is in state ownership in the Au Sable State Forest.

Near the tail of these spreads the river is joined by Goose Creek, an excellent brook trout tributary for the bait fisherman. The main river has increased to about 60 feet wide. From this point south to Sharon stream banks rise up to 20 feet, supporting pine and hardwood forests.

Butts, an avid trout fisherman, has lived on the Manistee a mile north of M-72 for several years. He estimated the trout population in this area to be mostly browns, and occasional rainbows. There are few brookies.

Near M-72 the river is about 70 feet wide and generally two to six feet deep with some pools over six feet. Cover is supplied by deep pools and some log jams and undercut banks. Gravel areas above and below M-72 make it a good stretch for brooks and browns, with a few rainbows intermixed. Between M-72 and Sharon browns run from 10 to 16 inches.

Stanley Kostrzewski of Lansing often foregoes the fishing opportunity offered from his cottage on Houghton Lake to fish the Manistee below M-72. Here he catches mostly browns and rainbows and a few brook trout on both flies and spinners. Rainbow populations increase below M-72 due to increased stocking and the faster, deeper, riffly water which is more suitable habitat for them.

The stream bottom contains several gravel areas downstream to the Riverview Camp. This area offers excellent night fishing for browns with flies. Listening for the sound of feeding browns slurping insects from the surface is the best way to locate them.

Downstream several miles from Riverview Camp is Yellowtrees Landing, the upper boundary of a 7.5-mile Quality Fishing Area, better known to the angler as a "flies-only" stretch. Size limits for this particular area, which ends at CCC Bridge, are eight inches for brook trout and 12 inches for other trout with a total limit of five trout per day. Browns are most common, followed by rainbows with some brookies present. Butts said this stretch contains better cover than areas above and below it but is more difficult to wade due to the swifter current and deeper pools.

Just below Yellowtrees Landing, Portage Creek joins the river—a good brook trout stream which originates from Lake Margrethe near Grayling.

The entire upper Manistee accommodates the fly fisherman well with its excellent caddis and mayfly hatches from mid-May through July. Good Hendrickson hatches in late April and early May are followed by Dun hatches in late May and early June, which overlap Brown Drake hatches in June.

Marion Wright of Grayling, Trout Unlimited chapter president, said hatches of Borchers and Cahills also occur between Hendrickson and Brown Drake hatches.

Giant burrowing mayfly (**Hexagenia limbata**) hatches, commonly misnamed "the caddis hatch," occur in late June and early July. Butts said the excellent **Hex** hatches on the Manistee surpass even those on the Au Sable, with the exception of the

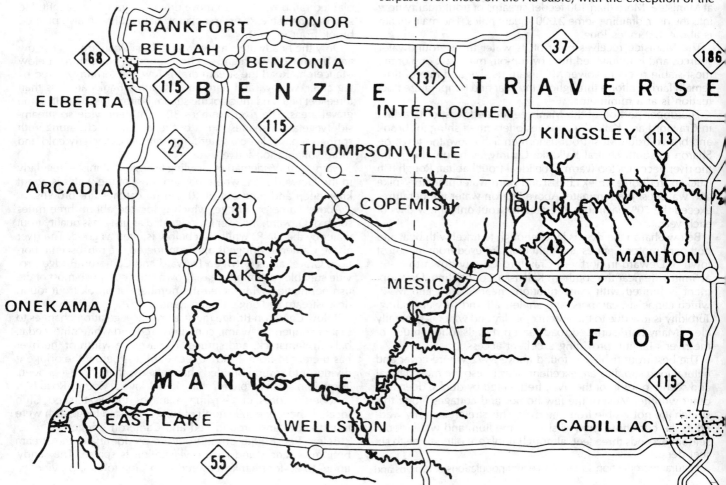

South Branch. He said the Manistee also had heavy caddis hatches and that the water was never so cloudy that fish couldn't be attracted with dry flies.

Andrus said the two main hatches above Long's Canoe Rental were the **Hex** and Brown Drake hatches, with the increased gravel areas downstream producing better and more varied hatches. He said the entire system offered good summer hopper fishing.

Below CCC Bridge brook trout become scarce, but rainbows increase in number. Below this bridge and particularly near Sharon, gravel areas become more frequent, but little natural reproduction of trout occurs except in the tributaries. Much of the water in this stretch is waist-deep with deep holes. The river is joined by a number of feeder creeks and increases steadily in speed and width until at Sharon it is from 80 to 100 feet wide and the current is swift. Below Sharon browns run from 12 to 20 inches.

Joined by the North Branch Manistee and several tributaries near Sharon, the river is more than 100 feet wide when it reaches Smithville. Many of these feeder creeks are of good quality for brooks and browns, particularly Big Cannon, Little Cannon, Filer, and Ham creeks, which contain excellent spawning areas. The North Branch offers good trout fishing except for the tributary draining Manistee Lake, which is too warm for trout. Hopkins Creek in Missaukee County offers excellent fishing for both brooks and browns.

Forest campgrounds are located at M-72 and CCC bridges and at Smithville.

Although fishing pressure is low below Smithville, the river does produce some large browns and rainbows. It travels through the northeastern corner of Missaukee County before entering Wexford County. Browns are planted annually in the mainstream throughout this stretch. Numerous creeks flow into the river and most are of good trout quality.

The Big Manistee contains two major dams: Hodenpyle, on the eastern Manistee County line, and the famous Tippy Dam known throughout the Midwest, located just north of M-55 in Manistee County. Both are hydroelectric dams owned by Consumers Power Company and their impoundments offer good walleye, smallmouth bass, and pike fishing. (The Pine River, which enters the south arm of the Tippy Backwaters, is considered a major tributary to the Manistee River and is discussed in a separate report.)

The lower river between Tippy Dam and Manistee Lake, including Bear and Pine creeks, is managed for coho and chinook salmon, steelheads, lake-run browns, and walleyes. Many fishermen travel several hundred miles each year to fish this area where some of the largest numbers of trophy steelheads and salmon are taken in Michigan. The river consists of large, deep pools connected by gravel-sand riffle areas with many log jams near the banks. These rifle-pool areas provide good spawning grounds for spring and fall steelhead runs and for fall chinook, coho, and brook trout runs.

Excellent steelhead runs in late April and May produce fish averaging eight to nine pounds, with many in the 10- to 15-pound class taken. Spawn bags produce good results and are commonly used. Casting with streamer flies, Little Cleos, jointed Rapalas, spinners, and small, wobbling plugs, such as Flatfish, Fire Plugs, and Heddon Tadpollies, also take many fish.

John Rokos of Traverse City, who fishes many of Michigan's rivers, works the Manistee from the Coho Bend landing near the Manistee County Airport. He said the river is awfully big with most pools 12 to 14 feet deep and must be fished with a boat. The most successful way to catch salmon, he said, was to anchor above a big hole and fish with two rods using the drop-back method. A chartreuse or silver Tadpolly is cast into the middle of the hole and allowed to wiggle in the current to attract fish. Spawn is used on the second rod, cast into the head of the pool and dropped back a foot or two at a time through the entire pool. Rokos said this is also the method used by most successful guides.

A Liberalized Salmon Fishing Area extends from Tippy Dam to signs posted about one mile downstream. Snagging of cohos and chinooks is allowed in this area from September 10 through October 25. The trout and salmon fishing season is open year-around in the mainstream from US-131 to the mouth.

In early September excellent boat fishing for salmon develops below the mouth of Bear Creek and salmon fishing below Tippy Day remains good into November. Steelhead fishing begins in October and remains good until mid-May. Fishermen willing to brave winter weather have lots of room and little competition to catch good numbers of hefty, fighting steelhead.

Chinooks average 12 pounds with some monsters larger than 25 pounds taken. Coho salmon averaging seven pounds are also common. Both are taken with bait and lures similar to those used for steelheads. There is significant natural reproduction of both species and of steelhead as well. A few lake trout are also caught below Tippy Dam.

Bear Creek, arising from a group of spring-fed creeks near Copemish in northern Manistee County, is an excellent trout and steelhead stream and enters the Manistee near the end of Kettle Hole Road off M-55. Most of the stream bottom is gravel and provides excellent spawning areas. The fishing

season is open year around upstream to County Road 600.

Dick Kuiper of Onekama, an avid fly fisherman, fishes Bear Creek for both steelheads and browns, the dominant species. Brook trout are found in the upper stretches and in the tributaries. Kuiper caught a chunky, 25-inch brown in the creek a few years ago and has taken brookies up to 16 inches.

Kuiper fishes for steelheads with either spawn or sponge pieces treated with Vaseline and anise oil. He heats the sponge pieces, Vaseline, and anise oil to liquid form, then drops them in cold water so they gel. This effective bait drifts a few inches off bottom.

Several public access points are found on both Bear Creek and the mainstream. Below Tippy Dam on the mainstream access is available at High Bridge, near Blacksmith Bayou, off Indian Village, Horseshoe Bend and Kettle Hole roads, at the Sickle Creek public fishing site, and off Peterson Road. The Udell Rollways Camp and Picnic Grounds, operated by the U.S. Forest Service, is located at the mouth of Pine Creek, another excellent trout tributary.

The Tippy Dam access site receives extremely heavy use and a user-fee system has been in effect since 1972. In 1978 access was improved on the north side of the river when Consumers Power Company upgraded the two-track trail leading from Tippy Dam Road to the crest of the hill overlooking the "Sawdust Pile Flats," which is also the downstream boundary of the liberalized fishing area. On the south side the Wellston Tourist Association improved the fire trail leading from Old House Road to the level terrain across from the Sawdust Pile Flats. About 30 parking spaces and public facilities were provided. The 150-site campground near Tippy Dam accommodates only a fraction of the fishermen who enjoy one of Michigan's most exciting fishing opportunities.

THE LITTLE MANISTEE RIVER
By WILLIAM H. BULLEN, Fisheries Biologist

Nine-Mile Bridge, Bear Track, Indian Club, Sawdust Pile, Old Grade, Carrieville—when mentioned to Michigan's inveterate trout fishermen, bring back fond memories of magnificent steelheads, wily brown trout, and surprising brook trout. Almost 100 years of waters have flowed past anglers' waders since the Little Manistee River first etched its reputation as "some of the finest fishing water in Michigan."The fish species involved have changed, the surrounding lands have changed, and the fishermen's waders have changed, but the reputation still stands.

Lying between the headwaters of the nearby Baldwin and Pine rivers in east-central Lake County, the Little Manistee arises as a group of small spring-fed tributaries joining near the once-famous lumbering town of Luther. Brook trout are fairly abundant in these headwaters and provide opportunity for the brush angler. All of the riverfront lands above Luther are privately owned and should be respected as such.

Two small coldwater creeks entering immediately below the dam counteract any warming effect from the dam overspill. Brook trout inhabit the stream in fair numbers from Luther downstream as far as M-37 where they finally give way to browns and rainbows.

Approximately 20 miles of 15 to 25 feet wide, brushy river exist between Luther and M-37 with nearly half of the frontage in public ownership. Canoeing is practically nonexistent in this stretch due to the river's physical characteristics, thus allowing a disturbance-free fishing experience.

Natural cover and stream-improvement devices provide fishable hides for the resident populations of brown trout in the 10- to 14-inch range and brookies up to 12 inches. The late-June caddis hatch above M-37 is fair and draws nighttime fishermen familiar with the stream in hopes of catching the larger browns in a careless mood.

Twin Creek, with its two branches, enters the Little Manistee from the north approximately two and a quarter miles above M-37. Good public ownership along this 10 to 20 feet wide, shallow tributary makes it ideal for the September grouse hunter who likes to fish for sizable brook trout while camping among large whispering pines.

From M-37 to Johnson's Bridge lies what many consider the heart of the Little Manistee system. Good access, either across public lands or private lands open to fishermen, is one reason why this is one of the most popular pieces of water. An abundance of gravel, interspersed with pools, attracts spawning steelheads during March, April, and May. Although fishing isn't allowed until the last Saturday in April to protect these spawners, sufficient steelheads are normally present when opening day arrives to provide good action. The modest size of the stream and its clear and often shallow water make these trophy fish extremely wary and difficult to approach, but once hooked, the fight of a big fish is long remembered.

Seven miles of river, between Spencer and Johnson's bridges, have been designated as "flies-only" waters and offer the fly-rod fan a wide variety of trout fishing experiences. Fair to good caddis hatches occur in selected areas above Indian Bridge with limit catches of 14- to 16-inch brown trout being the reward for the good nighttime angler.

The brown trout population in the Spencer to Johnson's bridge area is excellent. Electrofishing surveys disclose healthy numbers of brown trout of all sizes. Admittedly, good fishing success rarely comes to the casual midday angler, but in contrast the skilled early-morning or evening fly-caster can return home with glowing memories and a heavy creel.

One of the many sidelights to fishing the "Little River," as it's sometimes called, is the enjoyment of being among stately red and white pines that escaped the lumberjacks' saws. Logging drives, log rollways, and river clearing that accompanied timber harvest on other Michigan streams largely were absent along the Little Manistee because of its small size. Narrow-gauge railroads were used to move timber to local sawmills and therefore much of the streamside pine was left standing. The "sawdust pile" on the Indian Club property is all that remains of one of these local mills. The absence of sunken timber logs and old eroded rollways again makes the Little River unique among northern streams.

Johnson's Bridge marks the upstream limit of water open to early spring and late fall steelhead fishing. Public ownership is somewhat limited from this point downstream, but access is available to most areas by foot travel. No major tributaries, other than Cool Creek near Eighteen-Mile Bridge, enter the stream beyond Johnson's Bridge, and the river remains wadable for its entire length.

In spite of the stream's small size, canoeing is becoming more and more popular in the lower half. Beginning or novice canoeists have little trouble navigating most of the lower stream until the stretch between Nine-Mile Bridge and Six-Mile Bridge is reached. Here swift current, sharp bends, and numerous log jams keep even experts on their toes. This stretch has a good gravel bottom and is an important steelhead spawning area.

Most fishermen speak reverently of the good ol' days when fish numbers and sizes were greater than those found today, but at least in one respect the Little Manistee appears to be as good as it was in the past. Several times over the last 50 years this stream has been the source of wild steelhead eggs used to stock other waters. Records kept as part of these operations are about the only historical data available on fish-stock abundance. Fox Bridge was the site of such a spawn-take in 1926-29 when an attempt was made to capture the maximum number of spawning steelhead during March, April, and May each spring. The total number caught ranged from 1,123 to 2,274, with an average of 1,688. A comparable average of 5,249 have been captured at the present spawn-taking station in Mansitee County during the years 1970-73. Obviously, some of the 1970-73 steelheads would not reach Fox Bridge, but it still indicates a healthy population. All Little Manistee steelheads result from natural reproduction or straying since the Little Manistee has not been stocked with steelhead smolts.

One disadvantage of this small stream producing large numbers of steelheads has been the increased attraction and overcrowding of anglers in recent years. Literally thousands of people, many from out of state, descend on the lower river during early April and supersaturate the public areas. Overflow onto private lands and subsequent disrespect for private property have led to much posting, fencing, and other efforts to control trespass.

The upstream limit during the early spring and late fall season was extended in 1973 from Eighteen-Mile Bridge up to Johnson's Bridge in one attempt to spread out this pressure.

Recent numbers of steelheads passed upstream during the fall salmon egg-take have exceeded or closely equaled the numbers migrating during the spring run. These fall fish are in good fighting and eating condition and offer excellent success for dedicated steelheaders.

The stream area near the Lake-Mason-Manistee county lines was some of the favorite fishing water of William B. Mershon, one of Michigan's first and foremost sports fishermen and conservationists. In his book, "Recollections of My Fifty Years Hunting and Fishing," he tells of reaching the Little Manistee via logging trains and teams of the 1880s. In his first trips, fishing was only for grayling since brook trout had not yet become established. Grayling in this stream were among the largest he caught anywhere in Michigan, including the Pere Marquette and Au Sable systems, with the biggest ranging from one and one-half to one and seven-eighths pounds. Apparently the grayling fishery lasted only a relatively short time and was almost immediately replaced by outstanding brook trout fishing.

Brown trout fishing below Eight-Mile Bridge is not as rewarding as above except in scattered areas. Sand becomes more noticeable, particularly below Six-Mile Bridge, and natural reproduction appears limited. In addition, the intense spring steelhead fishery takes fair numbers of brown trout incidentally, which decreases the legal population left for a summer angler.

The Department of Natural Resources spawn-taking station, located about five miles upstream from Manistee Lake, is the site used for obtaining Michigan's supply of steelhead trout and chinook salmon eggs for hatchery production. Although operated on a time schedule which depends on fish migrations, the station is open to the public whenever Fisheries Division personnel are present. Usually the month of October and the first two weeks of April are best for observing the operations.

A permanent weir installation blocks all upstream migration when activated during the months of March-April and September-December, but all trout are passed into upstream waters via an underground return tube as the egg-take proceeds.

Many new or inexperienced fishermen are often curious about the relative size of their first catches of steelheads in Michigan. The average "steelie" returning to the Little River over the past several years has been increasing in size but appears to have leveled off in the eight- to nine-pound range. The majority of returning fish are four and five years old with five to 10 percent being trophy six-year-olds ranging from 13 to 20 pounds. Each year at least one or two topping the 20-pound mark are seen and provide the potential for a once-in-a-lifetime trophy, achieved by only a small handful of Midwest anglers.

Sandwiched between the traditionally famous Big Manistee and Pere Marquette rivers, the Little Manistee established an early and enviable reputation among these giants, which it has held ever since. It managed to escape many of the ecological horrors common to other streams in the early days. The niche carved by the Little Manistee in Michigan's angling history and its role in improving fishing in other Midwest waters have been immense. With today's ever-increasing awareness of the value of such resources, with the continued establishment of sharp-toothed laws designed to protect such irreplaceable values, and with keen fisheries management foresight, the Little Manistee will continue to supply steelhead fishing par excellence.

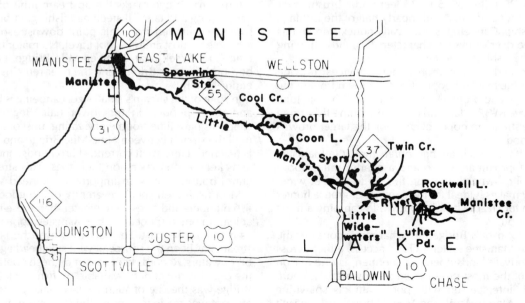

THE BOARDMAN RIVER
By JANET D. MEHL

The Boardman River is one of Michigan's top trout streams and one of the few in the state in which natural reproduction alone sustains high-quality fishing. Although brown trout dominate the entire system, excellent brook trout populations are found in the tributaries. Most of the tributaries contain excellent spawning areas and the more sizable ones offer considerable fishing in themselves. Substantial runs of steelheads and salmon and small runs of lake-run browns and lake trout occur from the mouth of the river to the Union Street Dam in Traverse City, about one mile upstream, the last of five dam sites on the mainstream.

The North and South branches arise in western Kalkaska county and flow westerly into Grand Traverse County to form the mainstream, which is 26 miles long. The mainstream continues west before swinging first northwest and then straight north, through Traverse City and into the west arm of Grand Traverse Bay. The river flows through three impoundments and Boardman Lake, a natural, 340-acre lake.

Bill Prisk of Traverse City, a Trout Unlimited board member, fishes the entire Boardman below Scheck's Bridge regularly. "The Boardman is for the fisherman's satisfaction of catching fish, not catching pounds of fish," he said. "Fish rarely exceed 20 inches, but the Boardman is still very much appreciated for the fine fishing it offers."

John Rokos, Jr., of Traverse City owns 80 acres on the Boardman near Ranch Rudolph, where he takes from 300 to 400 legal browns every year by spin fishing. He spin-fishes only in cloudy or rainy weather as bright sunlight reflecting off the spinner scares the fish. Rain also washes feed into the river, putting the fish in feeding frenzies and causing them to bite better.

In 1981 Rokos caught a whopping 25.5-inch brown in this area. "That fish was a lot more exciting than fighting the 15-pound steelhead I catch in the Boardman every year," said Rokos, who had taken more than 40 steelheads during the first six weeks of the 1981 fall run, most of which weighed about 10 pounds.

Wildlife abounds in the forested hills overlooking the narrow floodplain along the river. Deer, small game, ducks, geese, and fur-bearing animals offer considerable hunting and trapping opportunities, and an occasional black bear is seen lumbering into the woods. The Boardman River and the Grand Traverse Bay region provide wintering areas for the mute swan. Boardman Lake does not freeze over entirely in the winter and from 200 to 300 swans can be seen at a time at Logan's Landing. Canada geese, mallards, and black ducks winter here as well.

The Boardman offers excellent trout fishing from its headwaters all the way down to Boardman Pond and this entire stretch—practically the entire river—is easily waded. Most canoeing is done between the "Forks"—the area where the North and South branches meet to form the mainstream—and Boardman Lake, with portages necessary around Brown Bridge, Sabin, and Boardman dams. Narrow or shallow channels, overhanging brush, and fallen trees make canoeing difficult in portions of the North and South branches.

Although only a few developed public fishing sites exist on the river, about 50 percent of the river is publicly-owned, particularly that portion above Brown Bridge Pond, and access is provided by many county roads and trails and at most bridges. The number of campgrounds on the river is limited, with Brown's Dam, Scheck's Place, and Forks campgrounds all located between the Forks and Brown Bridge Dam. Scheck's Place provides 40 campsites, while Forks Campground provides only eight. However, three campgrounds with large numbers of sites are located on Arbutus Lake near Brown Bridge Pond and numerous private campgrounds are located near the river. Ranch Rudolph, about a mile upstream from Scheck's Place, has a restaurant and motel and offers a variety of activities, such as horseback riding and canoeing. It is ideally located for the fly-fishing schools it hosts each year, conducted by the Michigan Council of Trout Unlimited.

Although the entire Boardman contains excellent trout water, the fishing above Brown Bridge Pond is superior. Log jams, overhanging brush, undercut banks, tree roots, and pools provide excellent cover. Shaded banks and a swift flow over firm sand and gravel provide a very cold, well-oxygenated trout habitat of prime quality. About 70 percent of the land adjoining this stretch, which is known as the upper Boardman, is state-owned. Except for Ranch Rudolph and a few cottages near the Forks, few developments are visible from the river. Most of the river is contained in the Pere Marquette State Forest.

The North Branch originates in the Mahon Swamp northeast of Kalkaska and is almost as long as the mainstream of the river—nearly 24 miles. It is about 25 feet wide below Kalkaska and relatively shallow, averaging one to two feet deep with three- and four-foot pools. It drains several lakes, but the warm water the stream receives from these lakes is soon cooled sufficiently by groundwater springs.

Below Kalkaska the North Branch is wide enough to fly-fish and excellent caddis, mayfly, and stonefly hatches from mid-May through mid-July produce choice fishing all the way down to Brown Bridge Pond. Browns large enough to shake the composure of even the most veteran fishermen are taken here. Ten- to 14-inch browns and eight- to 12-inch brook trout are abundant. Much of the stream bottom is gravel, as much as 80 to 90 percent near the Forks, and extensive spawning takes place in most tributaries as well as in the North Branch.

The South Branch arises just south of South Boardman and US-131 and flows northwesterly to the Forks. Its 10 miles of mainstream contain extremely productive trout water, particularly for browns. The stream bottom is primarily gravel and extensive spawning occurs. It is about 25 feet wide and from one to four feet deep when it enters the Boardman mainstream.

From the Forks to Brown Bridge Pond the river is about 40 feet wide and from one to four feet deep with pools as deep as six feet. Ten- to 16-inch browns and eight- to 12-inch brook trout are common. Characterized by many riffles, this stretch produces the best fly hatches. Prisk said **Hexagenia** hatches were excellent in late June, particularly in the stretch between Scheck's Place and Brown Bridge Pond and below Sabin Dam. He said fishermen were often lined elbow-to-elbow during this hatch, but during the rest of the fishing season the Boardman was only moderately fished.

Rokos said he enjoys fishing the true caddis hatch near Ranch Rudolph in late July and has his best success fishing from about 9 p.m. to midnight. He said the "after-dark" hatches seem to bring out fish which average two to three inches longer than usual.

Near Scheck's Place, Twenty-Two and Carpenter creeks enter the main river, both of which provide good fishing for brook and brown trout.

In June 1984 the Traverse City Light and Power Department (TCL&P), city of Traverse City, and the Department of Natural Resources signed an agreement forming a partnership in fisheries management of the Boardman River. By the following year the DNR began annual plantings (200,000 to 300,000 spring fingerlings) of chinook salmon in the Boardman River system to enhance the Grand Traverse Bay fishery and issued all permits necessary to produce hydroelectric power at the Boardman and Sabin dams. Boardman and Sabin dams began producing electricity in 1986 and like the Brown Bridge Dam operate on "run-of-the-river" mode. The TCL&P Department constructed a fish ladder at Union Street Dam and a fish trap and transfer/harvest facility between the Union Street Dam and the mouth of the Boardman River.

The fish trap and transfer/harvest facility is located 0.8 miles upstream from Grand Traverse Bay and is within the city of Traverse City. This facility is named in honor of James P. Price, who was the first chairman of the Traverse City Light and Power Board and was instrumental in the agreement that was signed in 1984. Construction of the facility began early in 1987 and was completed by October. The fish ladder at the Union Street Dam was completed about the same time as the harvest facility. Cost of both facilities, including the land, was about $1 million dollars.

The 1984 agreement also created the Grand Traverse Area Fisheries Advisory Council. The council consists of 10 representatives from various interest groups and advises the DNR on various fisheries issues in the area.

Pacific salmon are to be harvested at the weir each fall (September and October). The trout and Atlantic salmon are permitted to migrate upstream (through the fish ladder at Union Street Dam) to Sabin Dam. The fish ladder at Union Street Dam is operational year around. Each spring (April-July) metal plates with an overhanging lip are installed in the ladder to block the migration of adult sea lampreys.

The Boardman River is open to year-around fishing from the mouth upstream to Union Street Dam with the exception of a year-around closure 300 feet upstream and 300 feet downstream of the harvest weir. In addition, the river from the mouth upstream to the weir is closed during September and October. To mitigate this closure, the river from Union Street Dam upstream to Sabin Dam was opened to the extended season (April 1 to the last Saturday in April and from October 1 to December 31).

Beginning in 1986, Skamania (summer strain) steelhead have been planted in the Boardman River. Plants have ranged from 15,000 to 20,000 and all have been marked for identification.

The river between Brown Bridge Dam and Boardman Pond,

referred to as the middle Boardman, is also considered classic trout water. The stream bottom is almost entirely gravel and sustains excellent brown trout populations as well as an occasional rainbow or brook trout. A few browns in the 18- to 24-inch class are landed. Barely dimpling the water, they effortlessly rise to the surface to suck in a fly with a quiet blurp, unlike the sudden splash of a small brook trout darting to the surface. Also unlike a small trout which thrashes near the surface, a big brown lunges for dark cover, bending a small spinning rod or fly rod over double.

The middle Boardman is about 50 to 60 feet wide and from three to six feet deep. Many individual homes are found along this stretch, most of which are occupied seasonally. This portion of the river is also characterized by riffles and supports good fly hatches. Access is more limited in this stretch, but a favorite among fishermen is the Shumsky's landing site on Shumsky Road, a short, gravel road leading south of River Road near Sleights Road.

Gary Marek of Traverse City, a Trout Unlimited regional director, fishes the middle Boardman at least three times a week. He said that although there are some areas in this stretch with deeper pools, there are considerable areas of "flat water"—relatively shallow, riffling water of quite uniform depth. This makes the Boardman easy to wade at night while fishing for browns. The largest brown he has taken from this stretch was a five-pound, 22-incher in 1979.

Less than a mile downstream from Brown Bridge Dam, East Creek enters the river, which along with its tributaries, provide good fishing and spawning areas. Much of East, Bancroft, and Jackson creeks are gravel-bottomed, containing plenty of 10- to 12-inch browns and eight- to 10-inch brookies. Parker Creek also offers good fishing. It contains a sand bottom and drains two lakes which make it too warm for good trout water until it receives colder spring water downstream. East Creek is nearly 20 feet wide when it enters the mainstream, with pools up to five feet deep.

Just down from the mouth of East Creek, Swainston Creek joins the river, another good spawning and fishing tributary predominated by browns with some brook trout present. The millpond at Mayfield is stocked with rainbows. Joe Nied of Mayfield lives on Swainston Creek and said that although browns are taken on bait from the creek, the fishing is rough. Nied fishes the middle Boardman nearly every day.

There is a public access site on River Road about two miles downstream from the mouth of Swainston Creek.

Jaxon Creek, not to be confused with Jackson Creek, joins the river about midway between Brown Bridge Dam and Boardman Pond. Although it drains four lakes, it is about 50 percent gravel and provides spawning areas for browns in its lower reaches.

Prisk said that except for their lower reaches, most of the tributaries were too overgrown with brush to fish except for "worm dunkers" after brookies.

Although fly hatches on the Boardman do not match those of the Au Sable or perhaps the Manistee, they are not to be scoffed at by any means.

"A guy could probably catch a fly hatch at any time during the entire season if he was up on flies," Prisk said. "He could get his 20-incher during the **Hex** hatch if he puts his time in."

Bob Summers, a Trout Unlimited board member who lives on the river near Sleights Road, said the Boardman is a challenging river to fly-fish because the faster water requires fishermen to pay their line out better. He said the deeper, faster holes also provide good wet-fly fishing, particularly with the classic imitation Muddler.

Summers builds custom bamboo fly rods, one among a handful still in the trade.

The Boardman supports excellent hatches of Hendricksons very early in the season although the water is often high and riley at this time. Stoneflies provide lots of action in late May and early June, particularly above Brown Bridge Dam. Little Sulfur hatches occur about the same time as the **Hexagenia** hatch which are good some years and occur throughout the whole system. Brown Drake hatches are often good as are hatches of White-winged Blacks. True caddis hatches, particularly black and cream, provide good fishing in July and August. Blue-winged Olives continue to provide fishermen with hatches in late summer and early fall.

The remaining seven miles of river—the lower Boardman—is dominated by impoundments, with the Keystone Dam site located about seven miles upstream from the mouth. In addition to these impoundments, millponds still exist on the North Branch at Kalkaska, on the South Branch at South Boardman, and on Swainston Creek at Mayfield.

Another important aspect to consider was the Boardman Natural River Management Plan. In 1976 the Boardman and most tributaries from just above Sabin Pond to US-131 were designated as a natural river to be managed as such by local governance. It subjected an area 400 feet wide on both sides and the designated river and tributaries to local zoning which restricts development in hopes of preserving the natural character of the watershed. Among the plan's objectives were to maintain the existing free-flowing conditions of the river and to manage the river for the existing fishing species—namely brook and brown trout.

From 5,000 to 20,000 yearling steelheads have been planted in the Boardman below Union Street Dam since 1977, in addition to those planted in Grand Traverse Bay. Substantial runs of steelheads and lake-run browns go up to Union Street Dam

in Traverse City, but this stretch is very short (one mile) and highly developed. The Keystone Dam site was eliminated from the renovation proposal because the entire dam was removed in 1969 and the river allowed to resume its normal flow. Reconstructing the entire site and the altered environmental effects were deemed too costly. Because Boardman and Sabin impoundments already existed, the increased water temperature and decreased oxygen content problems usually associated with creating impoundments would be minimal. Fish passage at Brown Bridge Dam will not be implemented to preserve the quality of trout fishery above.

All of the impoundments, including Boardman Lake, offer good fishing for warmwater species, such as smallmouth bass, northern pike, and panfish. From 500,000 to 750,000 walleye fry have been planted in Boardman Lake each year since 1976, with 1,750,000 planted in 1980.

Steelheads in the Boardman rarely weigh more than 13 or 14 pounds but may weigh as much as 16 or 18. Rokos catches most of his on spawn—single eggs—or corn which he said works almost as well. He also catches menominees this way during October. He throws corn into the river to chum the fish in, then baits a small single hook with corn. Often the water is clear enough to see the fish hit it.

Chinooks approach 30 pounds and are caught primarily on spawn and Mepps and Colorado spinners. Most cohos run about eight to 10 pounds with lake-run browns ranging from four to eight pounds.

Just above the mouth, the river is joined by Kid's Creek, which originates west of M-37. This was once an excellent spawning stream for brook and brown trout, but only the upper reaches now produce trout up to 14 inches. Extensive development and construction along the creek, particularly during the 1970s, destroyed bank vegetation and stream cover along the lower half of the creek. Tons of sand and silt eroded into the stream, making it unsuitable for spawning.

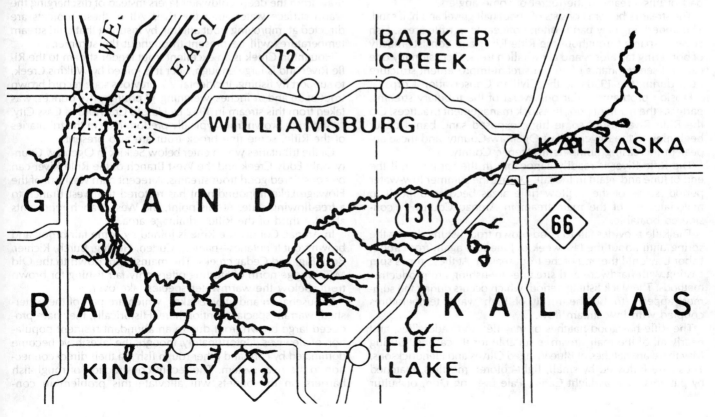

THE RIFLE RIVER

By RUSSELL LINCOLN, Fisheries Biologist, and
STEVEN SENDEK, Fisheries Biologist

The Rifle River originates in the northeastern part of Ogemaw County at the outlet of Devoe Lake. Several tributaries join it in this area, which is rich in artesian wells. Precipitation is not readily absorbed in the headwaters area due to an extensive clay pan. The resulting rapid runoff makes the Rifle one of Lower Michigan's least stable trout rivers.

The upper 10 miles of the Rifle flow through the Rifle River Recreation Area and the Ogemaw State Forest, both public lands. The remainder of the river, as it flows southward, is bordered by private lands except for one state-owned forty containing a public access site (about five miles south of M-55).

North of Selkirk the upper Rifle, unlike its tributaries, tends to be slow moving. Its gradient steepens near the village and most of the river below is characterized by fast shallow riffles with few deep holes. A notable exception is a three-mile stretch of placid water just north of Ogemaw-Arenac county line.

The land bordering most of this stream system is generally rolling upland forest typified by aspen in the northern portion and aspen, jack pine, and oak south of M-55. Lowlands are forested with elm, basswood, black ash, and soft maple with cedar, spruce, and balsam occurring in the swamps. Prickly ash borders part of this stream to the regret of some anglers.

The stream's bottom consists of about half gravel and half sand. The underlying clay pan is often noticeable in riffle areas. Fish cover is sparse throughout the Rifle River and consists mostly of bordering tag alders and a few fallen trees. Occasionally one can still see remnants of an old stream-improvement structure built during the 1930s by the Civilian Conservation Corps.

Erosion problems occur on several of the tributary streams, partly as the result of poor livestock management practices. On the Rifle River itself, some high, exposed sand banks occur beginning in the lower half of Ogemaw County, and these appear in increasing numbers in Arenac County.

· The Rifle River is readily canoeable in the spring, until the end of June and again in the fall. During the summer low-water period, some of the shallow riffle areas become difficult to negotiate. All of the mainstream in Arenac County is considered boatable.

The Rifle provides fair to good brown trout fishing during the spring until about the last week of June and again from about Labor Day until the end of the trout season. At these times spin casting with hardware and streamer fly-fishing are productive methods. The slack fishing period, which occurs during the summer, appears to be the result of high water temperatures coupled with low stream flow.

The Rifle has good hatches of mayflies and caddisflies, and nearly all of the mainstream is suitable for fly-casting. During May there are hatches of Blue-Winged Olives and Hendricksons. These are followed by small, light-colored mayflies, matched by patterns such as Light Cahill, Pale Evening Dun, or Sulfur

Dun. A few giant mayflies do hatch on the Rifle River but not enough to stimulate general feeding activity. In August a substantial evening hatch of mayflies known locally as white millers takes place in the upper reaches of the river.

The Rifle River system, however, is mostly bait-fishing water with anglers taking advantage of the fishing that occurs during the rainy seasons. This is especially true of the tributary streams since most are small and brushy.

Except for Skunk Creek and Ammond Creek, all the tributaries north of Selkirk can be described as good to excellent trout streams. Of these, Klacking, Houghton, Gamble, and Wilkins creeks are the best. Klacking Creek has an excellent population of brown trout with many fish larger than 14 inches and with some going over 20. Fishing is usually a challenge on this stream due to its extreme clarity.

Gamble Creek is a fine coldwater brown trout tributary of the Rifle River which enters it via two diversion ditches, one around Mallard Pond and the other around Devoe Lake. The first diversion was constructed by the old Conservation Department in the 1950s around Devoe Lake and the second was constructed around Mallard Pond in 1988 through a group effort by the Department of Natural Resources, Trout Unlimited, and the Frankenmuth Conservation Club. In addition to these projects, a deep-water discharge system was installed in Devoe Lake to draw from the deep, coldwater layers instead of discharging the warm surface waters into the river. All of these projects are directed at improving trout angling by insuring that cold stream temperatures will be present throughout the summer.

Houghton Creek is an excellent trout feeder stream to the Rifle River and is large enough, after it is joined by Wilkins Creek, to support fly fishing. Incidentally, a previous state record brown trout of 36 and 5/8 inches, weighing 17 pounds, five ounces, was taken from this stream in 1952 by Harold Crawford of Cass City.

Although brown trout typically predominate in the tributaries of the Rifle, some fine brook trout are also present.

Of the tributaries which enter below Selkirk in Ogemaw County, only Eddy Creek and the West Branch of the Rifle River can be considered good trout streams. A recent dam washout of the Flowage Lake impoundment has restored the West Branch to a free-flowing state. At this point, the West Branch represents about a third of the Rifle's drainage area.

In Arenac County the Rifle is joined by some fair brook and brown trout tributaries—namely, Curten, Hetting, Burch, Richter, Bear, Big, and Cedar creeks. The mainstream down to the Old M-70 Bridge north of Sterling offers only fair fishing for brown trout. Below the warmwater species take over.

Grousehaven and Devoe lakes, which are part of the watershed, warrant special mention here. Historically, they have produced large brown trout due to an abundant resident population of alewives. Unfortunately, though, the lakes have become dominated by carp and other rough fish via their direct connection to the river system. The recent construction of rough-fish barriers on the outlets will alleviate this problem in con-

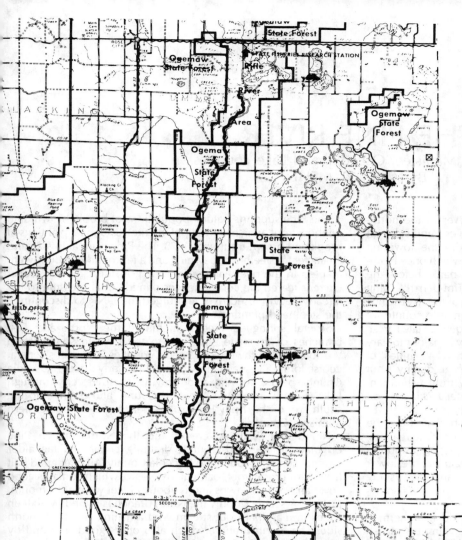

junction with various fisheries management techniques. Trout management for the lakes will then be divided between brown and rainbow trout.

The Rifle River has recently been gaining notoriety as a top steelhead and salmon stream. Past plants of fall fingerling steelheads are now being added to by significant natural reproduction. The fishery created is mainly confined to the spring since the steelheads do not enter the system until late fall/early winter and the bulk of the river is covered over with ice for the remainder of the winter. Anglers have considerable success throughout its upper reaches from Greenwood Road north.

Beginning in September, a moderate to large run of chinook salmon and a few coho salmon enter the river. The fish are the result of natural reproduction or straying from other stream plants since the Rifle River has not been stocked with salmon. There are no dams or impoundments to block their migration, so the fish are able to spread out over a large area.

Fly-fishing has become a very popular method of angling for these fish with streamers, wet flies, and various egg patterns.

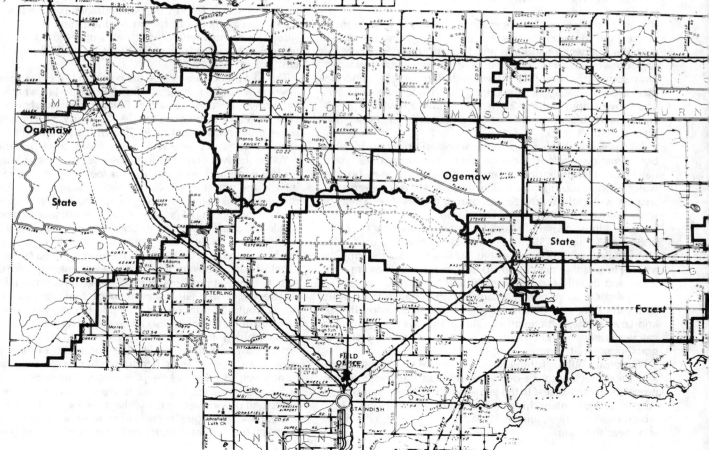

THE PINE RIVER
(Wexford, Manistee, Osceola, and Lake counties)
By JANET D. MEHL

The Pine River in the north-western Lower Peninsula got its name from the towering white pines which once loomed above its banks before the cries of "Tim-berrrr!" rang through the forests a century ago. Today most of the river winds through the pines, cedar, birch, aspen, and maple country of the Manistee National Forest and the Pere Marquette State Forest. A cold, first-class trout river, the Pine is actually a major tributary to the Big Manistee River. With more than 40 miles of mainstream and several hundred miles of high-quality trout tributaries, the river is fished extensively by trout fishermen. Many canoeists also enjoy the fast, rippling water, lacking in portages and shallow sand bars.

While ardent fly-fishermen entice elusive browns from the depths of shaded pools in the Pine's upper and middle reaches, bait and "hardware" fishermen lure rampaging rainbows from long riffles in the middle and lower reaches. The lower portions of the Pine are better suited for bait and spin fishing where snags are less numerous and the current slows somewhat as the river widens.

John Zakrajsek of Cadillac has been an avid fly-fisherman of the Pine for several years. He takes large numbers of fish each year between Skookum and Peterson bridges, where he says browns and rainbows occur in nearly equal numbers with some stretches near Peterson holding more rainbows than browns. Each year he catches 10- to 12-inch rainbows and browns approaching 20 inches, "quite a few" in the 15- and 16-inch range, a few 18-inchers, and usually one or two that hit the 20-inch mark.

Zakrajsek said that hatches below Skookum Bridge are variable but sometimes good. He said there are sometimes good hatches of Hendricksons in late April and early May, but the water is often too high for much success. He has the greatest success with little Yellow Stones during the first two weeks of June, followed by hatches of little Sulfurs.

Mark Miltner, owner of Marrick's Canoe Livery near the junction of M-37 and M-55, fishes this "super trout stream" from Dobson Bridge, which carries No. 50 Road across the Pine, to M-55. He says that nine out of 10 trout that he catches are rainbows and usually run between 10 and 12 inches.

Tim Kartsen, an employee at Larry's Sport Center in Hoxeyville, fishes the Pine at least once a week between Dobson Bridge and Low Bridge, which carries Old M-55 across the river. He catches rainbows and browns up to 18 inches on crawlers and grasshoppers all summer long

Numerous public fishing sites and the many county roads and trails that approach or follow most of the river's length provide excellent access to the entire system. These can be reached via several major highways, including M-55 and M-37, which cross the river, and M-61, M-115, and US-131, which run very near the river.

The Pine supports natural populations of brook, brown, and rainbow trout, which were supplemented by annual plantings of brook and brown trout until 1978. The Pine is ideal in size and character for steelhead spawning and a few hundred adults were planted in the river each year from 1974 through 1976. Local citizens feared the consequences of additional pressure to the already heavily used river and urged the DNR to discontinue the steelhead plantings.

Several spring-fed creeks, including the North and East branches of the Pine, give rise to the river in southeastern Wexford and northwestern Osceola counties. The river's general course forms a U-shape, flowing southwesterly through Osceola County before turning and flowing northwesterly through Lake County. It reenters Wexford County and drains into the south arm of the Tippy Backwaters near M-55 in southeastern Manistee County.

Negro and Spalding creeks and the North Branch Pine originate in Wexford County, draining cedar and tag alder swamp, and flow south into Osceola County. All offer good bait fishing for brook trout, particularly Negro, which contains good cover and some browns and is about 15 feet wide at its mouth. Just into Osceola County the North Branch is joined by Sixteen Creek, a marginal trout stream with a fishing site on its north side. The North Branch, which also offers good spin and fly fishing, flows for several more miles before it is joined by the East Branch near M-61.

The East Branch arises near the northern Osceola County line. There is a public fishing site just below US-131 where brooks and browns become numerous. Below the point where the Rose Lake outlet joins the river, the river is nearly 20 feet wide with pools four and five feet deep. Browns running eight to 12 inches are common here with a few brook trout present.

When the two branches join, the river becomes about 30 to 35 feet wide and from one to four feet deep. Some rainbows inhabit the gravel areas. Good cover is supplied by log jams, undercut banks, and overhanging brush. A public fishing site exists at the mouth of Sprague Creek, with another located about a mile and a half downstream. Good populations of legal browns from 10 to 14 inches are taken here, as well as brook trout and increasing numbers of rainbows. The river is joined by Big Beaver Creek, a good brook trout tributary, before entering Lake County.

As the river approaches Edgetts Bridge, it is from one to five feet deep and over half of the stream bottom is gravel. Excellent brook trout and rainbow trout fishing begins here, with some browns up to 18 inches also taken. The river banks are fringed with tag alders and cedar, which give way to hills of maple and aspen. Beyond Edgetts Bridge, the remainder of the river is a continuous series of sharp bends, forming excellent pools, many from seven to nine feet deep. Public fishing sites are located at Edgetts and Meadowbrook bridges, with two more in between. All provide access to excellent fishing for all three species of trout. Near Meadowbrook Bridge, most of the stream bottom is gravel, the current is rapid, and deep pools provide excellent cover and spawning areas. Eight- to 10-inch rainbows and brook trout are common, with browns running up to 20 inches.

Coe Creek, a good spawning tributary, joins the river just downstream from Meadowbrook Bridge, supporting good brook trout numbers until browns predominate near the mouth. Between Coe and Skookum bridges rainbows are numerous. Browns and rainbows are found in nearly equal numbers from Skookum Bridge to Walker Bridge, where cover and spawning areas are abundant.

Portions of the river between Skookum and Peterson bridges are too deep to wade and fishermen must get out of the river and go around them. Foot trails along the relatively low, sloping banks make bypassing these areas quite easy.

The 29-site Silver Creek Forest Campground is located just downstream from Walker Bridge near the mouth of Silver Creek. Silver Creek contains browns and a few brook trout.

Near the Lincoln Bridge site the stream bottom becomes predominantly sand and brown trout are the prevailing species, with some rainbows and a few brook trout present. The Lincoln Bridge Forest Campground contains a canoe-launching site and nine walk-in campsites only. Two public fishing sites are located just downstream from the Lincoln Bridge site.

Near the northern Lake County line the river is joined by Poplar Creek, most of which is contained in Wexford County.

It is a major spawning tributary for brown and rainbow trout and contains brook trout as well. Poplar Creek and its tributary, Dowling Creek, drain hilly country covered by pine, aspen, and hardwood forests, which provide a beautiful setting for the Ravine Forest Campground on the north side of Poplar Creek on No. 17 Road. Since 1975 the DNR and U.S. Forest Service have maintained a sediment basin on Poplar Creek to remove sand and sediment which would otherwise flow downstream over gravel spawning areas. Significant increases in the size and number of brown and rainbow trout present in Poplar Creek after the first few years indicated that the basin improves spawning conditions substantially.

Just into Wexford County the river is joined by Hoxey Creek, another spawning tributary for brooks and browns.

Rainbows remain the prominent species throughout the remainder of the mainstream to the Stronach Dam area, with some browns, a few brook trout, and increasing numbers of rough fish present. The Peterson Bridge Forest Campground is located on the Pine at M-37 in Wexford County, where the river is about 35 feet wide and from one to seven feet deep with some gravel areas. The river increases a little in size before reaching the Stronach Dam site just south of M-55 in Manistee County. The dam was built in 1912 by Consumers Power Company but was abandoned many years ago when the area behind the dam silted in completely.

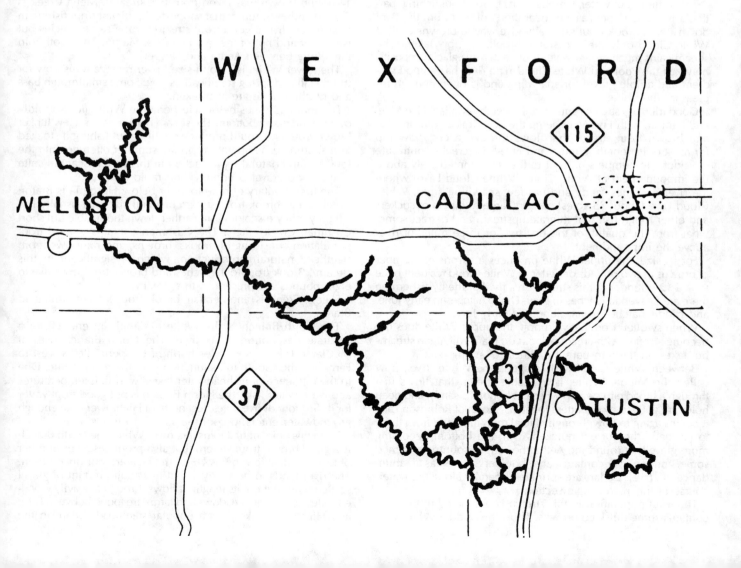

THE WHITE RIVER
By DAVID P. BORGESON, Fisheries Biologist

The White River rises from the extensive Oxford Swamp in north-central Newaygo County, the same swamp that feeds the headwaters of the famous Little South Branch of the Pere Marquette. Whereas the Little South flows north from its source, the White flows south toward the county seat of White Cloud.

Between the "Pool" and White Cloud the upper White is bordered with scattered cedar, old fields, pine stump fences, aspen groves, and white pine and is a beautiful stream that ranges from 20 to 40 feet wide. Excellent stream-improvement work, utilizing natural pine stumps and fieldstone, was done on this stretch of the river.

This is fine trout water, famous for its brook trout fishing, particularly in the upper reaches near the Pool, but from the Pool downstream brook trout gradually give way to browns until at White Cloud only the occasional brookie is now taken. The stream gains much groundwater (from extensive glacial deposits) between the Pool and White Cloud. The river has a good gradient and ample gravel for spawning and is open enough for pleasant fly-fishing.

Good tributary streams enter in this stretch—Mullan, Five-Mile, and Flinton, with Five-Mile being the best. It is a cold brookie and brown trout stream that flows through a cedar swamp for most of its length. Flinton and Five-Mile creeks contribute considerable numbers of trout to the river immediately above the impoundment at White Cloud (White Cloud Lake) where the river becomes sandy and has few spawning areas. White Cloud Lake (about 35 acres) harbors large numbers of suckers and other rough fish that migrate upstream and detract somewhat from the quality of the first two or three miles of river above the impoundment.

For its size, the upper White produces a surprising number of browns of two pounds or better. A White Cloud resident once took a 12-pounder in this stretch on a fly. For the fly-fishermen there are Beaverkill hatches in May, Drake hatches in early June, and caddis hatches in late June and early July.

When swollen from heavy runoff, the upper White does not become a coffee-with-cream color as do many Michigan streams but takes on the transparent darkness of strong tea.

Between White Cloud and Hesperia the White River, now called the Middle White, is a sizable stream that flows first through a broad elm swamp where its bottom is sandy, and deep holes are gouged by countless log jams. North of Robinson Lake it begins again to flow through glacial moraines, and from there to Hesperia the current quickens with the bottom becoming more gravelly. Around the Aetna the rolling country is farmed some, and the river contains large boulders as well as an abundance of gravel. Cedars are sprinkled liberally along the watercourse of this picturesque section.

The trout population in this stretch is only fair, but the river contains some outsized browns. Thus, the Middle White warrants the attention of the "big-fish" fishermen, particularly in view of the fine caddis hatches that occur from mid- to late-June.

In the White Cloud-Robinson Lake area an abundance of chestnut lamprey prey heavily on trout, and creek chubs become so evident after this first month of the season that bait fishermen are discouraged from fishing this section of the stream during the day. The stream is very well suited, however, for fly-fishing, particularly in the area around Aetna.

Several tributaries enter the Middle White, but by far the best is Martin Creek. The Martin is a fine brook and brown trout stream in its own right and is a favorite among some fly-fishermen even though it is quite brushy. It has a good drake and caddis hatch during June. The Martin produces not only good numbers of browns and brooks but fish of excellent average size also (a 14-pound brown was taken from this stream). Mena Creek is the only other tributary that supports significant trout fishing in this stretch. It is a good trout stream for the same species but is smaller and not of the quality of the Martin. They both join the White between Aetna and Hesperia.

The lower White is a good-sized river most famous now for its fine fall and spring steelhead fishing. Some smallmouth bass and northern pike are also taken.

For about 15 miles below Hesperia the White flows rapidly over a good gravel bottom. The stream here contains a few lunker brown trout and could produce quality trout fishing if stocked as it should be. Temperatures in the summer often get into the low 70s, and natural reproduction in this area is scant in spite of the good gravel conditions and rapid flow.

The first tributary of note to enter below Hesperia is Braton Creek, a fair brook trout stream of small size that usually has a lightly milky discoloration. Farther down the sizable but short Cushman Creek enters. The Cushman contains a good trout population consisting of brooks, browns, and rainbows (from steelhead natural reproduction, which is significant in this stream). Brook trout to 17 inches and brown trout from five to eight pounds are present in this stream.

Skeels Creek is another fair brook trout stream similar to Braton.

The North Branch of the White is significant enough for a separate description of its own. The North Branch rises at McClaren Lake, a few miles north of Hesperia, flows west to Ferry and then south to its junction with the main White. Due to the influence of its headwater lakes (warming temperatures and warmwater fish), the North Branch is not good trout water for its first four or five miles. Just north of Hightower Lake enough groundwater enters to cool the stream to trouts' liking.

From this point until it joins the lower White, the North Branch is a good brown trout stream that also produces a fair number of brooks. Sizable browns (16-22 inches) are not uncommon. The river tends to be sandy, but it has a fair amount of gravel scattered throughout its length. It flows through a heavily wooded valley, and some meadows and farms are found between Ferry and Hightower Lake. It is a popular steelhead stream in the spring and fall in the area below Arthur Road. The North Branch also offers good fly-fishing during the June drake hatches.

Several small but excellent cold tributaries enter the North Branch—Robinson Creek, Cobmosa Creek, Newman Creek, and Knudsen Creek—all of which contain brooks and browns of respectable size.

Downstream from the mouth of the North Branch, the tributaries of the White are notable in that they are sizable streams in themselves that contain almost 100 percent brook trout. These are Carlton, Sand, Silver, and Cleveland creeks. Carlton is the largest and best with Silver and Sand ranking above Cleveland. These are hard fished by local anglers from Muskegon and Whitehall, but they are excellent producers of brookies. Small impoundments on Sand, Silver, and Cleveland flood some good water but produce quality trout fishing themselves when rough fish are kept in check.

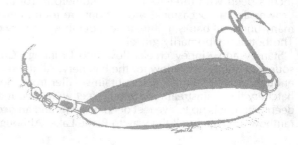

THE PLATTE RIVER
By JANET D. MEHL

The crystal-clear water of the Platte River in Benzie County has made it one of Michigan's most famous rivers since the turn of the century, historically for its brook and brown trout and more recently for its brown trout and anadromous fish, particularly coho salmon and steelheads. It is a favorite among many anglers because the clear, shallow water allows them to see the fish more easily than in most rivers. This makes it difficult to fish, however, as the fish tend to be spooked more easily and angling pressure is extremely heavy. Anglers catch resident browns from eight to 18 inches between Burnt Mill Road and Platte Lake but generally only on very overcast days as these fish are very elusive.

Nearly one million coho salmon are planted in the river and Platte Bay each year, producing tremendous runs in September. The fall salmon run in 1981 was the best to date, with 166,305 coho salmon, 2,172 chinook salmon, 682 steelheads, and 78 anadromous brown trout counted at the lower weir during September and October, according to DNR reports. There are two weirs located on the river for fish passage, fish harvest, and egg-taking operations. The Platte River State Anadromous Fish Hatchery provides the coho salmon smolts to be planted in Michigan and has supplied eggs to virtually every other Great Lakes state. Only about 50 percent of the eggs collected are used in-state, while the remaining 50 percent are given to other states in exchange for other species.

In keeping with a ruling by the Ingham County Circuit Court in 1989, all trout are passed through the lower weir but only the first 20,000 salmon to reach the weir are passed plus 1,000 per week thereafter until October 15, when no more salmon may be passed. A variety of special fishing regulations apply. The rest of the fish are used for egg-taking operations, harvested, and sold to the highest contract bidder.

The Platte arises in Lake Ann in northwestern Benzie County, flowing southwest until midway through its course it swings northwest, entering and exiting Platte and Loon (Round) lakes before emptying into Lake Michigan. The headwaters drain several small lakes and the river is generally too warm to support trout until it reaches Burnt Mill Road below Bronson Lake. Most of the river frontage is state-owned land from here to US-31. The stream is 20 to 40 feet wide and averages only 10 inches deep with three-foot pools. Numerous 10- to 12-inch browns and an occasional brook trout are found beneath the many undercut banks in this stretch, but they are very evasive. The bottom is primarily gravel.

Stanley and Kinney creeks flow into Brundage Creek, the source of coldwater inflow for the hatchery. All three are large enough to hold bait fish and contain smaller trout. Below the hatchery the mainstream is 30 to 50 feet wide, about one foot deep with pools up to five feet deep. Browns and an occasional rainbow are caught all the way to Platte Lake. Although cover is lacking in some areas between US-31 and Honor, the stream is very accessible and easily waded, the fish are generally a little larger, and the river is more easily fished. Access is available where US-31 crosses the river, at the Veterans Memorial Forest Campground just downstream, at Hayes Bridge at Brownell Road, at the Platte River Forest Campground on Goose Road, and at Case Bridge at North Pioneer Road. At Case Bridge the river averages knee-deep with pools up to six feet. The bottom is nearly all gravel.

Long-time anglers claim fly hatches on the Platte have declined in recent years due to sea-lamprey-control treatments every four years and heavy public pressure. The river does host several of the more common hatches, however, including the **Hexagenia limbata**, particularly below Honor, smaller mayflies such as Hendricksons, Brown and Gray drakes, and smaller stoneflies. Small streamers and bucktails also produce strikes.

Below Indian Hill Road the river flows through the Dead Stream Swamp to Platte Lake. The river is quite deep and the bottom is very soft, making wading very difficult in places. The North Branch of the Platte enters the mainstream just above Platte Lake and drains Little Platte Lake. The upper part of the creek flows through a tamarack and cedar swamp and can be fished for brook and brown trout. But below Indian Hill Road (County Road 671) most of the stream bottom is so mucky it can hardly be waded.

Below Platte Lake the river is void of cover and water temperatures become too warm for trout during the summer. Highway M-22 marks the boundary of the Sleeping Bear Dunes National Lakeshore through which the rest of the river flows. Walter Houghton, former Platte River Hatchery supervisor, said migrating cohos usually hold in Loon Lake for three to 10 days, providing an excellent trolling fishery.

The lower weir is located one-quarter mile below Loon Lake and about one-and-a-half miles above the mouth, while the upper weir is located at the hatchery. The remainder of the river is generally wadable and the bottom is sandy. Access is available at the M-22 Bridge and off Lake Michigan Road.

Fishing is permitted from the river mouth to Platte Lake year round except that the stretch from a point 300 feet downstream from the lower weir to the mouth is closed to fishing September 1 to October 31 and no fishing is permitted within 300 feet of the lower and upper weirs at any time. The stretch from Platte Lake to the bridge east of Honor is open April 1 to December 31, and the portion above the bridge is open only during the regular trout season extending from the last Saturday in April to September 30.

Steelhead runs have been heavy in the Platte in recent years. The number of steelheads counted at the lower weir is not indicative of the size of the fall runs because most of the steelheads enter the river after counting has ceased. November 1 finds hundreds of steelheaders flocking to the river below the lower weir when the season reopens. The best fishing occurs during the first two hours of daylight before the fish become spooked. At times other than during the regular trout season, or more simply, during the steelhead runs, only an unweighted single hook may be used which is not more than three-eighths of an inch from point to shank. Single salmon eggs or cut spawn are commonly used in the clear water.

Spring runs usually peak the second or third week in April—about the time the ice is leaving Platte Lake. The steelheads usually travel to the spawning gravel found between US-31 near the hatchery and Honor, while the salmon often hold below Honor. The majority of steelheaders fish the river below M-22, however. About one-half mile above the mouth the river nearly parallels the Lake Michigan shoreline, forming a long sandy point where many anglers enjoy surf fishing for steelheads.

Steelhead reproduction in the river is excellent and steelheads and chinooks are not planted.

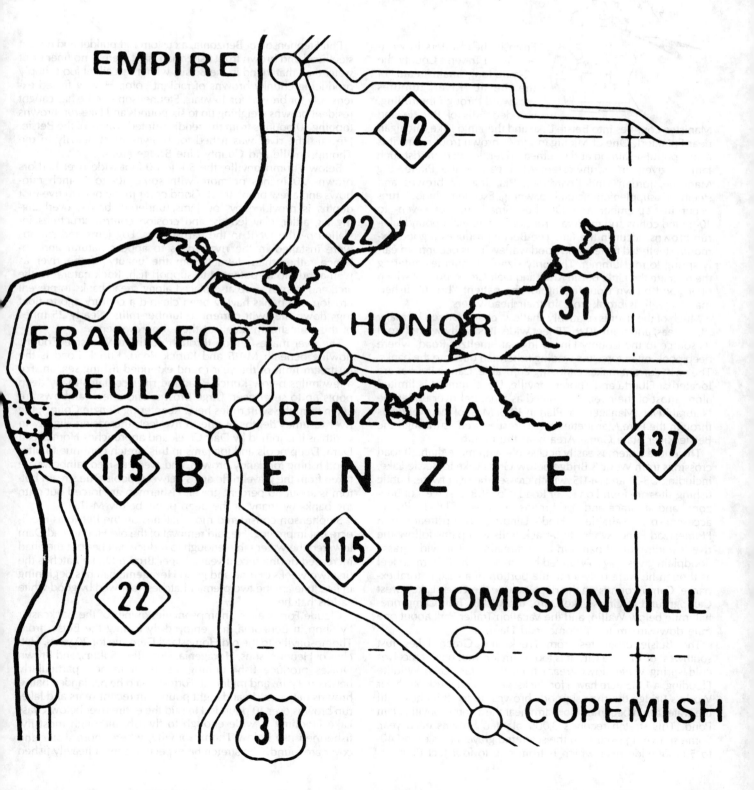

THE BETSIE RIVER
By JANET D. MEHL

From its headwaters in western Grand Traverse County, the 52-mile-long mainstream of the Betsie River tumbles westward through the rolling, wooded hills of Benzie and Manistee counties into Betsie Lake and then into Lake Michigan near Frankfort. One of Michigan's finer brown trout rivers, it is also a popular salmon and steelhead river, located amidst such famous rivers in northwestern Michigan as the Platte, Big Manistee, Jordan, and Boardman. Plantings of browns and steelheads supplement natural spawning. Excellent chinook runs occur in September and October. Small runs of seven- to 10-pound cohos and moderate runs of four- to eight-pound lake-run browns occur in the fall. The Betsie produces a good six-month steelhead fishery and good walleye runs occur from early spring to midsummer. The only sizable tributaries entering the river are the Little Betsie River and Dair Creek, both of which offer good brown trout fishing for the patient "brush" fisherman as well as brook trout in their headwaters.

Much of the river is relatively shallow, characterized by many riffle areas, and from 40 to 75 feet wide. It is easily waded from its source to the County Line Bridge at Smeltzer Road, where deep pools often force the wading fisherman out onto the banks. The swift current makes canoeing enjoyable. Canoe liveries are located at Elberta and Thompsonville. Development is limited along most of the river, designated as a natural river under the Natural Rivers Management Plan in 1973. Most of the river flows through the Pere Marquette State Forest as well as through the Betsie River State Game Area near the mouth.

The entire system is easily accessible with more than 20 road crossings from World's Bridge below Grass Lake to Betsie Lake, including US-31 and M-115, which crosses the river twice. Public fishing sites are found on River Road (Co. 608) just west of Benzonia and at Grace and Pond roads just west of US-31. Public access also is available at Fred's Landing just upstream from Homestead Pond, where two-track trails and paths follow the river's undeveloped banks in both directions. The wide grassy floodplain gives way to wooded hills making the fisherman feel as though he were only a minute portion of a vast, natural expanse. Campgrounds on the river include the Grass Lake Forest Campground at Grass Lake Dam, the Wallin Trail Camp one-half mile below Wallin, and the Vacation Trailer Park about one mile downstream from Homestead Dam.

The Betsie originates from Duck and Green lakes just southwest of Traverse City. It is too warm for trout until it receives cold spring water downstream from the Grass Lake Wildlife Flooding, a 1,145-acre haven for ducks, geese, and muskrats. Near World's Bridge the river supports browns up to 18 inches until the water again becomes too warm near the Thompsonville Dam Pond. This stretch receives 3,000 planted browns each year. Some spawning occurs on the scattered gravel areas of the 40- to 50-foot-wide river which is from one to four feet deep.

Phil Stephenson of Benzonia, a custom rod builder and devout steelhead and brown trout fisherman, said there is no finer trout water than that found in the Betsie, with its excellent food supply producing chunky browns of radiant color. Having fished extensively for browns for 15 years, Stephenson said he has caught resident browns weighing up to six pounds and lake-run browns topping 10 pounds from the reddish-tinted waters of the Betsie. He said the river was fished for browns most heavily in the Thompsonville and County Line Bridge areas.

Below Thompsonville, the 50- to 60-foot-wide river harbors browns 20 inches or more with some 10- to 12-inch rainbows and a few brook trout. Good cover in the one- to five-foot depths is provided by log jams, undercut banks, overhanging tag alder, clay ledges, and erosion control structures installed by the DNR in the early 1970s. Log jams and stumps were installed in the river so as to appear natural and enhance rather than detract from the beauty of the river as well as add to its potential to support fish. Rock natural to the area and stumps were also placed along streambanks to prevent erosion, the banks having been cleared a century ago to float logs down the swift current to lumber mills. Nearly 25 miles of the mainstream received these improvements.

The river makes a loop through northern Manistee County, flowing beneath M-115 and Kurick Road. Kurick Road is the upstream limit of the year-round extended fishing season. For a few miles below Kurick Road the river contains many deep pools up to seven feet. Large browns and a few rainbows are taken from the swift riffles here. Reentering Benzie County, the river resumes depths of one to five feet, increasing slightly in width as it is joined by Dair Creek and approaches Homestead Dam. Deep pools and log jams in this stretch continue to offer good fishing for dandy browns, and average-sized rainbows are taken from the gravel-riffle areas between pools. The stream bottom is about 60 percent gravel. Fishermen are forced out onto the banks by many of the deep pools below M-115.

Stephenson considered most hatches on the Betsie as mediocre but improving. He said removal of the old Homestead Dam lowered the water table enough to reduce hatches but they had increased during recent years. Super Brown Drake hatches the first two weeks of June and good **Hexagenia** hatches beginning in late June are the two premier hatches, followed by good white caddis hatches.

Claude Forrester of Thompsonville, owner of the Backcaster Fy Shop in Benzonia, has enjoyed fly fishing the Betsie from Thompsonville to the old Homestead Dam site for 20 years. Hatches of Hendricksons, **Hexagenia**, stoneflies, Sulfurs, and Brown Drakes produce fish running 12 to 18 inches, particularly between 9 p.m. and midnight. Forrester said he has landed native browns between six and eight pounds in recent years and lake-run browns over 10 pounds. He said the entire river below Grass Lake Flooding is wide enough to fly-fish, although most fly-fishermen fish below Thompsonville, where more water and cover are found. The stretch he expected is most heavily fished is that from the "T-ville" Dam to Lindy Road, with access at Red and Black bridges. Next most heavily fished is the stretch of wide, looping bends between Lindy Road and M-115. Good fishing and hatches continue throughout the season. He added that a few brookies were added to the catch between M-115 and Homestead Pond.

Robert Rommell of Elberta floats the Betsie from M-115 to the mouth for both browns and steelheads. He said there are many more fish in the Betsie than in the Platte River but more people fish the Platte because the fish can be seen in the clear, shallow water. Rommell catches one- to six-pound browns fly-fishing the **Hexagenia** hatch in late June.

Once a famous brook trout river prior to the 1920s and 1930s when brown trout became established, the Betsie River has also become a famous salmon and steelhead river in the last decade. Good steelheading is found from the mouth all the way to Kurick Road. Homestead Dam, located just off US-31 and M-115 near Benzonia, attracts fishermen from all over the Midwest for its steelhead runs each year. Fishermen are often lined elbow to elbow between Homestead Dam and Grace Bridge during late October when runs usually peak. Formerly a hydroelectric dam for Consumers Power Company, the dam was removed in 1974 and replaced with a low-head dam which acts as a sea lamprey barrier over which anadromous fish could pass, opening an additional 35 miles of river to anadromous spawning. Although steelhead formerly spawned only as far upstream as the Thompsonville Dam, the dam washed out in April 1989, extending the spawning water for anadromous fish to the Grass Lake Dam. The season is open only as far upstream as Kurick Road. Most fishermen fish the 10 miles of river between Homestead Dam and Betsie Lake, particularly at the dam, at the public fishing sites on Grace and River roads, at US-31, and at Lewis Bridge. Many steelheads are planted in the river each year.

Jim Mattis of Benzonia, steelhead fishing guide and owner of the Homestead Resort on the river, said steelheading remains good until Christmas, with most fish running six to 13 pounds. He said the river's tinted color and excellent cover and gravel spawning areas produce better steelhead fishing than many of Michigan's rivers as the fish are not as spooky and hit better. His favorite baits are spawn and yarn flies in the fall. Mattis said most fall steelheads are not spawning but follow salmon in to feed on their eggs and therefore hit more aggressively in the fall.

Mattis is not a light-line advocate, saying he uses at least six-pound-test monofilament, even in the slower, clearer stretches of the river. He says he catches as many fish on 10-pound-test line as the light-liners do—that the key to catching steelheads is achieving a smooth drift without the bait banging bottom too hard.

Mattis, also owner and charter captain of the Tam Boo Charter Service, said trolling for steelheads and browns with Rapalas in Betsie Lake is excellent until freeze-up.

He said winter steelhead fishing is often very good, especially during a mild winter, using spawn and spinners. His favorite winter baits are wigglers or imitation wiggler flies fished in deep holes.

Spring runs peak in mid-April. An increasing number of fishermen are discovering the excellent fishing upstream from the dam. The stretch between Fred's Landing and Kurick Road provides some very enjoyable fishing as it is largely undeveloped, contains excellent spawning and holding water, and, nearer Kurick Road, receives little steelhead fishing pressure.

John Rokos, Jr., of Traverse City, an avid steelhead fisherman, said steelheads average two to three pounds larger in the Betsie than those he catches in the Boardman. The largest steelie he has taken from the Betsie is a 17-and-a-half-pounder, although he has lost even larger fish. Rokos said spinners and spawn bags are best suited for the murky waters.

Rokos said his success is the result of carefully studying the steelhead's spawning habits. He climbs trees to spot the spawning fish on beds with the aid of Polaroid glasses. He may spend as much as 60 minutes catching a single fish, watching the fish for the first half hour or so until he thinks it is about ready to hit. Fish will generally not strike until they are nearly ready to spawn, Rokos said, and having carefully studied the spawning behavior, Rokos is able to recognize this stage of the ritual.

Rokos also fly-fishes for browns up to six pounds about one-half mile above Homestead Pond where the river is deeper, narrower, and slower, making it easier for the fish to see the flies. He said the many mud banks along the river's edge produce good hatches.

From Fred's Landing to the mouth, the Betsie flows through the Betsie River State Game Area, a refuge for waterfowl, beaver, and other wildlife, part of which is a sanctuary closed to hunting and trapping. Walleyes are also found in the river below Homestead Dam. Fair warmwater fishing exists in the Grass Lake Wildlife Flooding and the headwaters above and in Betsie Lake.

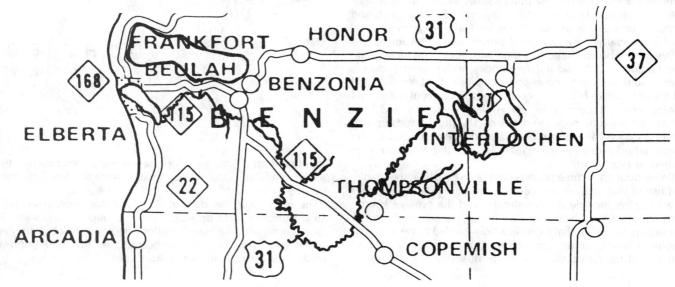

THE MAPLE RIVER
By WILLIAM J. MULLENDORE and
MASON F. SHOUDER, Fisheries Biologist

One of the northern Lower Peninsula's better brook trout streams, the West Branch of the Maple River, originates as the outlet of several small pothole lakes in the Pleasantview Swamp area of Emmett County. Augmented by several small tributary creeks, it meanders southeastward to cross US-31 south of Pellston. Half a mile east of the highway, it is joined by the East Branch (the outlet of Douglas Lake), and from there the mainstream flows on down into Burt Lake.

A 60-acre impoundment just below the junction of the two branches marks the lower limit of the high-quality brook trout water on the West Branch. The privately-owned impoundment holds a mixture of stocked rainbow trout and warmwater fish. The East Branch is marginal for trout, offering some fishing in spring and fall but dropping off during the summer when the source water from Douglas Lake warms up.

The lower mainstream at one time provided good fishing for brown trout and for spring and fall migrations of rainbows from Burt Lake. In recent years, however, this stretch has become badly silted and sanded from several ill-advised private development projects, and the fishing has deteriorated accordingly. Complicating the problem is a swampy delta at the Burt Lake mouth where the river spreads into many small shallow channels. Many believe this discourages rainbow runs from the lake except in years of high water. Past attempts by stream-improvement crews to confine the river to a single deep channel failed when spring floods washed out the structures. Dredging has been suggested as one possibility to create a permanent channel.

The West Branch of the Maple, where the good brook trout fishing is to be found, winds along a course of alternating swamp, farmland, and forest country. The bottom is generally sandy with stretches of gravel and some mucky spots which can give trouble to an unwary wader. Width varies from 20 to 40 feet, and depth is surprising with many holes five feet deep or more. Current is generally slow, and most portions can be canoed.

Streamside brush challenges the fly-fisherman on most of the West Branch, but the skillful fly-rodder who is patient, picks his spots, and doesn't mind occasional hangups in the trees can creel a limit of brookies here. However, at least 75 percent of the total fishing effort is exerted by early-season wormers and spin fishermen. Angling pressure drops off sharply by midsummer, although good catches can be made until season's end by the angler who knows the river, its trout, and the techniques required to take them.

Brook trout up to three pounds have been caught in the Maple, but fish of that size are, of course, extremely rare. A 13-incher is a bragging brookie for this stream, and the average keeper runs about eight inches. There are enough good-sized trout in the stream, however, that a conservation-minded angler can self-impose a 10-inch minimum size limit and reasonably hope to bring in at least a couple of fish on most days.

The West Branch of the Maple is peaceful, scenic, and fun to fish if you don't mind coping with brush. However, portions of it are beginning to show damage from large-scale beef cattle grazing which is developing into a major agricultural industry in the Maple River watershed. The animals trample the banks, destroy streamside vegetation, and provide a source of enrichment which shows up in increasingly lush growth of water weeds. In the minds of many who fish the Maple, this threat is much more serious and immediate than the possibility of

pollution from oil drilling which has recently been raised in the public mind. Steps to fence cattle away from this fine little river are necessary.

The reach from the dam to Burt Lake has been aided by a stream improvement project. Two sand traps are operated in cooperation with the Hagen Miller Chapter of Trout Unlimited in the lower reaches. It is expected that this will improve anadromous trout runs out of Burt Lake.

THE MUSKEGON RIVER

By JANET D. MEHL

The mighty Muskegon, with its 227 miles of mainstream, several river systems, and hundreds of miles of tributaries, draining numerous floodplains, sloughs, bayous, and lakes, supports the most diversified menagerie of fish and wildlife imaginable. Be it rainbow, brook, or brown trout, steelhead or salmon—whatever type of fishing the trout fisherman seeks— some portion of the Muskegon is sure to offer it and some of the very best. The 250- to 300-foot-wide river below Croton Dam in Newaygo County produces some of the largest runs of steelheads, browns, cohos, and chinooks in Michigan, as well as some of the largest fish.

The Muskegon earns its fame as a trout and salmon river below the town of Evart, particularly the 70 miles of river between the famous Croton Dam and Muskegon.

Phil Spring of Muskegon, who has fished the river regularly from Croton Dam to Muskegon for many years, said, "I think I could limit out on one-and-one-half- to two-pound rainbows any day of the season. Fish them light. That's the whole trick— light line."

Spring said these trout are called "football rainbows" because they grow so fast that their heads appear stunted in size and their bodies are very deep. Fish growth potential in the Muskegon is very great.

Among the many attributes which make the Muskegon a classic trout and salmon fishing river is its large size.

"I've never seen it where I didn't have a good stretch of river to myself on any given day," said Spring, who no longer fishes the Platte and Betsie rivers because they have become too crowded. "A guy can do more than just toss a spawn sack out in front of him because he's got more room."

Although a larger river doesn't necessarily mean larger sizes and numbers of fish, it does seem to hold true for the Muskegon. John Trimberger, district fisheries biologist at the Grand Rapids office, said the DNR estimates that an average of 25,000 chinooks, 10,000 to 15,000 steelheads, and 2,000 cohos are harvested by anglers on the Muskegon annually. He said chinooks generally average 18 pounds, cohos eight pounds, and steelheads eight to 10 pounds. Russell Lincoln, fisheries biologist at the DNR's Grand Rapids office, said the very small coho runs amidst such heavy runs of chinooks and steelheads was an issue not entirely understood.

"I think we have Michigan's best runs right here on the Muskegon," Spring said, although he fishes a number of Michigan's other prime rivers, such as the Pere Marquette, White, Pentwater, and Manistee. "It may be a toss-up between the Muskegon and Manistee rivers, but I prefer the Muskegon because there are less snags and I lose fewer fish in log jams."

Originating in the North Bay of Houghton Lake in Roscommon County, the Muskegon mainstream flows southwesterly through seven counties before emptying into Muskegon Lake

and then into Lake Michigan. Several river systems flow into the Muskegon, including the Clam, Hersey, and Middle Branch and Little Muskegon rivers, as well as tributaries that flow through additional counties, most of which offer some degree of trout fishing. The upper 100 miles of the main river are largely undeveloped and support warmwater fish, such as smallmouth bass, northern pike, channel catfish, and a few walleyes. Tiger muskies are planted from Leota to Temple each year. In January and February pike and suckers are speared through the ice on the bayous south of M-55. Most of the tributaries flowing into the river in Roscommon, Missaukee, and Clare counties are only marginal trout streams at most, except Butterfield Creek, which contains fair numbers of brook trout, and the Clam River, which in its upper reaches is one of Michigan's premier brook trout streams.

CLAM RIVER

Lake Cadillac gives rise to the Clam in Cadillac in southeastern Wexford County, although the river is too warm to support trout until it reaches the eastern Wexford County line. It flows southeasterly through Missaukee County and into northwestern Clare County before joining the Muskegon just above Church Bridge on Pine Road.

The Clam is peculiar in that only the portion of the river flowing through the western half of Missaukee County contains significant numbers of trout. In central Missaukee County several warm tributaries coupled with the dam at Falmouth make the Clam too warm for trout. Not until the river enters Clare County does it support trout again, where brook trout are found only rarely and 2,000 brown trout are planted each year.

When the Clam enters Missaukee County, it is about 25 feet wide and from one to two feet deep, draining low, brush-covered banks surrounded by cedar, birch, and aspen. Here the river begins supporting excellent numbers of brook trout, many 10 to 14 inches long. Jack Robbins of Lake City has taken 16-inch brookies and seen even bigger ones taken in the stretch between LaChance and Dickersen roads. He said this stretch is wide enough for the experienced fly-fisherman to fly-fish but the banks are lined with brush. Most of the stretch is only a couple feet deep with pools up to four feet, he said.

From the western Missaukee County line to M-66, the Clam contains good cover and many gravel areas and supports good fly hatches. The river increases in depth up to three feet and continues to offer good brook trout fishing down to M-66. Public fishing easements are located on the trail between LaChance and Blodget roads, accessible via M-55 and M-66.

In Clare County the Clam is about 50 feet wide and up to four feet deep, with many gravel areas supporting 10- to 14-inch browns and a few warmwater fish. Howard Flowers of Harrison fishes the swift stretch from the landing at Keehn Road where he said he nearly always limits out with 10- to 12-inchers. Portions of this stretch are deep enough to force a fisherman out of the water and around deep pools, he said.

Below the mouth of the West Branch, the Clam contains primarily warmwater fish.

MIDDLE BRANCH RIVER

Shortly after the Muskegon leaves Clare County and enters Osceola County, it is joined by the Middle Branch River, a good brown trout river with some brook trout. It originates from Hicks and Lost lakes in central Osceola County and flows northeast toward Marion. Near Marion the river swings to the east and then flows south to the Muskegon.

The river bottom is predominately gravel throughout the entire system. Good natural reproduction occurs upstream from Marion. The river below M-66 is stocked with 2,000 brown trout each year.

Near the mouths of Franz and Crocker creeks, both brook trout tributaries, the Middle Branch contains browns up to 14 inches long, although cover is poor. Between M-115 and Marion the river is from one to four feet deep, draining woodlands intermixed with farms. This stretch supports excellent numbers of browns up to 20 inches with an occasional eight- to 12-inch brook trout. As the river approaches M-61, stream-improvement structures, overhanging brush, logs, and some deep pools provide good cover. North of M-61 the river becomes wide enough to provide good fly-fishing. Two public fishing sites exist between M-61 and Marion.

Below Marion the river is a marginal trout stream. The trout population consists almost entirely of browns with an occasional brook trout. The West Branch of the Middle Branch does contain fair numbers of brook trout for the bait fisherman. The country surrounding the river is increasingly farmland toward the mouth, where the river is about 50 feet wide.

Below the mouth of the Middle Branch the Muskegon receives some good brook and brown trout tributaries, such as Kinney, Whetstone, Grindstone, and Hoffmyer creeks, all of which contain some spawning areas. Below Evart the Muskegon mainstream is managed for trout and smallmouth bass, with several thousand browns, rainbows, and smallmouths planted annually. An increasing number of farms are found along the river, which is about 200 feet wide and from one to eight feet deep with many gravel and rocky areas. Twin, Thompson, and Cat creeks also provide good spawning areas for brooks and browns, while Proctor and McKinstry contain brook trout.

HERSEY RIVER

Hersey and East Branch Hersey creeks arise in western Osceola County and join to form the Hersey River, which flows south along US-131 to Reed City before turning southeast and flowing into the Muskegon near the village of Hersey. It is primarily a brown trout river with some brook trout in the headwaters above Ashton. Natural populations are supplemented by plantings of 3,000 browns annually.

Below Ashton the river averages one to two feet deep with pools three and four feet deep. Many of the tributaries are too warm to support trout. The river is from 15 to 30 feet wide between Ashton and Reed City and is most easily fished with bait. It contains browns averaging 10 to 12 inches, with some as long as 18.

Below Reed City the Hersey flows through open pastures and supports occasional browns 20 inches or more as well as some warmwater fish. It is about 50 feet wide when it flows into the Muskegon.

Through Mecosta County the 200-foot-wide Muskegon supports fair numbers of rainbows, browns, and smallmouth bass maintained by annual plantings. These fish are taken with Mepps spinners, Rapalas, crayfish, flies, and worms. Some good hatches of mayflies occur, although they tend to be unpredictable. Roger's and Hardy Dam ponds offer good fishing for walleyes, smallmouths, and channel catfish. Tiger muskies were planted in Roger's Pond in 1980. Below Hardy Dam in Newaygo County the Muskegon soon spreads to form Croton Pond, backwaters of the famous Croton Dam. The Little Muskegon River system flows into Croton Pond.

LITTLE MUSKEGON RIVER

Winding its way southwesterly through Mecosta County, the Little Muskegon River drains a number of lakes. The East Branch is a good brook trout stream with brown trout in its lower reaches. It merges with the warmer West Branch to form the mainstream south of Schoolsection Lake. Natural populations are supplemented by plantings of browns each year. Dye, Shinglebolt, Sylvester, Quigley, and Big creeks are the major feeder creeks and contain mostly brook trout.

The entire Little Muskegon is easily waded and good canoeing water is found between the largely undeveloped banks from US-31 to the mouth. It is from 20 feet wide near the mouth of the East Branch to 60 feet wide where it flows into Croton Pond. The current is moderate, with many shallow riffle areas which produce good hatches. The river is classified as a trout stream down to Rustford Pond, where warm water temperatures limit trout habitat.

The Little Muskegon flows across northwestern Montcalm County before entering Newaygo County. Here it contains primarily smallmouths and a few browns and rainbows which have come from Tamarack Creek, its major tributary, which is 42 miles long.

TAMARACK CREEK
By Melvin Bonham, former fisheries biologist

From its headwaters in southern Mecosta County, this beautiful stream winds across northwestern Montcalm County to the Little Muskegon River in wooded eastern Newaygo County. Above Howard City overhanging brush and the small stream size make fishing difficult, contrasted to the reach below Howard City, which is easily fished. Water temperatures above Howard City are high during summer months. Only a portion of the river downstream from Howard City is canoeable with some difficulty.

The portion of Tamarack Creek west of Howard City has long been known as excellent trout water. The native trout fishery is supplemented by plantings of brown and rainbow trout each year. The stream contains excellent pool areas, many riffles, adequate cover, and is well-shaped. Bottom types consisting of sand, gravel, some clay, and very little silt are vital to the abundant insect production. Numerous springs reduce the marginal water temperatures found east of Howard City.

Tamarack Creek was chemically treated in 1979 to remove competitive fish and restocked with browns and rainbows.

The Muskegon River from Croton Dam to the mouth contains an even greater assortment of large fish, offering nearly any type of trout or salmon desired. All except brook trout are planted heavily each year, although some natural reproduction of all species occurs. A few lake trout are also taken near the mouth. Walleyes have been planted heavily to restore the once-famoius Muskegon walleye runs of the 1950s and walleye two feet or more are taken regularly.

In 1969 the dam at Newaygo was removed, opening an additional 14 miles of river to anadromous fish runs, as well as Bigelow Creek, an excellent spawning tributary for steelheads and brook and brown trout. Attempts to transfer fish over Croton Dam via a fish ladder were unsuccessful as it proved to be too steep.

Below Croton Dam the river is from two to 10 feet deep, from 250 to 300 feet wide, extremely swift, and portions contain huge rocks. From Croton Dam downstream to Newaygo the river bottom is all gravel and rock and most trout and salmon are taken in this stretch. The river is too deep and swift to wade early in the spring and many fishermen fish from boats throughout the season. Spring said the ideal boat is a 14-foot, flat-bottomed john boat which draws little water, with about a 15 h.p. outboard, short-shafted to help avoid rocks.

Craig Engweiler, owner of the Angler Archer Sporting Goods store in North Muskegon and avid Muskegon River fisherman, said the river offers good brown and rainbow trout fishing throughout the summer. He reported nearly 90 percent of the fish are taken on wet flies.

Tom Seroczynski of North Muskegon has fished the Muskegon regularly from Croton Dam to the mouth for more than 20 years. He said many of the browns and rainbows taken run between 14 and 16 inches with 18- and 20-inchers not uncommon. He said their flesh is fire orange due to the great number of crustaceans they eat. He uses wet flies and streamers imitating muddler and sculpin minnows to catch browns in deep, quiet stretches, floating the river from about 10 p.m. until daylight. During late winter and early spring he fishes for browns with minnows. One excellent spot for browns is the Cottonwood Flats area two to three miles below Newaygo, Seroczynski said. During the fall he catches browns and rainbows on spawn when they drop back about 20 feet behind spawning salmon to pick up their spawn.

Spring fishes for browns by going to riffle areas at night and listening for the fish to rise. Wet flies, crawlers, wigglers, and small crabs are among his favorite baits.

"The best bait late in the summer is a small crab less than an inch long that I catch with a smelt net," Spring explained.

For browns and rainbows Spring uses four-pound test line with a three-way swivel to which he attaches an eight-inch pigtail with weights and a long leader tapered down to four-three-, or even two-pound test. He uses enough weight so that his bait drifts along the bottom, including wet flies. During spring steelhead runs he uses the same setup with 10-pound test line and a leader tapered down to four-pound test. He uses a nine- to 11-foot rod with stripper guides and an open-faced spinning reel.

Seroczynski said there are some hatches of small flies on gravel beds, fished with dry flies with hook sizes 14 through 18. Since there are virtually no mud banks, there are no **Hexagenia** (giant mayfly) hatches, he said.

Many of the river's tributaries offer good fishing for all three species of trout, including Penoyer, Bigelow, Sand, and Minnie creeks.

The fishing season in the entire Muskegon mainstream is open all year long. Liberalized salmon fishing areas in which regulated snagging is allowed have existed from Croton Dam to the Pine Avenue public access site in Newaygo County and in the middle channel of the Muskegon from the causeway to Muskegon Lake in Muskegon County. Salmon runs begin in September and usually peak in mid-October, followed by steelhead runs which continue through May. A few lake-run browns are taken during salmon runs.

Salmon and steelhead are taken on spawn, Cleo spoons, Flatfish, Mepps and Colorado spinners, Tadpollies, Hot Shots, and wet flies, with wet flies being most popular. The two most effective flies are the Wiggler Fly-Special in brown, cream, gold, and green colors to imitate the wiggler, and the Doctor Tom, a bright orange and lime green fly which is effective particularly in the spring when the water is high and riley. Both are fished near bottom. About 5,000 of each are sold at Spring's Sporting Goods in Muskegon each year. Although these two flies were developed in the Muskegon area around 1973, they are becoming more popular throughout the state.

Nothing sets the adrenaline flowing quite like hooking a 10- to 15-pound steelhead, and many eight- to 10-pounders are taken from the Muskegon as well. Runs are heavy with steelheads up to three feet long and weighing as much as 20 pounds.

Spring prefers to fish from Croton Dam down to about two miles below Thornapple Road where much of the spawning occurs. This area, one of the most heavily fished, can be reached via M-46 and M-37. Engweiler said the area between Maple Island and Bridgeton is also heavily fished as it contains some gravel areas and deeper pools.

Numerous points of access exist in Newaygo County at Croton Dam, Pine and Thornapple avenues, High and Sand rollways, Newaygo, on both sides of Old Woman's Bend via Felch Avenue, and at Bridgeton. In Muskegon County public access is available at Maple Island, Mill Iron, at the end of Creston off Giles Road, and at the causeway.

Soon after the river crosses into Muskegon County it enters the Muskegon State Game Area, dividing into three channels which join again at Muskegon Lake. The state game area contains prime wetlands and a walleye rearing pond where about 150,000 walleye fingerlings are raised annually to be stocked in the Muskegon River, Muskegon Lake, and the surrounding area.

Engweiler said smallmouths are caught primarily in the flats between Newaygo and Bridgeton where there is little gravel. There are also small numbers of sturgeon in the river, he said, which are occasionally caught on spawn or night crawlers.

CEDAR CREEK

Seroczynski said Cedar Creek is one of the best brook trout streams in Michigan. It originates north of M-20 and the village of Holten in northern Muskegon County and joins the Muskegon near US-31. Nearly the entire creek flows through the Manistee Naitonal Forest and the Muskegon State Game Area; hence it is largely undeveloped. Natural reproduction sustains good populations of brook and brown trout.

Between Holten and M-120 (Old M-20) fishing pressure is light due to the small stream size, although nice brooks and browns are taken here. The area most commonly fished is that between M-120 and River Road, where brookies up to 18 inches are taken. Overhanging tag alders provide good cover but make fly-fishing difficult. The entire creek can be waded. Below River Road the creek flows into the Muskegon floodplain and trout became scarce, but those caught are usually large.

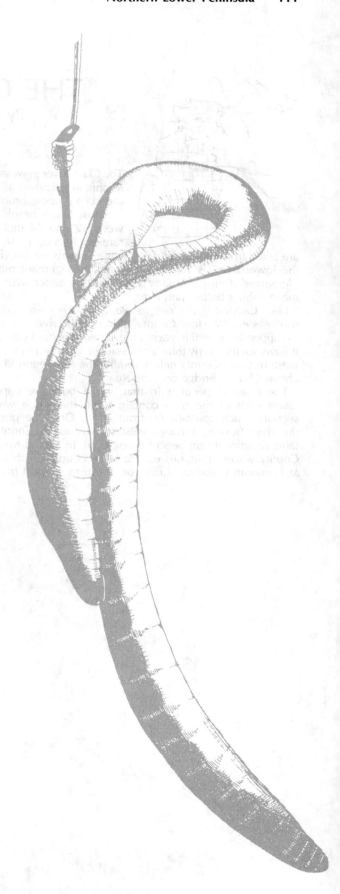

THE CLAM RIVER

By JANET D. MEHL

The Clam River in west-central Michigan is known as one of the state's finest brook trout streams. Many brookies between 12 and 14 inches and rare trophies up to 18 inches are taken from the upper river, while browns are caught from the lower river. A variety of special management plans implemented during the early 1980s on the upper river should make fishing better than ever.

Lake Cadillac gives rise to the Clam River in Cadillac in southeastern Wexford County, although the river is too warm to support trout until it reaches the eastern Wexford County line. It flows southeasterly through Missaukee County and into northwestern Clare County before joining the Muskegon River just above Church Bridge on Pine Road.

The Clam is peculiar in that, while both the upper and lower ends of the river contain trout, there is a vast midsection which contains no trout at all. Only the portion of the river flowing through western Missaukee County contains significant numbers of brook trout. In central Missaukee County warm tributaries east of M-66 coupled with the dam at Falmouth make the Clam too warm to support trout. Not

until the river enters Clare County does it support trout again. Here brook trout are found only rarely and browns are the angler's quarry with 2,000 planted annually.

When the Clam enters Missaukee County it is about 25 feet wide and from one to two feet deep, draining low brushy banks covered by cedar, birch, and aspen. Here the river begins supporting excellent numbers of brook trout, many 10 to 14 inches long. It is wide enough to fly-fish and supports good hatches, but the brush-lined banks make fly-casting tricky. The first mile-and-a-half of the river cutting through Missaukee County flows through state land, and trail roads parallel both sides of the river. The state land extends just past the mouth of Gunnerson Creek. A waterfowl flooding was proposed for this portion of the river, but trout anglers defeated the proposal as it would virtually destroy the Clam's potential to support trout.

Jack Robbins and son Jeff of Lake City have landed 16-inch brookies and seen even bigger ones taken from the section between LaChance and Dickersen roads, the most heavily-fished portion of the upper river. Most of this stretch is calf- to knee-deep with pools up to four feet deep.

From the western Missaukee County line to M-66, the Clam contains many gravel areas and good cover provided by log jams, overhanging and submerged brush, and undercut banks.

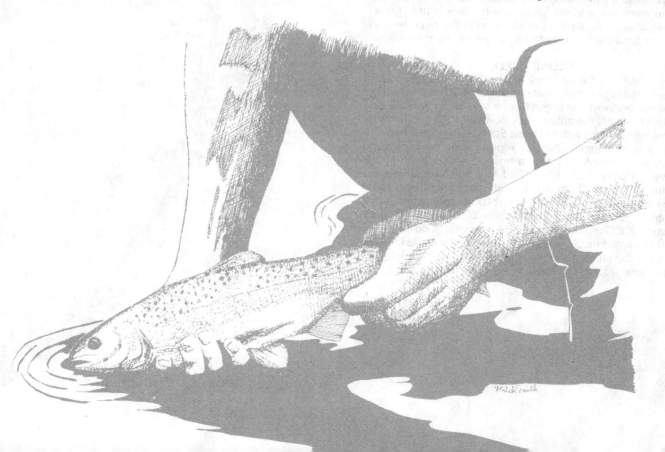

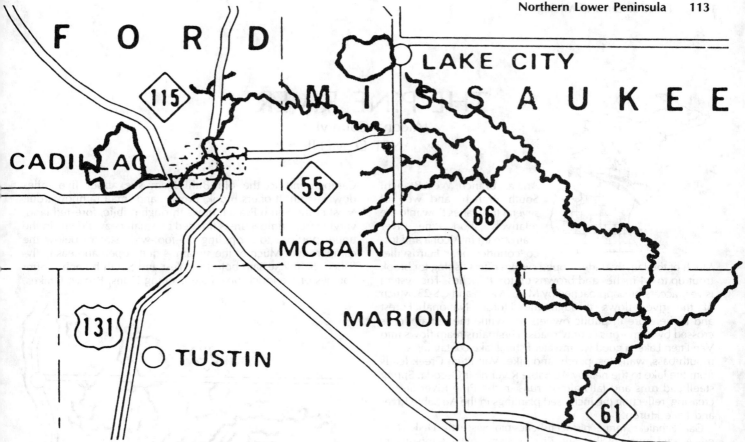

The river continues to offer good brook trout fishing down to M-66, increasing to an average depth of three feet. Access is available at many county road crossings.

Despite the Clam's reputation as a superb brook trout stream, however, avid anglers began reporting to the Department of Natural Resources that the fishery was declining. Their concern led to three major management programs to be implemented on the upper river during the 1980s: special quality fishing regulations, construction of three sediment traps, and habitat improvements and erosion-control work.

In response to anglers' complaints, the DNR conducted electro-shocking surveys to compare trout populations to those recorded during previous surveys. Data showed that reproduction and growth rates in the river were still excellent. Therefore, biologists concluded that the declining numbers were due to heavy angling pressure, particularly from early-season bait fishermen. To help relieve overharvest, quality fishing regulations became effective with the 1982 trout season opener for a three-mile stretch of the river between LaChance and Blue roads. Only single-hooked flies and lures may be used. Brook trout must be 10 inches long with a limit of five fish per day.

The DNR also constructed three sediment traps in the river in 1982, a new tool used in trout management. Gaylord Alexander, DNR fisheries researcher, has experimented with sediment traps for years and shown dramatic increases in trout

populations by reducing a stream's sediment load. A sediment trap is merely a trench dug across the river bottom where sediment collects and is periodically removed with a dragline. The Clam's first sediment trap is located about one-half mile below Seeley Road, the second just below LaChance Road, and the third between the old and new M-55 bridges.

The removal of the stream's sediment will create more pools and expose more gravel and cover. After the traps have been maintained for two to three years and the river bottom becomes more stable, biologists will determine which areas are still lacking cover and stream-improvement and erosion-control structures will be installed.

In Clare County the Clam is about 50 feet wide and up to four feet deep, with many gravel areas supporting eight- to 14-inch browns and a few warmwater fish. Howard Flowers of Harrison fishes this stretch from the public fishing site at Keehn Road where he nearly always limits out with 10- to 12-inchers. Portions of this area are deep enough to force a fisherman out of the water and around deep pools, he said. Anglers wishing to float this stretch can rent canoes from Duggan's Canoe Trips, Inc., west of Harrison on the Muskegon River at M-61.

The West Branch of the Clam, joining the mainstream a few miles above its confluence with the Muskegon, is too warm to contain trout. Below the mouth of the West Branch the mainstream contains primarily warmwater fish.

THE PINE RIVER

(Alcona County)

By JANET D. MEHL

An East Branch, West Branch, South Branch, and web of several tributaries flow into the relatively short Pine River mainstream in Alcona and Iosco counties near Harrisville. Much of the largely undeveloped system offers fishing for brook trout up to 14 inches and browns up to 18 inches. The system is very accessible, approached by M-65, M-72, and US-23. Much of the river flows through the Huron National Forest and is therefore in public ownership, while the remainder is crossed by numerous county roads. The mainstream flows into Van Etten Lake, a good warmwater fishing lake containing small-mouth bass, walleyes, perch, and pike. Van Etten Creek leads from the lake to the nearby Au Sable River near Oscoda. Spring steelhead runs and fall salmon runs in the Pine River are increasing, reflecting the increased plantings in the Au Sable River and Lake Huron.

Gary Schnicke, former district fisheries biologist at the DNR's Mio office, said much of the Pine River system contains top-quality trout water, particularly the West and South branches. Exceptions include the East Branch and Van Etten Creek both above and below Van Etten Lake. The East Branch arises in the Lincoln Swamp north of the village of Lincoln and is soon joined by several small feeder creeks as it flows south to join the mainstream near Mikado-Glennie Road. Above Killmaster the East Branch contains a few brook trout but water temperatures are generally too warm to support trout. Van Etten Creek arises near Lincoln and flows south through Mikado to the mainstream but is too warm and silty to support trout. Below the mouth of Van Etten Creek, the main river is also marginal trout water, although it does support a few large brown trout as well as warmwater fish and steelheads and salmon during runs. The mainstream is open to fishing year-round below County Road 171.

The West Branch of the Pine originates in central Alcona County and flows easterly to join the mainstream at Mikado-Glennie Road. Although it drains some small farming areas and contains some small beaver dams, it is generally a good brook trout stream, rippling over firm sand and rock and gravel bottom. It attracts many bait and spin fishermen and is wide enough to fly-fish below Hubbard Lake Road, where it is about 25 feet wide. It is accessible from Stout Road, Bean Hill, Fowler, Hubbard Lake, and Cruzen roads. There is a long gravel stretch near Cruzen Road two miles west of County Road 171 which is heavily fished.

Backus Creek, a small but lengthy stream draining Jewell Lake, flows into the West Branch from the north. It receives much cold groundwater inflow below the lake and soon becomes a good brook trout stream for the "brush" fisherman. It is about 15 feet wide at the mouth.

Biologist Schnicke said the most productive stretch of the Pine River system is that on the South Branch from the Pine River Forest Campground to the old Buhl Dam site about five miles downstream. It offers brook, brown, and small rainbow trout. Most of the South Branch flows through public, forested land, varying from timber areas flooded by small beaver dams in the upper portions to a rippling, 25-foot-wide stream below the campground. Much of the stream is quite open and easily fly-fished. Schnicke said both the West and South branches offer hatches of Hendricksons, Pale Evening Duns, Brown Drakes,

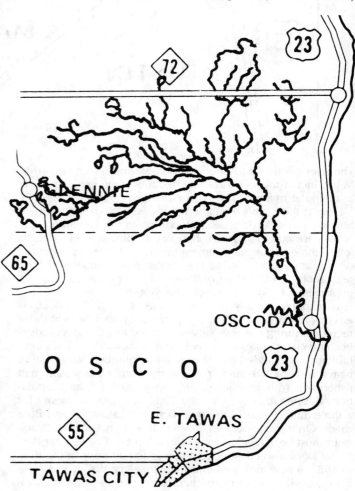

and **Hexagenia limbata,** or the giant burrowing mayfly. The best **Hex** hatches occur on the lower South Branch.

Bryant and Wallace creeks join to form the South Branch in southern Alcona County. Both drain lakes and are too warm to support trout until they receive cold groundwater inflow in their lower reaches. A few miles below their confluence, the South Branch is joined by Kurtz Creek draining Indian Lakes and North Lake, a stream too warm for trout until it is joined by Samyn Creek, a small brook trout tributary. Across the South Branch from the mouth of Kurtz Creek is the Pine River Forest Campground located just off USFS 4121 Road. From here downstream the South Branch holds good trout populations, and most of the bottom is rock and gravel to the old Buhl Dam site. United States Forest Service trail roads approach or parallel much of the river.

Cover is somewhat lacking in the stream. Below the old Buhl Dam site, the swift current slows and the bottom contains some clay and little gravel. Areas of the stream bottom formerly consisting of gravel were covered by sand after the Buhl Dam was removed several years ago. McGillis, Gimlet, and McDonald creeks empty into the lower South Branch, all cold, clear brook trout streams containing some gravel areas. McGillis Creek drains Tubbs, De Lap, and Sprinkler lakes and is too warm for trout until it reaches Bean Hill Road. The South Branch flows into the mainstream about two miles south of Mikado-Glennie Road.

Patrick Reames of Mikado has fished the Pine regularly for about 35 years. He said portions of the lower South Branch are waist-deep and some pools force wading fishermen out of the river.

Long-time local anglers claim the fishing has declined steadily since the early 1970s due to the increasing public pressure. Natural reproduction is not supplemented by DNR plantings, although many of the steelheads and salmon in the river come from Au Sable River plantings.

Biologists reported that during the 1940s—when natural steelhead runs peaked in Michigan before their devastation by the sea lamprey—the Pine River was considered Lake Huron's finest steelhead spawning tributary. Much steelhead reproduction still occurs in the river, particularly in the gravelly South Branch, and attracts a larger following of steelhead chasers each year. Although the river above County Road 171 is not open to fishing until the regular trout season opener, steelheads generally remain in the river until about May 1.

Below the mouth of the South Branch, the Pine River mainstream is about 35 feet wide and contains a few large brown trout. It is joined by Roy and Duval creeks, brushy streams which are bait-fished for brookies.

THE CEDAR RIVER
By JANET D. MEHL

The Cedar River originating in northern Clare and Gladwin counties hosts some fine brown trout fishing for both the "brush" fisherman and the fly-fisherman. Most portions of the Middle and North branches are narrow enough that a fishing rod laid across the stream will touch both banks. Much of the West Branch and mainstream, however, are big enough to fly-fish and offer a rich variety of hatches. The river flows southeasterly to Gladwin. Chappel Dam, owned by Consumers Power Company, impounds 345-acre Wiggins Lake near Gladwin. Flowing through Gladwin, the river winds its way southward to Ross Lake, impounded by the dam at Beaverton on the Tobacco River. Brown trout fishing is also found in the field-lined Tobacco River system lying just to the south.

Many Tri-City area anglers have discovered that the Cedar's fine trout habitat is close enough to home to fish in an evening, accessible via US-10 and M-18 in an hour or less. Main roads lead to the system from all directions. M-61 crosses the river in Gladwin, providing access to east and west, and intersects US-27 just south of Harrison. Although the Cedar flows through little state land, it is very accessible from the many county road crossings.

The Martuch chapter of Trout Unlimited of Midland installed stream improvement devices and monitored trout populations in cooperation with the Department of Natural Resources in 1975. Dr. George Lane of Midland, research director of the studies and Cedar River fisherman for 25 years, said the chapter has installed split log cover structures in the North Branch above Bard Road. The logs are split lengthwise and pinned above the bottom with steel rods. The structures were also installed on 2,000 feet of the West Branch through Trout Unlimited's 26 acres of Leon T. Martuch memorial property near Bailey Lake and Townline Lake roads.

Dr. Lane said the Midland chapter conducts electro-shocking surveys on the West and North branches using the DNR's equipment. Captured fish are plotted on maps to determine which of the installed cover structures they prefer. The chapter has also conducted a systematic angling program for several years, Dr. Lane said, in which anglers record catches and insect hatches.

He said the population in the North Branch has decreased in recent years and suspects the sedimentation covering gravel spawning areas may be contributing to the decline. Leo Mrozinski, district fisheries biologist at the DNR's Cadillac office, said about 4,000 browns are planted in the North Branch each year because it is of lesser trout quality than the other branches.

The West Branch contains the finest quality trout water and is the biggest of the three branches. While one might expect that the West Branch becomes the mainstream once it is joined by the Middle Branch, this is not so. The West Branch is considered to extend all the way to the confluence of the North Branch, commonly known as "the Forks," in Gladwin County.

It is a very productive stream and natural reproduction sustains excellent brown trout populations. Although very small, the Middle Branch is also productive and fish plantings are not necessary in the Cedar in Clare County.

The West Branch originates in northeastern Clare County, draining five small lakes, and flows south to Townline Lake

Road before swinging east to the Forks. Near the headwaters above Arnold Lake Road it contains brook trout and is joined by Popple Creek, a small brook trout tributary flowing through

cedar swamp. Popple Creek flows through state land west of Athey Avenue.

Athey Avenue crosses the West Branch four times, and local fishermen often fish the deep pools formed by the culverts beneath the road. The stream is from six to 20 feet wide above Cranberry Creek and select portions can be fly-fished with difficulty. It is a peaceful little stream to fish, flowing through cedar and popple lowlands interspersed with a few meadow areas. The ankle- to waist-deep waters ripple over gravel stretches and swirl beneath undercut banks and log jams. Cabins are found on the stream along Athey Avenue, but an angler will generally have the entire stream to himself to catch his limit of 10- to 16-inch browns.

Cranberry Creek draining Cranberry Lake enters the West Branch one-half mile north of Townline Lake Road. It contains brook trout and browns up to 14 inches near the mouth. It increases the width of the West Branch to about 25 feet. Cover remains excellent and the rest of the stream contains pools up to five feet deep.

The Cedar's finest fishing is found on the West Branch from Bailey Lake Road to Bard Road in Gladwin County. The DNR surveys a 1,000-foot section above Hoover Avenue and data from several years show high numbers of 10- to 14-inch browns and fish over 20 inches every year. The entire stretch is wide enough to fly-fish and supports good hatches. Below the confluence of the Middle Branch near Hoover Avenue the West Branch is 35 to 40 feet wide and contains great numbers of bigger browns. Cottages are found on the river near Hoover Avenue and below Bard Road, while much of the remainder of the frontage is undeveloped and owned by the Gladwin Rod and Gun Club. Overall, the West Branch contains a good pool-riffle ratio, excellent cover, greater trout populations, and the best fly-fishing water on the Cedar.

Originating in northeastern Clare County, the Middle Branch is a very small, brushy stream—only three to five feet wide at Arnold Lake Road and about 10 feet wide at the mouth. The stream is seldom fished except near the mouth and contains brookies and sizable brown trout. Gravel stretches and cold water temperatures support natural spawning.

Braided creeks draining several lakes in the northwestern corner of Gladwin County form the North Branch in the Tittabawassee River State Forest, commonly known as the field trial area. Some brook trout and a few browns are found in the headwaters, although the lake surfaces and beaver dam activity above Blue Lake raise water temperatures to marginal levels by midsummer. Forest campgrounds on House and Trout lakes offer 41 and 35 campsites, respectively.

The North Branch flows through wooded country interspersed with grassy areas. The stream bottom is primarily sand down to Renas Road. Below Renas Road the 15- to 20-foot-wide stream no longer contains brook trout. The water is ankle- to waist-deep and the banks are primarily brush-choked down to Schmidt Road, where the river begins flowing through more open farm areas. Below M-18 the bottom contains scattered gravel areas where limited spawning occurs.

Below Schmidt Road about a three-quarter-mile stretch of the North Branch flows through property owned by the Campfire Girls. The next winding mile of the stream flows through state land down to Sage Road.

Dr. Lane said most of the North Branch between Sage and Bard roads is about 25 feet wide and fly-fishable. From Bard Road to the Forks only about half of the stream is open enough to fly-fish, he said. The Forks is contained in a sizable chunk of state land straight west of Pratt Lake. The state land is accessi-

ble from a dirt road leading west from Shearer Road, a north-south road ending about one-half mile west of Pratt Lake. There is a small parking area on the state land.

Don Peterson of Clare, recently retired district fisheries biologist from the DNR's Gladwin office, said the mainstream from the Forks to Wiggins Lake contains some tackle-busting browns, particularly above Eagleson Road, the lower limit of trout stream designation. Since the river below Eagleson Road is not a designated trout stream, it is open to fishing year-round. There is a public fishing easement just above Wiggins Lake near the mouth of Smith Creek, a nontrout tributary. Another non-trout tributary draining Mud, Pure, and Contos lakes enters the mainstream below Eagleson Road.

Biologist Mrozinski said the river below Gladwin was chemically treated in 1976 and replanted with browns and smallmouth bass. Although browns have been stocked annually in this stretch ever since, Mrozinski said he expects the plants will soon be discontinued as the section is dominated by warm-water fish and brown trout numbers are low.

The West Branch contains most of the Cedar's fly-fishing water and generally hosts the best hatches. Good hatches of **Ephemerella subveria** (Hendrickson) occur on the West Branch during the first two weeks of the season, while those on the North Branch are poor to fair. Dr. Lane said hatches of **Adoptiva** (tiny Gray Mahogany) from mid- to late May are excellent in both branches. At least one of two hatches of **Stenonema** in late May is always good, particularly on the North Branch, he said either **vicarium** (March Brown) or **suscum** (Gray Wolf). Hatches of **Ephemerella dorothea** (Pale Evening Dun or Sulfur Dun) vary from year to year but are usually good on the West Branch. Hatches of **Ephemerella simulans** (Brown Drake) and **Hexagenia limbata** (giant burrowing mayfly) are only fair at most, but both are best on the mainstream near Eagleson Road.

Isonychia (Giant Mahogany) hatches in July are not real good but offer opportunity for anglers who like to fish big flies (size #12), Dr. Lane said. While hatches of **Stenonema integrum** (White Mayfly) are insignificant on many streams, they are extremely good and consistent on the Cedar from July through October, he said. Sporadic hatches of **Baetis vagans** (Blue-winged Olive) and **Trichorythodes** (tiny White-winged Black) also occur on the river.

Excellent stonefly and caddis hatches occur on both the West and North branches, particularly yellow stones and little black caddis (**Chimarra**).

THE ROGUE RIVER
By DAVID W. SMITH and
DAVID P. BORGESON, Fisheries Biologists

The Rogue River is a medium-sized stream of moderate flow lying almost entirely in Kent County but originating in Newaygo County. It has its headwaters in a series of ditches that drain the old Rice Lake bed. The stream in this area has been dredged and straightened to drain the productive vegetable fields east of Grant. The ditched conditions extend a short distance into Kent County and into the Rogue River State Game Area. The river flows south through the game area, through flooded timber and swamp lands, downstream to Sparta. Below Sparta the river makes a sweeping curve northeastward through wooded terrain and then swings south again through Rockford and on to its confluence with the Grand River at Grand Rapids.

There are approximately 42 miles of mainstream with an average width of 55 feet and an average depth of 30 inches. The water is light brown and well oxygenated. Flowing through low swampland and agricultural land, it is rich in nutrients but rarely exceeds 74°F in water temperature. Rogue River browns and rainbows put on weight in a hurry and reach good size. Above Sparta sand and silt are the predominant bottom types. Below Sparta the bottom has more gravel and rubble.

The Rogue boasts several top-quality trout tributaries: Spring Creek, Duke Creek, Cedar Creek, Stegman Creek, Shaw Creek, Rum Creek, and Becker Creek. All are clear, coldwater streams containing healthy brook and brown trout populations. These streams are very important to the Rogue because of the cold water they contribute and the natural trout spawning they provide.

Prior to 1969 the Rogue's fish population was dominated by carp, suckers, and burbot while some smallmouth bass, northern pike, and brown trout were present. Extensive trout stocking had taken place since 1954 with fair results, and the fish that did survive the competition and predation grew well.

In 1969 all fish were eradicated from the Rogue and the stream was restocked with browns and rainbows. Excellent growth and survival of the planted fish have provided top-notch trout fishing ever since, although additional chemical reclamations are necessary to keep rough fish in check.

The bottom fauna of the Rogue includes a wide variety of insect types. Local entomologists claim that the insect species diversity is equal to that of the Au Sable River.

Between the state game area and 13-Mile Road conditions for wading and floating are poor, but below 13-Mile Road they are excellent. Fly-fishing, bait, and spin casting are all effective, although through the game area streamside brush and fallen timbers make fishing a challenge.

The stream section from Algoma Avenue to 12-Mile Road near Summit Avenue is broad and hard-bottomed and is a fine, picturesque fishing area. From Rockford Impoundment to the mouth, steelheads are taken seasonally, and the water holds some nice resident browns and rainbows. This lower river is surprisingly remote and underdeveloped. It is a rocky and fast, handsome stream.

Public access is available at bridges, the state game area, county property at 12-Mile Road and Summit Avenue, and numerous parcels purchased by the Department of Natural Resources for access. Because of its nearness to Grand Rapids, the river serves a great purpose in providing high-quality fishing recreation for many people.

A thorough stream-improvement project was begun on the Rogue in 1972 with the objective of clearing up the congestion and damage caused by elm die-off in the upper swampy areas and to improve trout cover in the lower reaches above Rockford. This attention has improved Rogue River fishing.

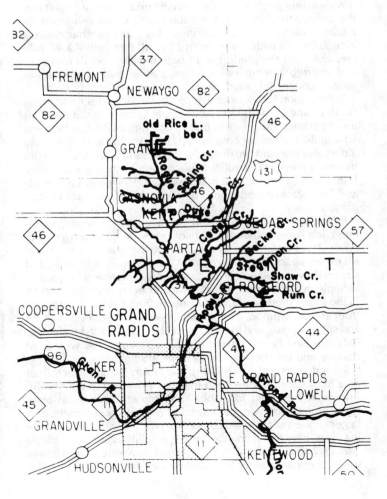

FISH CREEK
By DAVID W. SMITH, Fisheries Biologist

Whenever fine trout streams are discussed among Lower Michigan fishing circles, Montcalm County's Fish Creek is certain to be mentioned. Its popularity is based upon its healthy trout population and its proximity to populated areas.

Fish Creek originates in a cedar swamp in northeastern Montcalm County, southeast of Edmore. The stream flows south through farm and pastureland and eventually meets the Maple River below Hubbardston in Ionia County.

Situated in a nutrient rich, potato-farming area, the cool spring waters of Fish Creek are very fertile yet exhibit the aesthetic qualities of a northern stream. Farmers intensively irrigate their crops along its banks, but its bountiful supply of freshwater springs maintains its level continuously. Although its flow fluctuates with rainfall, it never diminishes to the extremely slow currents typical of many southern Michigan streams.

Alternating pools and riffles provide excellent trout habitat in the upper stretches above Stanton Road. Good fish cover includes undercut banks, watercress, logs, and overhanging tag alders. Stream widths vary from 10 to 30 feet with gravel, rubble, and sand the predominant bottom types. Small minnows and invertebrates such as mayflies, caddis, and stoneflies provide abundant fish food. Stream flow is moderately swift.

Expect good brook trout fishing above McBrides Road at the south boundary of the Vestaburg State Game Area. Below this area to Stanton Road brown trout predominate. Browns between 10 and 14 inches are commonly taken in this area. Thick tag alders and lowland brush border the streambanks, making spin fishing and fly-fishing difficult, but the entire stretch is wadable. Fishermen can gain stream access at bridges on county roads and from state-owned land on the Vestaburg and Stanton state game areas.

From Stanton Road to Carson City overhanging brush, watercress, log jams, and undercut banks provide good brown trout cover. The bottom type grades from small gravel to sand and silt downstream. The stream varies from 10 to 50 feet wide, and stream flow is moderately swift. Minnows and invertebrates provide plenty of fish food. Sizable brook trout are sometimes taken in the lower stretches, but downstream from Crystal Road brook trout are uncommon. This stretch is easily fished with both fly and spinning gear, and the stream can be easily waded or floated. Public access is by consent of riparian owners, as well as at bridges and on state-owned land near Stanton.

Several years ago a fish kill in the North Branch affected an area from Cannonsville Road in Ferris Township to the Middle Branch in Evergreen Township. Probably arising from a spray-rig cleaning operation, the mortality was nearly complete, and large numbers of trout and competitors were killed. In the following years, after replanting the stream, a fabulous fishery resulted.

In 1972 the stream from Colby Road downstream to Carson City was chemically rehabilitated by the Fisheries Division. The fishing history of this area indicates that it will grow good-sized browns readily. With competing species removed, this stretch again became a good producer.

Below the old dam site at Carson City to its junction with the Maple River, Fish Creek is dominated by large numbers of suckers and creek chubs along with warmwater game species such as smallmouth bass, bluegills, rock bass, black crappies, northern pike, and bullheads.

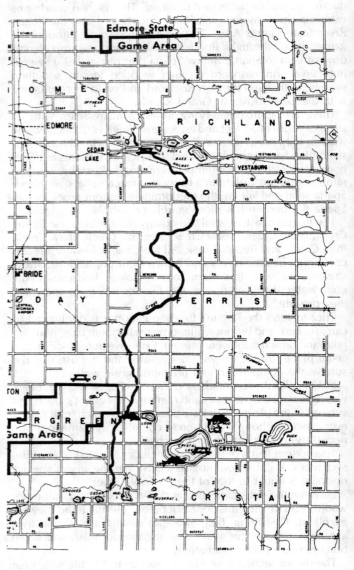

THE KALAMAZOO RIVER
By PAUL SCHEPPELMAN, Fisheries Area Manager

The Kalamazoo River, as it flows across southwestern Michigan from east to west, picks up water from quite a few good trout streams. The Kalamazoo itself is basically a warmwater stream, except the stretch below Allegan Dam in Allegan County, where coho salmon run in the fall. This same area has also produced some nice brown trout from three to five pounds. Spin casting with hardware is the best way to fish this area.

Starting on the east side of the area and working downstream, Augusta Creek is the first good trout stream. This stream, which empties in at Augusta, originates in Barry County but produces the best fishing after it enters Kalamazoo County.

Augusta Creek ranges from 15 to 20 feet wide, its bottom is predominately gravel, and it has ample cover and holes to create a good fishery. The surrounding country ranges from oak-covered ridges to tag alder and tamarack swamps. The stream lends itself best to bait and spin fishing, but there are also many areas where the fly-fishermen can work effectively.

Many good catches of brown trout are taken every year with some fish running two to four pounds. An occasional brook trout is also taken. From the opener through the second or third week, pressure is heavy, but after that the angler can have the stream pretty much to himself, as is the case with many of the southern Michigan streams.

The Kellogg Forest Area below M-89, which is managed by Michigan State University, is open to the trout fisherman. Officials ask that anglers keep the area clean and fill out a voluntary creel census report.

The DNR recently purchased a 244-acre parcel on Augusta Creek north of the Kellogg Forest. This parcel, with large amounts of stream frontage, will be jointly managed by the DNR Fisheries and Wildlife Divisions. A fisheries study is under way there in cooperation with Michigan State University. In order to assess existing conditions on this new acquisition, a five-year "No-kill" regulation was instituted in 1988 for a section of the stream from M-89 to the bridge in Section 3 of Ross Township.

Moving downstream, between Kalamazoo and Plainwell, Spring Brook, a quality trout stream, flows into the river just north of Parchment. This stream starts near the Barry-Kalamazoo county line. It is a relatively short stream of about eight miles, but it picks up a large amount of spring water in this distance. Average width runs from 10 to 18 feet with a 50-50 sand and gravel composition. The banks are mainly tag alder with most of the upland cover consisting of large oaks.

Good catches of brooks and browns are the rule rather than the exception on this stream. Browns predominate, but brooks are numerous enough that anglers will normally end up with a mixed creel. Browns will run to 15 inches and brooks up to 10 or 12 inches. Bait or spin casting is the most successful mode of fishing, but there are some areas open enough for limited

fly-fishing. All of the brook trout and many of the browns result from natural reproduction, as the DNR has not stocked brook trout in this district for several years.

The mouth of Silver Creek is about three miles upstream from Plainwell. Although this is a small stream, its contribution to the trout fisherman in southern Michigan is significant because of the brook trout fishing it provides in an area where this fish is becoming relatively rare. This fishery has held up so far, even though part of its headwaters in Allegan County is contained in Lake Doster, a man-made impoundment.

The stream is only four and a half miles long with a width of six to 10 feet. The upper portion flows through a somewhat swampy wooded area but has enough gravel areas to provide ample habitat for natural reproduction. The lower area is the pasture and small woodlot type of cover, the bottom mostly of sand.

Most of the brook trout are taken in the upper portion, with browns more numerous in the lower stretch. Most fish taken are not bragging size, but when the stream is a little high and colored, anglers should be able to get a few for eating. Live bait or spinners produce the best results.

The mouth of Gun River is located about halfway between Otsego and Plainwell. It is the largest trout stream tributary to the Kalamazoo River and starts at the Barry-Allegan county line as the outlet of Gun Lake. Within two or three miles it picks up enough cooling water to be suitable for trout. Although it was dredged many years ago as part of the county drain system, its banks have now grown over with brush. Despite its maintenance as a drain, it harbors some fine trout fishing. For the most part, it flows through rather low ground, consisting of soft maple swamps and muck farms. Most of these farms drain many springs into the river, and this contributes much-needed cold water. Good fishing in these feeders in the spring is also available. With the heavy growth along both banks, the fisherman gets the feeling of isolation as he fishes this stream.

Average width is 30 to 35 feet, and the bottom is predominately sand. Fishing is mostly in holes or along aquatic vegetation near the banks. To fish this stream effectively, waders should be used. Brown trout are the only species available, and they may be taken by most conventional gear. There are no large fly hatches to speak of, but most summer evenings will have a hatch large enough to show you feeding fish and fly-fishing is good. Most fish will run from sublegal to 14 inches long. Occasionally, fish in the two- to five-pound class are taken.

In the last couple of miles below US-131, the stream becomes deeper and slower. Warmwater species show up more in this area, including some large northern pike. A seven-and-a-quarter-pound brown trout was taken here, however, a few years ago.

About a mile and a half below Otsego Pine Creek joins the Kalamazoo River. It is known locally by three different names as it flows through three different counties.

In Kalamazoo County it is called Sandy Creek. As the name implies, it has a predominately sandy bottom, but there are some gravel areas. This is where the bulk of the natural reproduction for the entire stream system takes place.

It is a relatively small stream of six to 12 feet wide and flows through old abandoned and brush-infested farms. The fish are quite small in the upper portion, but as the stream becomes larger, the fish size increases. The last mile and a half, before it leaves the county, are the best for brown trout.

As the stream enters Van Buren County, it is called Mentha Drain, deriving its name from the once-prosperous community of Mentha and its many hundreds of acres of mint farms that it drained. These drains contribute a lot of good spring water to the stream and also increase its size.

Its width will vary from 15 to 20 feet and it is deep enough that anglers need waders to fish it effectively. The bottom is a combination of sand and silt in most areas, and this, combined with the many dead elms that have fallen into the water, make for hard wading and fishing. But good brown trout catches and fish surveys show this to be among the top brown trout waters in southern Michigan. For the fisherman who wants to accept the challenge for hard wading, mosquitoes, and numerous snags, the fish are there for the taking. Browns running from 10 to 16 inches are not uncommon, with some in the two- to five-pound class. Live bait and rising water is the best combination, but fish are also taken at other times on live bait, spinners, and in limited areas on flies.

As this same stream flows into Allegan County it is then known as Pine Creek. Shortly after it enters this county, warmwater tributaries from lakes begin to raise the temperature of the stream. Consequently, in the first mile or two the brown trout gives way to other fishes such as northern pike, bass, suckers, etc. However, in this area, the trout that are taken are larger due to the abundance of minnows for food and the bigger water. Probably the best way to fish here would be with minnows or hardware with an imitation minnow effect.

Moving downstream to the popular Highbanks goose hunting area, Swan Creek enters the river. Most of its trout water is in the state-owned Allegan State Game Area, so public access is assured.

The stream starts at Swan Lake in the southern portion of Allegan County. For the first few miles it is not trout water. Starting at 110th Avenue, an occasional brown trout is caught, and from there downstream it provides fair trout fishing. Most popular spots are the Iron Bridge on 115th Avenue and below Swan Creek Pond on 118th Avenue. There are also some good areas for the person who wants some peace and quiet, by walking into the more remote areas with the aid of a compass and county map. Campgrounds abound in the area for the fisherman who wants to stay awhile.

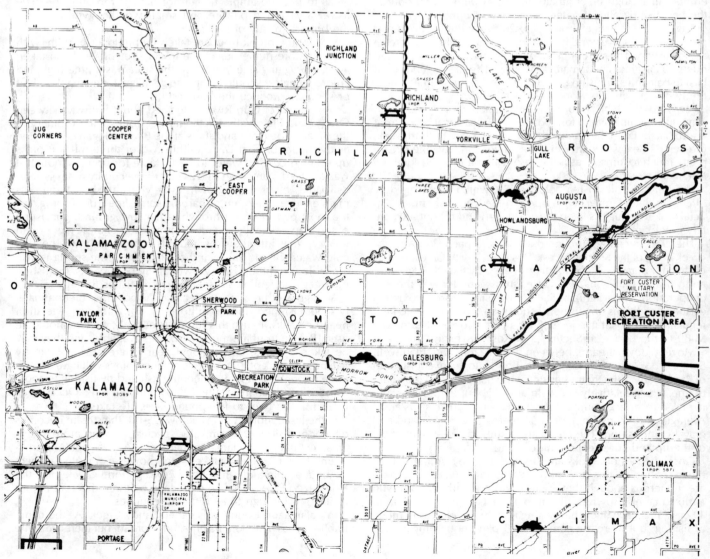

Swan Creek is an average-size stream of about 25 feet wide, and waders are nice to have but not necessary to effectively fish it. The stream banks are tag alder lined and the upland is predominantly oak forest with a few white pine here and there. The bottom is mostly sand, but there are some areas of nice gravel for spawning and food production.

Fair catches of browns are taken every year from this stream. During the spring the high water levels make for good fishing for steelheads from the mouth upstream to the dam at 118th Avenue. This section of stream is opened for the extended spring season. Fishing is by most conventional gear, but the fly-fisherman would be hindered in some areas because of brush. In fact, some of these hard-to-get-to spots are where the old lunkers are taken by the fisherman with the patience to work them out. Most fish will run from 10 to 15 inches and quite a few up to five pounds.

Sand Creek and Bear Creek enter the Kalamazoo River near M-89. They are both spring fed and their size increases rapidly, although the Bear is a larger stream. For the most part, they flow through state-owned land. These two are among southern Michigan's most picturesque streams, as they flow over countless rocks and riffles and through a steep-walled valley that is studded with large hardwood and hemlock.

Brown trout are numerous enough to make it interesting in Bear Creek, with the fish running up to 20 inches, and there is ample food, cover, and spawning grounds. Sand Creek is predominately a brook trout stream, but due to the small stream size, maximum size of brookies is around 10 to 11 inches.

The Rabbit River joins the Kalamazoo just above New Richmond. Steelheads run to the dam at Hamilton and provide a good fishery. Fishing from shore or a boat with hardware or spawn bags is the best method. Above Hamilton the stream was chemically reclaimed several years ago and restocked with brown trout.

The last trout tributary on the Kalamazoo system is Mann Creek, which enters the river at New Richmond. Although there is some state-owned land on the upper portion, the major portion of the stream is not publicly owned.

Brook trout are the main species in this stream, with occasional fish up to 12 inches. Stream width varies from eight to 15 feet and it is quite brushy. This limits fishing to bait or possibly small spinners. From the headwaters to below 54th Street, the bottom has many springs and is too soft to wade. Below this area, however, it changes to sand and gravel. Most of the surrounding country is scrub oak forest with tag alder swamps in the immediate vicinity of the stream.

Salmon, brown trout, and steelhead runs on the main stream are stopped at Allegan Dam northwest of Allegan, and good fisheries for these species exist from there downstream. Plans call for extending the runs upstream all the way to Battle Creek through dam removal and fish ladders.

THE PAW PAW RIVER
By PAUL SCHEPPLEMAN, Fisheries Area Manager

The headwaters of the Paw Paw River are in eastern Van Buren County. Its three major branches converge near the city of Paw Paw. The East and West branches converge at Maple Lake, an impoundment in the village of Paw Paw. The stream below the Maple Lake dam is marginal for trout, but it receives a good steelhead run each spring; fishing success is good there from February through April. Salmon also run the river in the fall and provide a fair fishery in September and October.

At the town of Lawrence, the stream has once again cooled by groundwater inflow to the high 60s in summer and is capable of supporting trout down to the dam in Watervliet. As larger numbers of brown trout become available, this stretch may be stocked to establish the species in this area. The lower section, down to Benton Harbor, is primarily a warmwater stream. However, salmon and steelhead runs are present and create an attractive fishery at Watervliet Dam.

The headwaters of the North Branch of the Paw Paw begin in some enormous privately-owned spring holes north of the Wolf Lake State Fish Hatchery near the eastern boundary of Van Buren County. Below these springs it is known as Campbell Creek.

Within a half mile, at 28th Avenue, the stream is 10 to 12 feet wide and has some nice holes below the road. Bottom is mostly sand and quite soft for wading. Brook trout dominate, but there are also some nice browns. Occasional brookies will run over 18 inches in length. Most of the drainage on this entire branch is broad elm and maple swamps, which causes the stream to overflow its banks quite frequently after a rain or during spring runoff.

Below Fish Lake Road it is then known as Whiskey Run, or the North Branch. From here downstream the stream is slower and deeper. In order to fish effectively, anglers should have an inner tube and waders or with some difficulty could use a canoe. The stream averages 25 to 30 feet wide and has a soft, sandy bottom. Many good catches of brown trout are taken, especially early in the season. There are a few caught every year that exceed five pounds. Fish may be taken on all conventional gear, including flies. The bait fisherman may become discouraged, however, at times because of the large number of chubs and suckers that move up from the lower section of the river. By the time one gets to M-40, the trout have given way to warmwater species.

The East Branch of the Paw Paw originates near the Kalamazoo-Van Buren county line in Paw Paw Lake, which is a good producer of rainbow trout. It ends in Maple Lake at Paw Paw, where it meets with the West Branch.

The East Branch is a fair producing brook and brown trout stream, with brooks giving way to browns about midway downstream. The stream is 25 to 30 feet wide and gives up an occasional large fish, browns to seven pounds and brook trout to three pounds.

The bottom is over 50 percent gravel, which makes for good food production and spawning. Surrounding country is mostly grape vineyards, farms, and small woodlots. The banks of the stream are pretty much covered with brush and trees. Fishing techniques are up to the individual as most gear is equally effective. The fly-fisherman gets some good fly hatches in May, June, and early July.

The West Branch starts in southern Van Buren County near Decatur. As it flows toward Maple Lake at Paw Paw through predominately farm country, it picks up a few nice spring-fed tributaries. These improve the stream as trout water in its lower four miles.

This entire branch was chemically treated many years ago to remove all rough fish and was restocked with brown trout then. Although there are some rough fish present, it provides some fair fishing for those who work at it. As part of the county drain system, it is quite straight and has a sandy bottom. Most of the cover consists of countless trees that have fallen in and dug holes in the sandy bottom.

A significant tributary which enters at the town of Lawrence is Brush Creek. Along with its two tributaries, White and Red creeks, it startles the unwary fisherman with the size of the fish that come out of it.

With much of the stream no wider than a living room, Brush Creek continues to give up browns 16 to 18 inches. This is partially due to the fact that the stream has many shallow, gravel riffles that drop off into deep pools and undercut banks. These riffles also produce aquatic insects for food. Most fish are taken on live bait, but other gear could probably be used to a more limited degree. Surrounding country is mainly farmland with wooded borders along the stream.

Inside Berrien County at Watervliet, Mill Creek enters. It starts in Van Buren County and flows through a heavily wooded area, draining many springs into its watercourse. The gravel bottom starts to change to sand as it flows through farmlands near the county line.

Most brown trout taken here run 10 to 14 inches, with the odd larger fish taken in the lower stretch. The upper end is bait water because of the heavy cover, but most types of gear could be used on the lower. A live grasshopper or one of the good imitations floated along the grassy banks in June or July is an effective technique. Brook trout are also present in the upper part of the mainstream and several branches.

The last trout stream to come before the river reaches Lake Michigan is Blue Creek. Its headwaters start above the site of the former Milburg State Fish Hatchery.

Although the upper portion isn't too large, Blue Creek yields a good number of eating-size brown trout. By the time it reaches Milburg, it has picked up enough groundwater that it now averages 15 to 20 feet in width. From here on it becomes a good stream for most types of gear. There are many deep holes and clay banks so that an angler would want waders to fish effectively. Fish become progressively larger downstream, with some reaching 16 to 18 inches.

Surrounding country is orchards, farmlands, and woodlots. The stream bottom varies from gravel riffles to clay shelves and sand.

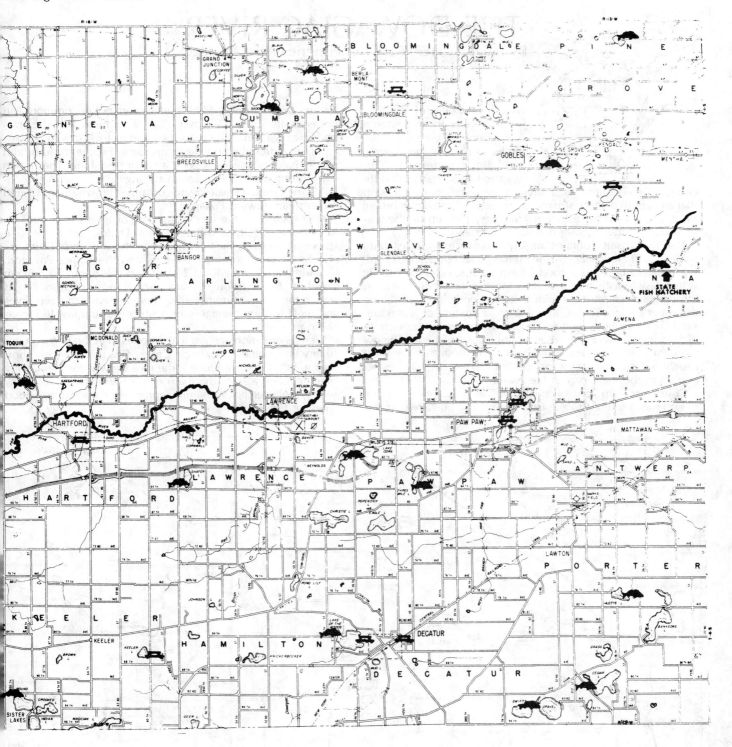

THE DOWAGIAC RIVER
By PAUL SCHEPPELMAN, Fisheries Area Manager

The headwaters of the Do-wagiac River lie in southern Van Buren County as the outlet of Lake of the Woods, and its counterpart, Do-wagiac Creek, starts in north-eastern Cass County as a drain system for many lakes in that area. Both of these streams produce good catches of brown trout, along with the tributaries that they pick up on the way to Niles and the St. Joseph River in Berrien County.

The river itself contains mostly warmwater species until northwest of Dowagiac. By then it has picked up enough cooling water to become a good brown trout stream. This is big water, easy to fish and canoeable. Most of the whole system is through farm country but with quite a wide belt of trees along the water's edge. The bottom is a good mixture of gravel and sand. The two best areas for large browns are in the vicinity of Sumnerville, where there is a public access site, and below the dam north of Niles. Fish of six to 10 pounds have been caught occasionally in these areas with some limit catches occurring in the early part of the season.

Going back up to Dowagiac, Dowagiac Creek joins the river. From Volinia to Lake LaGrange is the best area on this stream. Brown trout of 14 to 16 inches are not uncommon, and occasionally 18- to 22-inch fish are taken here. This stream is periodically chemically reclaimed and restocked with browns and is an extremely popular fishing area. Excellent caddis and mayfly hatches make it a good area for fly-fishing. The stream is not trout water below Lake LaGrange.

Peavine Creek, a small stream containing brown trout, is found downstream toward Pokagon.

At Pokagon, on the headwaters of Pokagon Creek, and on Kimmerlee Creek, a tributary near Dailey, are some fine spawning grounds for the browns in these waters. There are also brookies in Kimmerlee Creek and the Upper Pokagon. Its width varies from 10 to 20 feet and it is about 50 percent gravel. It flows through many farms and woodlots on its way to the river at Sumnerville. There are enough deep holes and most fish are average size, with some running 16 inches and over.

There is one more stream that empties in at the Berrien-Cass county line, namely McKenzie Creek. This is a relatively short stream, but it does produce some nice browns for the passing fisherman and also to the main river system. There are many good gravel stretches for natural reproduction and enough good holes for fishing.

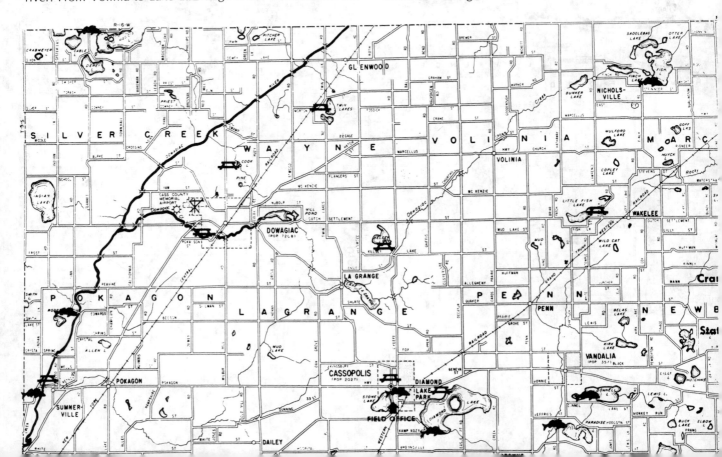

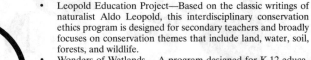

Michigan United Conservation Clubs

Protecting Michigan's Environmental and Outdoor Heritage Since 1937

The Michigan United Conservation Clubs (MUCC) was formed in 1937, and has grown to be the largest and most active statewide federation of conservation and civic clubs in the nation. For more than three generations MUCC has been in the forefront of efforts to protect Michigan's outdoor heritage; carefully manage its natural resources; fight for the conservation of its soils, forests, waters, wildlife and fish; and promote the right of all citizens to enjoy Michigan's outdoor opportunities.

Today, MUCC's membership of more than 120,000 people in combination with more than 480 affiliated clubs provides the foundation and strength of our organization. The vitality of MUCC lies in the diversity of its member's interests - ranging from fly fishing and hunting to bird watching and canoeing. And despite their varying recreational interests, our membership shares a strong interest in the enjoyment of the outdoors and a deep commitment to protecting the rights of present and future generations to clean water, clean air, thriving forests, and abundant fish and wildlife.

Through its publications, conservation education and environmental programs, and public policy stands, MUCC continues to work towards the goal of a sound environment and recreational future for Michigan.

Looking Out for the Public Interest

Because of their special interest in enhancing the quality of Michigan's out-of-doors, MUCC members play an active role in developing conservation and environmental policy. The association maintains strong liaisons with the Governor, state legislators, regulatory officials, and leaders in local government and commerce.

MUCC continually monitors the development of legislation and rules and regulations affecting conservation and outdoor recreation, and represents the conservation viewpoint before government agencies and elected officials at all levels of government.

You already know MUCC by some of our environmental victories:

In 1976, MUCC mounted the campaign to place before state voters a proposal for mandatory deposits on beer and soft drinks, and in 1986 went directly to the public for expansion of the "Bottle Bill," one of the most successful anti-litter and waste reduction programs in the nation. MUCC worked diligently for the approval of the Michigan Natural Resources Trust Fund, which sets aside royalties from oil and gas exploration for the purchase of valuable recreational lands and parks.

MUCC successfully led the fight to preserve Michigan's vital, but fragile wetland resources through the Wetlands Watch, a network of concerned citizen volunteers across the state. MUCC's door-to-door canvass has also rallied citizen's and legislative support for the Sand Dunes Protection Act - an act that protected Michigan's unique coastal sand dunes from overdevelopment.

In 1994, MUCC led the campaign that passed Proposal P, a state parks initiative that created the Michigan State Parks Endowment Fund. The fund established a permanent source of funding for the Michigan State Parks System, and was voted for by more than 75 percent of the voters in November 1994. MUCC also led the efforts in 1996 to pass Proposal G, which allowed the continued use of scientific management to regulate wildlife and hunting.

Providing Learning Opportunities for All Ages

Of all of MUCC's ongoing activities, it is the organization's education and training programs that set it apart. Each year, MUCC coordinates a wide variety of conservation and environmental education programs designed to instill in people from all walks of life, respect and appreciation for nature and living things, and to equip these people with the skills to use our natural resources wisely. Some of these education programs include:

- Wildlife Encounters—an exciting, live wildlife program offering children and adults a rare opportunity to come face to face with the birds and mammals of Michigan. Presentations on "Michigan's Valuable Wetlands" and "Michigan Birds of Prey" are available, ranging from 40 to 60 minutes, and can be arranged for schools, community organizations, and service clubs for a nominal fee.
- Tracks® Magazine—a national award-winning conservation and wildlife reader designed to teach elementary school children the principles of wildlife habitat, ecology, and the importance of conserving natural resources. First published in 1978, *Tracks* is distributed to schoolchildren across the U.S.
- Project Learning Tree—an environmental education program designed for educators working with students from pre-K through 12th grade. PLT uses the forest as a window into natural and developed environments, helping people gain an awareness and knowledge of the world around them, and their place within it.

- Leopold Education Project—Based on the classic writings of naturalist Aldo Leopold, this interdisciplinary conservation ethics program is designed for secondary teachers and broadly focuses on conservation themes that include land, water, soil, forests, and wildlife.
- Wonders of Wetlands— A program designed for K-12 educators interested in learning exciting hands-on activities about Michigan's most endangered wildlife habitat.
- The Great Lakes WISE Project—a comprehensive pollution prevention and solid waste management curriculum for grades K-12 and managed by MUCC. WISE (Waste Information Series for Education) is designed to teach the importance of individual action and that each of us shares a responsibility in protecting our natural resources. The notebook is complemented by fun and interesting student readers such as *The Trash Can Gazette* and *Slime Magazine*.
- Wildlife Discovery—an in-classroom program for elementary schoolchildren in which specially trained volunteers travel to elementary schools across Michigan teaching children about wildlife and the complex interrelationships that govern our natural world.
- MUCC Youth Camps—a series of one-week summer camp seminars for boys and girls between the ages of 9 and 14. Since 1946, the MUCC Youth Camp has attracted thousands of youngsters with programs focusing on wildlfe, the environment, and natural resources conservation.
- Weekend Courses—conducted in January and September at the Ralph A. MacMullan Conference Center at Higgins Lake, these weekend programs introduce adults to basic outdoor skills and a variety of natural history topics.
- Leadership Training—an annual training and development conference for members of MUCC-affiliated clubs who are seeking leadership roles in the conservation movement.
- In-Service Teacher Training—a series of lectures and training programs on the use of the outdoors as a classroom to help educators better relate Michigan's conservation heritage to children.

Taking the Conservation Message to People

MUCC believes that an educated and informed citizenry is the cornerstone of the conservation movement. When given ample information on conservation and the environment, Michigan citizens will make wise and thoughtful decisions on conservation. For more than 50 years, MUCC has educated, informed, and stirred to action three generations of citizen conservationists through programs like:

- *Michigan Out-of-Doors*—the official monthly magazine of MUCC. Each month, *Michigan Out-of-Doors* covers a wide variety of outdoor recreation and resource conservation topics ranging from the latest tips on hunting and fishing to detailed examinations of Michigan's conservation movement.
- Michigan Out-of-Doors Television—the official weekly television show of MUCC. This weekly magazine style television show features hunting, fishing, wildlife, outdoor recreation, and current event information from across the state. Check your television listing for show times on your local Public Broadcasting Station (PBS).
- Environmental Quality Index—a comprehensive, yearly analysis of Michigan's overall environmental quality, compiled by MUCC professional staff and published as an insert in *Michigan Out-of-Doors*.
- The Outdoor Library—a very popular selection of enjoyable and helpful books, maps, and guides that will provide useful information to anyone who enjoys outdoor recreation activities.

You Can Make A Difference

Membership in MUCC makes you an active part of the largest state conservation organization in America. You can either join as a member of an MUCC-affiliated club or as an Individual Associate Member. Both types of memberships include a monthly subscription to *Michigan Out-of-Doors*.

No matter which level of membership you choose, your support and contributions are helping MUCC fight the battle to protect the environment and ensure the rights of sportsmen and women across the state.

For a membership application or for information on the MUCC-affiliated club nearest you, call or write:

Michigan United Conservation Clubs
Membership Services
PO Box 30235 • Lansing MI 48909
Phone: 517/371-1041 • FAX: 517/371-1505
E-MAIL: mucc.org